Journey Into an Interfaith World

Journey Into an Interfaith World

Jews, Christians, and Muslims in a World Come of Age

KENNETH L. VAUX

WIPF & STOCK · Eugene, Oregon

JOURNEY INTO AN INTERFAITH WORLD
Jews, Christians, and Muslims in a World Come of Age

Copyright © 2010 Kenneth L. Vaux. All rights reserved. Except for brief quotations in critical publications or reviews, no part of this book may be reproduced in any manner without prior written permission from the publisher. Write: Permissions, Wipf and Stock Publishers, 199 W. 8th Ave., Suite 3, Eugene, OR 97401.

Hebrew Bible translations by Mechon Mamre, http://www.mechon-mamre.org/p/pt/pto.htm; Christian Gospel citations from New Revised Standard Version; and Qur'an translations by Yusuf Ali, http://www.islam101.com/quran/yusufAli/QURAN/3.htm.

Wipf & Stock
An Imprint of Wipf and Stock Publishers
199 W. 8th Ave., Suite 3
Eugene, OR 97401

www.wipfandstock.com

ISBN: 978-1-60899-540-0

Manufactured in the U.S.A.

Thanks to Sara and the children for their love and support,
to Melanie Baffes for assistance in research, writing, and editing,
and to members of the Spring 2009 "Jew, Christian, Muslim" class at
Garrett-Evangelical Theological Seminary.

Contents

Preface / ix

Introduction / xi
The Heritage of Israel • Nazi Science and Medicine • Interfaith Medicine • War and Interfaith Concerns • Fundamental Theology and Interfaith Matters • Cambridge (CARTS) • Al-Andalus • Common Theological Ground

I THEOLOGY:
THE COMMON GOD—AKEDAH / 1
An Interfaith Trialogue on Akedah • Akedic Readings in Judaism and Islam • The Akedic History of God • Akedah and the Human Condition • An Interfaith Theology of Akedah • Akedic Existence

II ETHICS:
THE COMMON GOOD—TORAH, THE LAW OF CHRIST, TAURUT / 35
Faith and Ethics—Starting Points • Sources of Ethical Principles • Ethics and Religious Identity • Themes Common to Judaism, Christianity, and Islam • An Applied Interfaith Ethic

III SCRIPTURE:
THE COMMON WORD—INTERACTIVE INTERFAITH READING / 81
Search for a Common Word • Hebrew Scripture • Christian Scripture • Muslim Scripture • A New Hermeneutic • Current Emphasis on Scriptural Reasoning • How Can Scriptural Reasoning Inform Public Action? • Chains of Scriptural Reasoning and Interfaith Dialogue

IV INTERFAITH ACTION:
THE COMMON WORK—CONFLICTS IN A GLOBAL WORLD / 163
City and Country: Two Cities • Life and Death: Akedah and Bioethics • War and Peace: Rumor and Rules of War • Three Interfaith Voices

V CORROBORATIONS:
EXPLORATIONS OF RELATED TOPICS / 196
The President and King: Interfaith Conciliation • Luther and Interfaith Dimensions: Gift of the Beloved Son • Luther, Jews, and Muslims: The Preeminent Commandments • Do Jews, Christians, and Muslims Worship the Same God? • Conversion and Religious Freedom • Into God's World • The Bread of Angels • Jews and Christians

Bibliography / 251

Preface

THIS STUDY SEEKS TO PROVIDE a theological rationale and a practical roadmap for interfaith exploration, dialogue, and programming. Colleges and seminaries attempt to bring this realm to new pastors, rabbis, and mullahs—and thousands of groups around the world are now forming to further interfaith awareness, scriptural sharing, and common social-ethical action. In developing a case for the urgently-needed tripartite consultation called for among the three faiths, I explore the common God, the common good, the common word, and the common work.

Introduction

Israel will restore the wholeness of human nature through the work of its people in the natural world of the countryside.[1]

Israel is delivered out of Egypt so that it may live before God as God's people on earth.[2]

THE HERITAGE OF ISRAEL

"IN THE BEGINNING WAS THE WORD (*Logos*) and the Word was with God, and the Word was God. . . . All things came into being through him (*egeneto*), and without him not one thing came into being. . . . in him was life (*zoe*), and the life was the light of all people (*anthropos*)." (John 1.1, 1.3–4)

"And they say: 'Allah has begotten a son. Glory be to Him—to Him belongs all that is in the heavens and on earth: Everything renders worship to Him. To Him is due the very origin of the heavens and the earth. When he decides on anything and He says to it: 'Be,' And so it becomes." (Qur'an, Sura 2:116–17)

Israel's heritage in the world beyond its own unique witness is found in Christianity and Islam—the two largest religions, each with a populace of nearly 2 billion persons. Israel (and its heritage), as Matthew Arnold implied, knows "where the world is going."[3]

Living in the world of 2009, one so threatening and so promising, presents a thrill in such a world known to Israel's interfaith family, where

---

1. Buber, *On Zion*, 156, 158.
2. Bonhoeffer, *Letters and Papers from Prison*, 336.
3. See Arnold, *The Great Prophecy of Israel's Restoration*.

God is creator, redeemer, and Lord. *Sub specie aeternitatis*, a phrase known to secular humanistic wisdom and monotheistic faith, describes the world we know, thanks to biblical insight. Here, God's grace and presence, command and faithfulness induce within the world's people common faith and ethics—the new humanity necessary to ground and found God's new world. We are all called to offer our unique and unprecedented gift to this God through service in the world.

Standing in the biblical-theological movement, I continue in this study, a journey into an interfaith world, specifically the cosmos and complex I explored in *Jew, Christian, Muslim*.[4] I begin by recounting the stages of my own journey into this new world.

NAZI SCIENCE AND MEDICINE

It began in 1966. I showed up at the office of Helmut Thielicke, professor of Systematic Theology and director of the Seminar in Social Ethics at the University of Hamburg, on the North Sea coast of still post-war Germany. Along with Dresden, the great ancient city of Hamburg had been leveled by the fire-wind bombing of the Allies that whipped down the great industrial avenues of the ancient cities. This fire bombing, together with Hiroshima, Nagasaki, Tokyo, and the Japanese cities, the first genocidal war crimes, would close the second world war with a show of force that would crush any reminiscence of Hitler's *Wehrmacht* and the frightening specter of a fascist domination.

Thielicke had invited me to join him as a doctoral student when he visited my seminary, Princeton, earlier in the 1960s. I wanted to work on the Jewish Holocaust, agonizingly fresh in the minds of the still-trembling German and world populace. I thought I could study Nazi medicine and human experimentation, since I had just begun work in the Great Texas Medical Center in Houston. I was a 27-year-old Presbyterian campus minister, assigned to the scientific world of Rice University and the renowned medical center across Main and Fannin Streets, in Houston's South Central City. It was the hey-day of advanced, experimental medicine. Andrew Ivy himself, the Chicago physician who had written the Nuremberg Code, had been involved in the questionable research and inadequate patient consent taking place at Northwestern's research center, the Cook County system of medical care, and prisons in the state of Illinois system.

4. See Vaux, *Jew, Christian, Muslim*.

My concerns were several: *then*, Judaism and the fate of this particular and peculiar people in mid-century European history; and *now*, the awesome power embodied in this world technological center; NASA and the Space Center; the petrochemical industry; and the wonder of new medicine—the home of DeBakey and Cooley heart transplants—a citadel of American monetary and military eminence in the world.[5]

But at this juncture of history, America also was bewildered. We had taken over the ill-advised and ultimately futile Viet Nam War from the French in Indochina. Protests for peace were starting in Germany and the U.S. Dr. Martin Luther King, Jr. was taking his civil-rights campaign from Georgia and Alabama into the North and to the more progressive parts of the old Confederacy, including Texas, where 10,000 new residents poured in each week from the frigid shores of Lake Michigan and Superior.

Deciphering and discerning the meaning of Israel, vis-à-vis the Christianity I had studied at Princeton Seminary earlier that decade, was my first interfaith endeavor.

GAZA: A LEAP TO THE PRESENT

It is Sunday before the new term begins. I rise early to compose my lecture for the two classes I am teaching: "War and Peace" and "Jew, Christian, Muslim." It is still ice and fire, snow on snow, and from tropical Tampa, the Super Bowl. Jennifer Hudson, in her recent tragedy, singing the national anthem—fire and metal—and Bruce Springsteen and those banned vegetable ads—fire and ice.

The rockets still fly from Gaza into southern Israel and fizzle harmlessly, yet the Israeli outrage fulminates. At Davos, Israeli President Shimon Peres castigates Turk Prime Minister Recep Tayyip Erdogan on the makeshift rockets, until Erdogan protests silently and walks out. The Israelis are sublimely silent on the 1,000-plus deaths and hundreds of phosphorus-burned women and children in Gaza.

No one could watch what has transpired in Gaza—only the bee or the coursing geese following the divine pathways they know by instinct. Only God can see Gaza and weep.

---

5. Dr. Michael E. DeBakey and Dr. Denton A. Cooley, two of the world's most renowned heart transplant surgeons, pioneered procedures at Baylor College of Medicine and Methodist Hospital in Houston in the 1950s.

The press was banned, and we weren't allowed to watch; only God could watch it—like the *Bhagavad Gita*'s "brighter than a thousand suns," like Auschwitz's iron-furnace encasement, only gas and ash from the exhausted lives of millions into the ether of the world. The fire bombing of cities—the next modern holocaust after Auschwitz and Buchenwald—sucks up oxygen from the air as fires sweep down the cities of tunneled buildings. Like Hamburg and Dresden, Tokyo, Hiroshima, and Nagasaki, Sodom and Gomorrah—fire and ash, frozen stone and ice, and phosphorous bombs now encase the 22,000 crumbled buildings and charred bodies of Gaza.

So this early Sunday morning, "With Heart and Voice" (WFMT) begins with The Sixteen, the world's finest song ensemble and Gabriel Fauré's Requiem, "Behold the Lamb of God/*Agnus Dei*." The program ends with Brahms's Requiem with words from Matthew: "Blessed are those who mourn—they shall be comforted." (Matt 5.4) Between the bookends of Requiem, the 7 a.m. news tells of the overturning of a gasoline truck in Kenya, Barack Obama's brief homeland, and hundreds of children rushing out to gather fuel in paper cups, trying to survive and often dying in the process. On Sunday morning, the thousand suns explode again with a cigarette butt; 200 children scooping up gas are killed and hundreds less fortunate suffering with terrible burns.

My reflections have remained irrepressibly interfaith. The interfaith textual chain of my morning devotion is called "The Bee," from the Qur'an, Sura 16:

> - **Judaism**—"I am the Lord. You shall keep my commandments, walk in my ways, and fear me" (Deut 8.6).
> - **Christianity**—"You cannot serve two Lords" (*oytheys thynatay thysy kyryoys thoyleyeyn*) (Matt 6.24).
> - **Islam**—"Allah sends down his Spirit. Proclaim there is no God but God. Follow my ways" (Sura 16.1).

So we turn to John (1.29), the great text of descending word ends on *Akedah*: "*Agnus Dei, qui tollis peccata mundi* . . ." (Lamb of God, who took away the sins of the world).

∼

INTERFAITH MEDICINE

After a career start in bio-ethics in Houston, I was called to Chicago in 1978 to an Ethics Chair at the nation's largest medical school, the University of

Illinois. The doctors, nurses, and patients came from all faith traditions. Muslim and Jewish physicians, along with the variety of Christian practitioners, were my teachers and clinical colleagues. It was at this time that I began to travel to the Middle East, becoming deeply concerned with the Israeli-Palestinian peace process and with the interface and interplay of Abraham's three filial peoples—especially in that spiritual epicenter of the world.

The last elective course I offered at the medical school explored interfaith perspectives in medicine. By this time, I had started in interfaith research and education projects—in the Institute of Religion in Texas and in what would be called "Project X" at the Park Ridge Center in Chicago.

Reflective of the thematic interests of these institutes (I also had helped found the Hastings and Kennedy Institutes of Bioethics), the course I offered had an equal number of Jewish, Christian, and Muslim students. We considered the issues that were the substantive themes of Project X: health, disease, suffering, pain, life, death, sexuality, and care—all from an interfaith perspective. The students were appreciative: "We've never had the chance to look at medical-scientific and care issues in light of faith traditions. To explore the experience of my patient meeting death and my own response was a challenge and joy—a valuable gift to my career as a physician." After 25 years of training medical and nursing students, I've witnessed thousands of these dedicated men and women enter their practice with deepened theological and ethical sensitivity.

Today, my professional passion involves awakening the same interfaith awareness in religious leaders—training Christian pastors to be adept in the disciplines of interfaith knowledge and programming: scriptural exegesis, inter-textual hermeneutics (Judaism, Christianity, and Islam), interfaith theology, Christology, Pneumatology, and ministry in the midst of progressive world issues such as health, war, politics, justice and the poor, the oppression of women and children. I return to this recent departure after further review of my background formation.

WAR AND INTERFAITH CONCERNS

While I was still in the medical school and had started the interfaith Project X relating to health issues, I began working on war issues.

The first of a series of books in interfaith contexts and war history was a 1991 sabbatical project, *Ethics and the Gulf War*. My medical colleagues were taken aback. "Look," I pointed out (employing the new linguistic comma, preferable to "like"), "there's a section on care of animals—" (*e.g.,* killing camels when igniting oil fields), "it's bioethics!"

In truth, my mind was turning to two new directions—to fundamental theology, theological ethics, and interfaith perspectives. I proceeded to write *Ethics and the War on Terrorism, Jew, Christian, Muslim* (especially its provocative section on war and evangelism), and then a reissue of *Ethics and the Gulf War* in 2005. The winter of 2009 brought forth *America in God's World*, which takes seriously Gandhi's charge that the most dangerous war is economic and political, what he calls the first of "seven blunders of the world."[6] My approach always is to see theology as a force for good and evil.

The series of war books followed the interfaith matrix. *Ethics and the Gulf War* traced Judaism through its phases of biblical holy war, pathways through medieval *pogroms* and crusades down to the series of wars establishing and defending the plantation of the state of Israel in Palestine (the 1948 Arab-Israeli War). The Gulf War was one chapter in this book of tears.

Ethics and the Gulf War also traced Saddam Hussein's resurgent Islam and the role that feigned theocentrism played in the invasion of Kuwait, the real goal of which was to stop Kuwait siphoning off of the great oil reserve that stretched under the Kuwait/Iraq border. It also traced President George Bush's (the first) appropriation of Christian "just-war" theory in his initiation, prosecution, and conclusion of the first war on Iraq.

In *Ethics and the War on Terrorism*, I struggled to decipher and describe the religio-ethical parameters of September 11th and the subsequent American-led war on terrorism against "militant-fundamentalist Islam." Although ostensibly the 2003 invasion of Iraq and Afghanistan was to find Osama bin Laden and to bring the "cohort of conspirators" to justice, it took the mistaken path of blaming Iraq for the events of September 11th. It also erroneously blamed Iraq for developing weapons of mass destruction and for harboring and nourishing *Al Qaeda*. Seven years later, as we disengage from Iraq and reengage in Afghanistan (against our old friends, the Taliban, who became known to us during the Afghan War against Russia)—*Shiah* Islam is now in resurgence, perhaps in the strongest way since the CIA toppled Mohammed Mosaddeq in Iran

6. See Vaux, *Ethics and the War on Terrorism; Ethics and the Gulf War; America in God's World.*

in the 1950s, imposed the Shah, and set the stage for Ayatollah Khomeini. Both *Sunni Hamas* and *Shiah Hezbollah* have been strengthened in recent wars with Israel, and *Al Qaeda* now is an "American-made" force in the world.

My studies of resurgent and insurgent Islam, Judaism, and Zionist Christianity in this sequence of conflicts (and in the suicide bombings) have sought to show religious causality in distorted faith and in hopes for efficacious justice and peace to heal and reconcile our religiously shattered world.

FUNDAMENTAL THEOLOGY AND INTERFAITH MATTERS

Jew, Christian, Muslim was an attempt to probe fundamental theological, ethical, pastoral (health care), and military/missional matters in their interfaith context. In Part One, I sought a common theological (Christological) matrix between the faiths of Abraham in the *Akedah*. The Abraham-Isaac-Ishmael complex is at the theological core of each faith:

- **Judaism**—*Akedah* lies behind Passover, Exodus, the New Year, and the theme of death and resurrection.
- **Christianity**—The cross of Christ/resurrection is grounded in the theology of the "beloved son" (*agapetos, monogenos, cf.* John 3.16).
- **Islam**—The theology of Islam found in *Qur'an* and *hadith* is a persecutorial theology based on the strenuous travail of the Ishmael tradition.

Part Two, on ethics, was focused on Decalogue and Torah (*Taurut*) studies. Part Three on health, pastoral, and Shephardic issues looked at life and death, health and illness matters, and, in the infamous Part Four, I talked about defensive and offensive faith. This section was euphemistically called "A Military/Christological History of the Apostle's Creed."

This phase of fundamental work has borne fruit in various essays: "Do Jews, Christians, and Muslims Worship the Same God?" and "Conversion and Religious Freedom" and in my budding interest in scriptural reasoning (SR) and developing *midrashic* (interpretive) chains of scriptures to guide interfaith dialogue.[7]

---

7. These articles can be found in Part V: Corroborations.

CAMBRIDGE (CARTS)

Beginning in 2005, I became a fellow at Cambridge University's Centre for Advanced Religious and Theological Studies (CARTS). This fellowship would become a background and context for all of my research and teaching, which had taken an interfaith turn and focus well before the events of September 11th. I had worked with Jewish scholars at Northwestern: Laurie Zoloth, a bioethicist and director of the Center for Bioethics; Jack Glassner, an amazing scholar fully proficient in Arabic, Islamic, and Hebraic traditions; Mark Sheldon; and Ben Sommer, recently called to Jewish Seminary in New York City, the heir apparent to Abraham Joshua Heschel's heritage in that splendid institution.

My Muslim colleagues at Northwestern University were headed by Souleymane Bachir Diagne (from Dakar, Senegal and trained at the Sorbonne), certainly the leading Islamic scholar-philosopher in this country, now at Columbia University. Joining us was Rashid Khalidi (the Edward Said chair of Middle East Studies at Columbia), our most eminent Palestinian scholar. Bashir, Sheldon, and I often led interfaith trialogue exercises with our students and neighborhood congregations. Dr. Sani (from Nigeria) and Rudgere Seesemann also were significant interlocutors for the Muslim faith tradition.

At Cambridge, I found myself in an environment dedicated to interfaith research and study. Peter Lipton, George Wilkes, Nicholas de Lange (among others) from the Jewish community, along with many Jewish scholars in faculties other than Divinity, provided foundations even in this very "Eurabic" culture—rich in Christianity and Islam, but rather strongly de-Judaized, as was all of post-*Shoah* Europe.

Tim Winter and Tony Street were wonderful guides to the richness of the Islamic heritage. The array of Christian scholars in biblical historical and theological studies was simply unparalleled anywhere in the world; with some 40 colleges (each with its dozens of fellows), one found himself among an embarrassment of riches. I felt like a kid in a candy store. I studied Hebrew Bible and ancient cultural studies, (*e.g.*, Hinduism), as well as New Testament, early Rabbinic Judaism, Jewish Christianity, and Early Christian Studies—topics salient and very important to my desire to find historical causalities and influences among the three Abrahamic faiths.

I wrote essays, presented seminars, and attended lectures, conferences, and workshops. Perhaps most importantly, I was a regular at choral evensong, Sunday worship, and special theological events—films, concerts, and student-discussion groups. Having a son who was a graduate tutor and fellow at Kings College opened many doors. Of greatest import to my research and development was the contact with students of all faiths. Men and women studying to be rabbis, priests and pastors, and mullahs—along with doctoral scholars preparing for teaching careers—became fast friends.

At the same time that I was doing fundamental theological work represented by essays on questions such as "Do Jews, Christians, Muslims Worship the Same God?" and "What About Evangelism?" I set out to participate in and facilitate new interfaith scriptural reasoning groups in Chicago, Evanston, the suburbs of Illinois, Cambridge, Antwerp, Paris, and other places my work took me. On the campaign trail for President Obama over the last two years, I undertook interfaith conferences in Indiana, West Virginia, Pennsylvania, and Wisconsin, among other places. In universities, councils of churches, union halls, and city offices, I led interfaith discussions of citizenship and public ethics.

AL-ANDALUS

An important chapter in my journey was my sabbatical research leave in southern Spain in 2003. In my teaching—the required Doctrine of God and Moral Theology courses and electives such as War and Peace, Economics, Medicine, Barth, Bonhoeffer, Jew, Christian, Muslim, and the like—I used interfaith approaches to probe basic questions relating to theism, Christology, Pneumatology, anthropology, axiology or ethics, eschatology, etiology (creation), and theodicy (good and evil).

In one or another interfaith setting—perhaps an audience of Jews and Christians—I would probe an expansive interpretation of what Christians call the second person of the Trinity, Jews, the second God in heaven, and Muslims, the *Mahdi*, the medium or mediator—redeemer. Taking off from our more expansive notions of Christology—where we considered Sophia, wisdom, *Logos*, *hikmah*, Messiah, Son—I sought a richer, more universal view of "God with us" (*Emmanuel*).

I was astounded by the resonances of the faiths, even at the rudimentary level. But we must remember that Judaism and Islam, in some senses, do not have doctrinal systems. Of course, in ethics, justice and economics, rich and poor, health and life, sickness and death, war and peace, there was profound common ground.

Al-Andalus

The faint lure of a *halvalero* over the Granada evening turned into a commanding staccato of flamenco after September 11th. Fratricidal animosity among Abraham's children—Americo-Israel vs. Arab-Europe—had the world on the brink of calamity in Palestine and Iraq. Where to look for peace and wisdom? What was ancient Andalusia? A pulsing center of the Roman Empire? An Iberian Peninsula jutting out like the Rock of Gibraltar toward the new world? The yearning, if not the sun setting, where the Apostle Paul concluded his ministry? Here beginning in the seventh century c.e., the Muslim world would gain a European stronghold as its poised mission, initially thwarted, toward the fragile dawnings of tribal peoples who would begin to become consolidated Europe under Charlemagne. Here in Granada, Cordoba, and Seville, Jews, Christians, and Muslims would interact with magnanimity and mutual edification until the Inquisition. Here Maimonides, Averroës, and Aquinas—all protégés of Avicenna of Isfahan—would find common insights in medicine, mathematics, philosophy, and theology. Here, Greek wisdom would synergistically intertwine with Judaic, Jewish-Christian, and Islamic monotheism to evoke the dawn of Western science. From the Crusades onward, a fateful trifurcation had set in. Recently, phenomena like global warming, weapons of mass destruction, and religious war have increased the breach of irenic truth and justice—the atmosphere of science.

So, on New Year's 2003, after 40 years absence from Spain, I return. Not only pan-Abrahamic peace, but also theology for science took its strong beginnings here in early medieval Andalusia. Here, devout theologians who laid the foundations not only for the modern age of science, but also for the concord and rapprochement among monotheistic theology, philosophy, and knowledge, more generally, are first found. In Avicenna of Isfahan, Iran and Maimonides and Averroës of Cordoba, the age reaches its zenith.[8]

---

8. From Vaux, *An Abrahamic Theology for Science*, 15.

COMMON THEOLOGICAL GROUND

This journey has led me to see what might be the common theological ground for such an interfaith project. My approach to the interconnection of Judaism, Christianity, and Islam is historical-ontological. I believe—as I contend in *Jew, Christian, Muslim*—that the three faiths will either abide in "faithful unification" or "fateful trifurcation." In other words, we will either "hang together or hang separately" (Ben Franklin). The three cognate faiths, I believe, are given by God for some purpose in God's universal history. The connections are historical, by which I mean their faith movements flow together from and into each other in derivative, idiosyncratic, and synergistic ways. At one point in history (first century c.e.), the Jewish and Christian faiths were still one. In a brief moment in the seventh century, Islam was still a part of Judaism and/or Christianity.

Ontologically, they are one, since they derive from and are anchored in the "reality" of the One God. In what senses are these faiths historic, ontic, and genetic in nature and character? Christianity springs from Judaism, and Rabbinic Judaism springs from historic Judaism and nascent (first-century Jewish-Christian) Christianity. Islam springs from Christianity (Abyssinian) as well as Diaspora Judaism—Alexandria, Egypt (Cairo). I also believe that each fraternal faith has "gone wrong" in its dissociation ("parting of the ways") from the others.

Spiritual genealogy is less important than spiritual ontology. The question of "from whom we come" in this perspective is superseded by "to whom do we belong." Within the divine being imparted to Abraham, Noah, Moses, and Jacob become Israel, is an ontology/constituting identity. The dimension of divine nature that coincides in the existence (*esse*) of Jews, Christians, and Muslims is found in what I call *Akedah*—the metaphor of the divine/human son—called in the Septuagint (LXX) *agapetos* (love-child) and *monogenos* (only-begotten). All three scriptures echo the same refrain: "Do we not belong to One Father?" This echoes Plato's profound assertion in the *Timaeus*: "the father and maker of all this universe is past finding out . . ."[9]

---

9. Plato, *Timaeus*, translated by Benjamin Jowett, http://classics.mit.edu/Plato/timaeus.html.

I

Theology

The Common God—Akedah

TO FURTHER SET THE CONTEXT OF THE INTERFAITH CONVICTION about "a common God," I now review a panel conducted by NPR before the events of September 11th. I was joined by Ingrid Mattson, from the distinguished Interfaith program at Hartford Seminary (she will be remembered as the Muslim reader in the first worship service of the Obama administration at the National Cathedral on January 21, 2009). Joining us was Jon Levenson from Harvard Divinity, whose salient work on "resurrection" in Judaism has deeply influenced my own perspectives.

AN INTERFAITH TRIALOGUE ON AKEDAH

The end of the *hajj* (pilgrimage) period in Islam culminates with the celebration of *Eid al-Adha*, the feast of Abraham's sacrifice. The story of Abraham—called on by God to sacrifice his son, then spared the horror by the substitution of a ram—is the foundational story in Islam, as well as in Judaism and Christianity. While Jews and Christians do not commemorate Abraham specifically, they do recall stories of the sacrifice of children. In this conversation, my colleagues and I explore how the founding story has shaped the three religious traditions that it engendered.

Moderator: The *Eid al-Adha* holiday celebrates Abraham's sacrifice specifically. How is the story remembered, and what are the themes associated with this holiday?

Ingrid Mattson: The theme of this holiday is really the theme of Islam generally, which is a religion of submission to the will of God, and the story of Abraham and his son both submitting themselves to the will of God by agreeing to go through with this sacrifice. Even though it was not carried out, this incident is an example for Muslims, and for all people, of the fact that we must all submit ourselves to the will of God. In the Qur'an, it is not only Abraham, but also his son who agrees to this. This is a distinction from how the story is told in the Jewish and Christian traditions—in the Genesis version, Isaac is the child being sacrificed, but he is silent and not consulted about the sacrifice.

Moderator: Many people who are not familiar with Islam think about the Prophet Muhammad and his central role in the faith, but where does Abraham fit into the whole tradition of Islam?

Ingrid Mattson: The Qur'an, the holy book of Islam, was revealed to Muhammad. In the Qur'an, you find Abraham mentioned many, many times throughout, and he is always given as an example of someone who refused to just follow along with the practices of his ancestors. He broke away from what they were doing—idol worship and immorality—and turned back to worshipping one God. Abraham is mentioned again and again in the Qur'an, reminding Arabs of that time—who were idol worshippers and placed a lot of emphasis on keeping up the traditions of their ancestors—as well as Muslims today that traditions are not necessarily good in and of themselves. It's good to follow a tradition, but it's not good to follow a bad tradition. And so we're told that even Abraham broke away from his ancestors in rejecting those idols and turning back to God. The Qur'an also appeals to Christians and Muslims to look to Abraham as their spiritual father and to remember his role in the formation of the faith.

Moderator: How does the Islamic version compare to the Abraham story in Christianity?

Kenneth L. Vaux: The Abraham story is basically the beginning of the story of humanity—a story of faith in the world. You have the other old stories about Adam and Eve, Noah, and so forth, but the saga of human history under God begins with Abraham. So, in a way, Abraham and Sarah are the proto-humans for Christianity.

Moderator: What does it mean for Christianity that the beginning story would be a story of sacrifice?

Kenneth L. Vaux: It's a complex story. It's the promise of life, the gift of life, the long wait for progeny. Abraham and Sarah are almost centenarians when they are finally given the gift of life, and then immediately after follows Genesis 22: "Take this son and sacrifice him." You have the wonderful story of the two sons, which often occurs in the Hebrew literature, but the notion of the beloved son and the call to give over the beloved son, the only-begotten son, becomes the very heart of the Jesus story and the Easter story. "This is my beloved son" is the cardinal verse of the New Testament: "God so loved the world that he gave his only son" (John 3.16).

Moderator: What does it mean within the Jewish tradition that this central or founding story is a story of sacrifice?

Jon D. Levenson: In the Bible, the story of the *Akedah*—which is the *binding* of Isaac because he isn't actually sacrificed—has to do with God's claim upon the first-born-son, which has to do with his claim on first fruits of the field, the flock, the herd, and the first fruits of human procreativity, namely, the first-born son. You also have Abraham as the paradigm of obedience to God. God commends him for his willingness to listen to His voice and not withhold his son. In the Jewish tradition, Abraham becomes a paradigm for obedience to Torah and *Mitzvah*—commandments in sacred scripture and most centrally in the Torah. You also have a connection in the late Second Temple period, around the second century b.c.e., that this is the origin of Passover, that the father's willingness to give up his son, who is then ransomed through the sacrifice of the ram in his place, is the origin of the *corbontessah*[1] of the paschal lamb. When you get

---

1. The literal meaning of the Hebrew term for sacrifice, *korban*, is "drawing near," because sacrifices were believed to restore the broken covenant relationship between the people and God.

a little further along in the Rabbinic tradition, the first to third centuries c.e., the Christian era, you find that this holiday is not associated much with Passover, but with *Rosh Hashanah*. This is the celebration of the new year in Judaism, and it has to do with the idea of radical dedication to God, dedication even, if necessary, unto death. But it also has to do with God's granting a reprieve, answering Abraham in his hour of agony and sparing the life of Isaac—just as Jews on *Rosh Hashanah* come into the divine courtroom knowing they are guilty but hoping for a second chance, just as Isaac is given a second chance.

Moderator: What sort of ethical or moral obligations does the Abraham story impose on people—their notions of virtue or morality—and how does it shape understanding of people's obligations toward others?

Ingrid Mattson: In the Muslim tradition, one of the things that's done on this holiday, the Feast of the Sacrifice, is that a lamb or some other kind of animal actually is slaughtered. Muslims are required to give one-third of the meat to the poor, another third to distribute among neighbors, and the remaining third people generally cook and invite others to share with them. So part of the symbolism of this day is to remember that you are part of a community, you have obligations to other, even those who cannot afford to themselves do a sacrifice. Even if you live in an affluent neighborhood, you may send the money to another country for people there to enjoy and share. This tradition goes back to the idea of unity, the unity of humankind, which is a very strong theme of *hajj*, the pilgrimage period that ends with this feast. People come from all over the world, dress the same, strip themselves of any kind of worldly sign of status, rank, or wealth. Now they are all there as human beings standing before God as they will on the Day of Judgment.

Kenneth L. Vaux: In all three of our faiths, this theme is used as the paradigm for suffering, for interpreting suffering and interpreting martyrdom. Jon Levenson can tell us more about this, but I think of the great *Akedah* texts of the Jews martyred under the Roman Empire, before Christ. They, along with the Christian martyrs under the Roman Empire and the Jewish martyrs of the 11th-century crusade, often use the *Akedah* text to interpret their plight. I draw on this theme for the Holocaust in our own time, and even today as we discuss genocide in places such as Kosovo. In all these crises, we hear reminiscences of *Akedah*. I heard a Serbian priest this morning talking of the crucifixion of his people, and I heard colleagues from the Albanian, Islamic side talking about the sacrifice those people are called on to offer. So *Akedah* becomes a paradigm for giving over one's life or being willing to lay down one's life for the Torah, for the good, for the Law, or for the beloved community.

Jon D. Levenson: As the story develops in the Jewish tradition, there is increasing emphasis on Isaac, not necessarily in place of Abraham, but alongside Abraham as a willing participant in what looks like will be his own death. So he becomes a kind of prototype of the Jewish martyr, someone put to death rather than renounce his faith, rather than refuse to observe the commandments of the Torah. In fact, there are traditions in Rabbinic or Medieval Judaism in which Isaac actually is sacrificed and is miraculously resurrected from the dead. But I would hesitate to see this story as primarily about virtue and morality; although a great deal of the Bible is, this story has a more foundational, fundamental significance. There is a tendency in the Jewish tradition to see Abraham as a paradigm of obedience to the commandments, so that you even have the notion of Abraham—who lived long before Sinai and certainly long before the Rabbinic tradition—observing in advance the entire Torah before it was given, including the commandments of the written Torah, but also the commandments elaborated in the Rabbinic literature from the *Talmudic* period thousands of years later. And, of course, *that* Torah is very much concerned with matters of justice and passion for the poor and fair dealing throughout society and among Jews and Gentiles alike.

Moderator: Can you talk about the links between the Abraham story and the call to monotheism?

Kenneth L. Vaux: Historically, we are talking about a wonderful period of human civilization with *Akhenaton* and Egyptian gods and pharaohs. Abraham is around that period, in the second millennium b.c.e. characterized by an enormous revolution in spiritual consciousness. It's at this time that humans first perceive God—and that singular God, that singular power or force who is the God of life and death also is the God of good and evil. So it is the moral deity that emerges.

Moderator: Jon Levenson, in *The Death and Resurrection of the Beloved Son*,[2] you talk about how the story of Abraham and Isaac becomes a paradigm for other stories in Judaism and becomes—even if the sons are not explicitly sacrificed—a template for certain themes that are retold over and over. Can you talk about that?

Jon D. Levenson: There are stories throughout Genesis of a father with a beloved son, or parents who have a son in whom they have invested a great deal. This is not merely the investment that all of us make in our children, but an investment in faith in response to a divine promise. To some degree, those stories tend to be about sibling rivalry and favoritism, which is troubling to many of us. Often the favored son is lost to the father and miraculously restored: one thinks of the favorite son Jacob, who is lost to his father Isaac and then restored. Or think of the favorite son Joseph, who is lost to his father Jacob. Jacob goes into mourning, assuming Joseph is dead and at the end of the story, we learn that Joseph miraculously is not only alive but ruling as the second to the pharaoh and saving the lives of his father and brothers in the years of famine. So while these are stories of sibling rivalry and parental favoritism that fractures a family, in the end, the family tends to be reunited and there tends to be reconciliation and reuniting. The unfavored son is able to graciously accept the fact that he is not favored, but this does not mean he is hated, despised, or read out of the family. The favorite son is able to learn, sometimes with great difficulty as in the case of Joseph, to act graciously and in a forgiving fashion toward the brothers who once, in rage and anger, tried to do him in. So that's a story that I think reverberates throughout the Bible and it is a paradigm. It's a foundational story for the people Israel themselves, for the Jewish people, in the particular trials in their history.

Ingrid Mattson: There is an important parallel to that story in Islam, but with a bit of a twist in that the Muslim tradition is not unanimous on which son actually was sacrificed or intended to be sacrificed. It's not important for the theology of Islam that one son or the other would have been the person selected for sacrifice, because this really is an example of submission or obedience to God. The fact is that the Muslim tradition does recognize that Isaac and Ishmael had different mothers and that,

---

2. See Levenson, *The Death and Resurrection of the Beloved Son.*

when Isaac was born, Ishmael did go with his mother to Arabia, and was sent off into an area that was a harsher and more difficult land. There now becomes a very interesting parallel to the sacrifice of Abraham and his son with the mother of Ishmael, who was left alone in the desert for some time with her son. It was hot, and she was desperately searching for water. She ran back and forth between two hills (*Safa* and *Marwah*), looking for water, and then God miraculously opened a spring under the heel or foot of the baby as he was lying there. This is a very similar theme, of a mother doing the best she can for her son and submitting herself to the will of God, but having to endure in a very difficult situation. In the end, God does save both the mother and the son through the miraculous spring that appears.

Jon D. Levenson: I might add that the story of the mother's near-grief as she sees her son about to die, in Genesis 21, is very powerful and there the focus is on the mother's grief and the mother's heroism. Whereas in the next chapter, Genesis 22, in which the story of the binding of Isaac takes place, the emphasis is on the father and we don't hear about the mother.

Moderator: Do you think that sets up two different models of parental roles? Or perhaps gendered ideas about obligation and duty? Certain critics of the Abraham/Isaac story have seen it as very patriarchal, very cruel, suggesting that the ultimate obligation to God means a willingness to sacrifice your very child, that it is not protection of the child that's lauded in the story, but rather willingness to sacrifice. But you're talking about a story where this tremendous effort is put forth to find water to protect the child.

Ingrid Mattson: In the Muslim tradition, both stories are remembered in the pilgrimage, which contains a number of different rituals, one of which near the end is the sacrifice of the lamb. But earlier in the pilgrimage, every pilgrim must repay that act of running back and forth between those two hills seven times. So both sides, both actions, both ways of obeying God must be remembered by both men and women.

Kenneth L. Vaux: The Jewish and Christian heritages accentuate this point. One of the wonderful *Akedah* texts in Judaism is in Maccabees, about

Hannah the mother and her sevens sons—and it's just as much saga about the mother as her seven sons are sacrificed, in this case, to the Roman authorities who demand an idolatrous expression. I think of Christianity and Palm Sunday, and the imagery there is so rich: you have the donkey, Jesus riding into Jerusalem on the donkey, which is a recapitulation of Abraham taking the donkey out to Mount Moriah. You have the crown of thorns in the passion. Pontius Pilate places a crown of thorns on the head of Jesus, and that is the bramble where the saving ram appears. There are so many rich images, but the maternal/paternal theme is strong because always in the background of the Christian text you have the mother of Jesus. The *Mater dolorosa*, the woman of sorrows. She is the powerful background of this whole saga.

Jon D. Levenson: In the Jewish tradition, God does intervene and call off the sacrifice, so we have a binding of Isaac, not a sacrificing of Isaac. Within the Jewish liturgy and the daily prayers of Judaism, Jews call upon God this way. We say that as Abraham suppressed his mercy, which was difficult for him to do, it is difficult for fathers and mothers to suppress their mercy, so God should suppress his anger and forgive. God should show mercy to correspond to Abraham's titanic struggle to suppress his paternal mercy and to obey the divine command. So again, you have both the element of radical self-giving and radical obedience to what seems like a very horrific command. You also have a notion of grace, forgiveness, and mercy at tempering the whole story.

Ingrid Mattson: I should mention that Muslims believe that Jesus is a prophet. His story is mentioned in the Qur'an in many places, and there's a very strong parallel between how Jesus' life and sacrifice is represented with that of Abraham and his son. Because just as God is said to have intervened and saved Abraham's son, so God is said to have intervened and saved Jesus so that although people intended to kill him, God miraculously at the last minute substituted someone who appeared to look like him, put him in his place and that Jesus is in fact still alive with God at this time. So there's a very strong parallel between the two stories.

Moderator: What is the effect of the sacrifice on Sarah? Isn't there a Jewish tradition that says the ordeal drove her to her death because she was so disappointed with what her husband had done?

Jon D. Levenson: There is a Jewish tradition that believes Sarah died because of the binding of Isaac. That is to say she dies in chapter 23, right after the *Akedah* in Genesis 22. I don't know that it's disappointment, she might be dismayed, it might be shock, or it might be the interference of some sort of demonic figure that some of the *midrashim* suggest approaches Isaac or Sarah. It's not a story with a completely happy ending. That is to say, it is undoubtedly a horrifying, dramatic story for all involved.

Moderator: There seems to be great good in the understanding relations between the different faith traditions that come out of this story.

Jon D. Levenson: Yes, especially between Judaism and Christianity. It's more complicated to include Islam, although Islam should be included. In other words, you do see the favored son, the favored son is Jacob, who is the son of Isaac, the favored son of Abraham. But Jacob is in fact also named Israel, and in a sense this is the paradigm of the origins of the people Israel. It's not simply biography, it's also natural history, with all the difficulties that come with parental favoritism, with God's election, singling out a particular family, a particular natural family in history and all the abuse and contempt and danger that that designation subjects the favored family to. We also have the internal temptation toward arrogance or severance from the larger community that has to be overcome. So it is a kind of relationship between Judaism and Christianity as to who is the beloved son. In Christianity, there's a strong tendency even in the New Testament to try to replace Isaac with Jesus as the favored son. So the seed of Abraham is in Jesus in the New Testament and even the *corbontessah*, even the paschal lamb is identified with Jesus himself. So you can see a certain intercommunal strife originating in a common text, which is the Hebrew Bible.

Moderator: How would Christianity frame that tension?

Kenneth L. Vaux: The great drama of human history is about the kind of struggle of the children Jon Levenson has mentioned. The burden of my own work is to try to find ways of rapprochement between these three great Abrahamic faiths. It seems to me that something very tragic happens in Christian history when it becomes anti-Semitic, when it rejects Torah.

When Paul moves against James, the brother of Jesus, and the Jewish Christians and becomes more Aegean, Greek, and Roman—more Eurocentric—and similarly when that great leap occurs in the emergence of Christianity, when it skips even the Middle East and ignores Arabia and becomes an occidental phenomenon, a serious distortion occurs. To me it's so important in the Christian tradition to recover Torah and recover Abraham. One of the most powerful images in Christianity, a paschal image, is in chapter 5 of Revelation, where there is the Lamb of God on the throne holding the scroll, the Torah, and that is the image in Handel's *Messiah*, the One to whom all power and majesty and might and wisdom belong. The rapprochement of these faiths, it seems to me, is very critical especially today.

Moderator: Is it reasonable to say that this story, the sacrifice story, also contains within it the notion of chosen ones and chosen people,, and this is one of the ideas that sort of keeps the three traditions apart? The idea that each tradition is the chosen one and the other ones have gone astray or are misled or missed the boat somewhere along the way is divisive, so does the story contain the seeds of division as well as of unity?

Kenneth L. Vaux: The peoples of God are chosen in particularity for universality. To me, that is the meaning of Abraham: his seed will be like the sands of the sea and the stars of the heavens. The Jews are to be a light to the Gentiles. I think that when we ethnocentrize it, when we make it us against them, we destroy the spirit of the Abraham tradition.

Jon D. Levenson: Would you agree that there is a tendency in Christianity and Christian literature, especially in the West, to see the Church as somehow universal and the Jews as somehow tribal or particularistic in a sense in which the Church is not? In other words, one of the things that gets lost in the identification of Jesus with Isaac over the centuries is a sense that it does involve a singling out, an act of favoritism—and is not simply an affirmation of primordial humanity, all children of Adam, but that there is a specific community with its own particular rights. Just as in the case of the Jews, there is a specific community with its own particular rights.

Kenneth L. Vaux: And when ethnocentrism or nationalism override the centrality of the faith and the ethical imperatives that come from that, I think danger ensues.

Jon D. Levenson: But what I'm asking is this: is there also a danger that comes from a kind of universalistic reading that misses the fact that it is a particular natural family that is mysteriously and bafflingly selected for this special destiny?

Kenneth L. Vaux: I think the biblical history of the Abrahamic tradition is both celebrative of a particular culture and particular faith, but also affirmative of our common humanity and of the destiny we have in the world to see one human community, that we are all the children of Abraham.

Ingrid Mattson: There is a chapter in the Qur'an that's actually titled "The Pilgrimage," that discusses many of these events we're talking about today. It is very interesting, because in that chapter, in connection with the story of Abraham, the Qur'an says that every people has its own rights and its own practices and that all of these were given to them by God. But there's also a very interesting verse in that chapter that talks about Abraham as neither Christian nor Jew but a Muslim. Now what does that mean? Obviously, it cannot mean Muslim in the sense of what we mean now by this community that follows the Qur'an because it obviously was not revealed at that time. But it means Muslim in the sense of someone who submits themselves to God. I think this is something that even Muslims themselves forget in making Islam a kind of birthright or an identity—that as long as you are born to a Muslim family somehow you've got it made, or as long as you call yourself Muslim, rather than actually being a person who submits themselves to God. So that Islam itself can become, with some people, this kind of special identity that is separate from their actions. This text means that you don't have any special privilege unless you actually follow—do the right things, do the right actions—submit yourself to God.

Moderator: But you're talking about an identity that is sometimes more familial or cultural or ethnic than one based on the demands of the faith?

Ingrid Mattson: Exactly. When a certain geographical community, for example, or neighborhood, identifies themselves as one religious community, so that it becomes a kind of communal identity rather than a faith commitment, then you have problems because then it's my group against your group. Even Isaac is mentioned after the story of Abraham as someone who was righteous, who submitted himself to God and had children, some of whom were righteous and some of whom were not. So there's not a real rivalry between Isaac and Ishmael and even the children of Ishmael—some can be good, some can be bad, there's no guarantee for either.

Moderator: If my understanding is correct, it was not uncommon for children to be sacrificed in the Near Eastern religions at that time. And so I have understood that part of the point of the story of Abraham and Isaac was that this God would not demand that kind of sacrifice. Rather than having your children be burned or killed, if you worshipped this God, your children would be saved and allowed to live. Is this accurate?

Jon D. Levenson: Generally speaking, child sacrifice was uncommon in the religions of the ancient Near East. The Torah sets itself uncompromisingly against child sacrifice. On the other hand, with the subject of the sacrifice of the first-born son, which is a kind of first-fruits offering, the picture is more complicated. In this case of Genesis 22, the sacrifice is called off, it's the *binding* of Isaac in the Jewish tradition, it's not the *sacrificing* of Isaac. On the other hand, God explicitly rewards Abraham and blesses him because he didn't withhold his son, his favored son. So he obeys the command and fortunately does not have to carry it out. Of course, the whole Jewish tradition in the Torah itself, certainly in a text like Leviticus 20, is unalterably opposed to the idea of child sacrifice.

Kenneth L. Vaux: The theological complexity is so profound. It seems to me that Christianity almost picks up more on the threads of Judaism that say Isaac actually was sacrificed, that tradition that picks up on the theme of the ashes. Granted, this could be the ashes of the ram's horn that were burned and so the *shofar*. But Christianity essentially says: in this God, with this son, they went all the way. The meaning of the Easter sacrifice is profoundly ambivalent, profoundly mysterious.

Jon D. Levenson: Would you agree that, to some extent, Christianity revisions God in the image of Abraham, that is to say the loving father who graciously donates his first-born son, that to some extent Christianity picks up on this story by putting God in the role of Abraham?

Kenneth L. Vaux: I do, and I also think you also have the obedient son. Paul has a passage in Romans that captures your point about Abraham and Isaac: "He who did not withhold his own Son, but gave him up for all of us, will he not with him also give us everything else?" (Rom 8.32) This passage keeps both of these themes together.

Ingrid Mattson: There is an important ethical message in this story as well, because even though no one is supposed to go out and slaughter their children for God, there are very difficult times where you may have to put your children in a situation where they may very well be killed for a certain ideal. I mean just think about what the American military is doing right now: parents are called upon to freely let their children go and fight for a higher cause and put them in harm's way. There certainly will be some people who will die. Here there is a message that, although our duty as parents is to protect our children and to give them everything we possibly can for their own good, sometimes what may be for the good of all humanity is that we might have to agree to see them off to go into harm's way.

Moderator: But that implies a certain tension in the story. In other words, you have to be willing to do that, but you also have to know that this is the ultimate sacrifice. In other words, that the cause for which it is being done is something as good as the fact of being asked by God to do it.

Ingrid Mattson: Then it becomes a good for them as well, because good is not simply the material goods of this world but something else, a higher ideal, a higher cause.

Jon D. Levenson: But sacrifice is not sacrifice if what is given up is not supremely precious.

Moderator: I have noticed that Abraham is not only a concept, but the very foundation for Muslims. The *hajj* to Mecca involves circling the *Ka'ba*, which is the temple-like black structure. Here, the Muslims circle around a structure that, in Islam, is believed to have been built by Abraham. In Christianity, Abraham does a parallel act—the ultimate in faith and love and devotion in sacrificing the son. And for Jews, Abraham symbolizes the leader of the oppressed who left Babylon for the Promised Land and the fertile crescent of Israel.

Jon D. Levenson: It's also the case for Jews, Abraham's binding of Isaac at Mount Moriah is seen as the foundational sacrifice for the temple. The temple in Jerusalem, as early as Chronicles, identifies Moriah with the temple itself. This becomes the original foundational sacrifice that I think carries over into Christianity and Islam in different ways.

Moderator: We've talked about mothers in this story, and sometimes the role of the mothers can be obscured in the retelling of the story. But I would like to raise a question of why there are no daughters in this story, of what the significance of that is. You've talked about the first-born son and his prominence, but is it significant that it's not a daughter?

Ingrid Mattson: Nothing is made of it, it's not significant. There's no emphasis put on the fact that it is a son. I think this simply reflects the culture of the time. Boys were the ones to be put in harm's way. It would be boys who were put in situations of battle, boys were the ones who carried the name of the family, who could take care of parents when they were older. Often girls, when they were married, would go on to live with another family. So there's a certain culture at that time that makes it more of a tragedy when the oldest son is killed. He is the one to carry on and take care of the family.

Moderator: Does it suggest that a son is a better, more worthy sacrifice than a daughter?

Jon D. Levenson: No, it doesn't say that. Again, there are traditions in the Bible that the first-born son—not to say a son in general, but the first-born, the one who opens the womb, who is the first fruit—is therefore owed to God and must be somehow rendered to God. Jews still observe this. Observant Jews follow this in the form of *Pidyon HaBen*—ransoming of the son from the priest through a gift of silver dollars.[3] I should add that there is in the Bible, in Judges 11, a story of the sacrifice of a daughter of the judge Jephthah. Jephthah has no son, only a daughter, and he knows that he'll sacrifice whoever is the first to come out to greet him when he returns from victory over the Ammonites. He ends up having to sacrifice that person at her insistence, and it is his only daughter.

Kenneth L. Vaux: One of the great Greek stories is when Agamemnon sacrifices his daughter, Iphigenia, to gain safe passage of his ships. I think also today of the women and children pouring across the border of Kosovo into Albania and Macedonia. Why is it women and children? Because the men and the sons are taken out and killed together. There's something cultural that compels that. But sons and daughters, men and women are drawn into this human significance, and the main story of Abraham and Isaac is God's rescue, "Do not lay a hand on the child." Your propensity is to kill, but the command of God is life and resurrection.

Ingrid Mattson: I would also say that it would really backlash in the context of the time to sacrifice a daughter, at least in the time the Qur'an was revealed. The Qur'an condemns the pre-Islamic Arabs for female infanticide—they demeaned women so much that they often committed female infanticide. So the intervention of God in the Qur'an for female babies is to save them from this terrible cultural practice.

Moderator: Picking up on the theme you mentioned about the patriarchal aspects of this, I think of the Pat Barker books that deal with World War I and explicitly suggest that patriarchal societies send off sons to be sacrificed in war as a way of reinforcing the patriarchy. And I wonder, are you familiar with these books—*Regeneration, The Eye in the Door, The Ghost Road*—one of which won the Booker Prize? These are powerful explanations of war in general and World War I in particular.

---

3. *Pidyon HaBen* means "redemption of the first-born son." In ancient times, the first-born son was dedicated to the priesthood; in the *Pidyon HaBen* ritual, the son is redeemed from the *Kohen* (priest).

Kenneth L. Vaux: You may know the poems of Wilfred Owen, the First-World-War poems. He was killed just hours before the armistice. His poem, "The Parable of the Old Man and the Young," became the offertorium in Benjamin Britten's *War Requiem*, and if you listen to that recording, you have Dietrich Fischer-Dieskau portraying a German solider and Peter Pears as a British solider singing this *Akedah* text. The Abraham goes forth to the mountain and, in his last few lines, sings of the father slaying "the seed of Europe" one at a time.[4] I think it's a powerful story of the continuing saga of human pain and suffering and deliverance.

Jon D. Levenson: I think it's dangerous to associate sacrifice with simply death and war and murder or genocide. I think sacrifice has a different motivation. I think the person doing the sacrificing loves what he sacrifices and resists wanting to give it up and does so in the selfless service of God. So that even though none of us would condone sacrifice today, I think conflating it with murder and bloodshed and killing in general—which are all around us and are more easy for us to relate to—is very dangerous and leads to very profound misunderstandings about what the *Akedah* is all about.

AKEDIC READINGS IN JUDAISM AND ISLAM

The Akedah in the Palestinian Targums

To begin a practical discussion of a common God, I recite the litany of the *Akedah* (the binding of Isaac) from Géza Vermès, the renowned Judaist from Oxford—his exposition of the interpretation of Genesis 22 in the Palestinian *Targums*.[5] The biblical account of Abraham's ordeal may be summarized as follows:

1. Abraham was ordered by God to sacrifice Isaac as a burnt offering on a mountain in the land of Moriah (vv. 1–2).

2. He departed the next morning accompanied by Isaac and two servants. On the third day of his journey, he saw the mountain and, leaving his servants behind, went on with his son. Isaac carried the wood for the sacrifice (vv. 3–6).

---

4. Benjamin Britten, *War Requiem*, op. 66 (1961).
5. Vermès, *Scripture and Tradition in Judaism*, 192–95.

3. To Isaac's question concerning the victim, the patriarch answered evasively: God will see for Himself a lamb (vv. 7–8).

4. Abraham built an altar, bound Isaac, and made ready to kill him, but an angel prevented him from doing so (vv. 9–12).

5. He discovered a ram and offered it in the place of Isaac and called the place *Yahweh Yireh* ("God sees") (vv. 13–14).

6. As a reward for Abraham's obedience, God renewed His promises to him (vv. 15–18).

7. Abraham returned to his servants and they traveled on together to Beer-Sheba (v. 19).

When the *Targumic* sources, which usually contain the simplest form of exegetical translation, are examined, they reveal two different types of exegesis. The primitive kernel is represented by the Fragmentary *Targum* and *Neofiti*, but Pseudo-JONATHAN and a *Tosefta* fragment of *Targum Yerushalmi* (Jerusalem *Targum*) give a secondary version of the original interpretation.[6]

The following is a translation of the Fragmentary *Targum*. (The variant readings of *Neofiti* affecting the meaning of the account are given in the footnotes.)

> *xxii.* 8. And Abraham said: The Word of the Lord shall prepare a lamb for Himself.[7] If not, my son, you shall be the burnt offering.[8] And they went together with a quiet heart.[9]
>
> *xxii.* 10. Abraham stretched out his hand and took the knife to kill Isaac his son. Isaac answered and said to Abraham his father: Bind my hands properly that I may not struggle in the time of my pain and disturb you and render your offering unfit[10] and be cast into the pit of destruction in the world to come. The eyes of Abraham

---

6. Ms. T-S, B 8/9, published by P. Grelot, *Une Tosephta targumique sur Genèse xxii dans un manuscrit liturgique de la Geniza du Caire*, in *REJ*, xvi (cxvi), 1957, 5–26.

7. *Neof.*: "A lamb for the burnt offering shall be prepared from before the Lord." The 2*TJ* reading is given in the margin of *Neof.*

8. *Neof.*: "You are the lamb of the burnt offering."

9. *Neof.*: "With a perfect heart." The 2*TJ* version is inscribed in the margin.

10. *Neof.*: "Bind me properly that I may not kick (resist) you and your offering be made unfit."

were turned to the eyes of Isaac, but the eyes of Isaac were turned to the angels of heaven. Isaac saw them[11] but Abraham did not see them. In that hour, the angels of heaven[12] went out and said to each other: Let us go and see the only two just men in the world.[13] The one slays, and the other is being slain. The slayer does not hesitate, and the one being slain stretches out his neck.

xxii. 14. Abraham worshipped and prayed the Name of the Word of the Lord, and said: O Lord, You are He that sees and is unseen.[14] I pray: all is revealed before You. It is known before You that there was no division in my heart at the time[15] when You told me to offer Isaac my son, and to make him dust and ashes before You. But I departed immediately in the morning and did Your word with joy and fulfilled it.[16] Now I pray for mercy before You, O Lord God, that[17] when the children of Isaac come to a time of distress, You may remember on their behalf the binding of Isaac their father, and loose and forgive them their[18] sins and deliver them from all distress, so that the generations which follow him may say: In the mountain of the Temple of the Lord, Abraham offered Isaac his son, and in this mountain—of the Temple—the glory of the *Shekhinah* of the Lord was revealed to him.

The distinctive features of this oldest *Targumic* narrative are:

1. Abraham told Isaac that he was to be the sacrificial victim.

2. Isaac gave his consent.

3. He asked to be bound so that the sacrifice might be perfect.

4. He was favored with a heavenly vision (omitted).

5. Abraham prayed that his own obedience, and Isaac's willingness, might be remembered by God on behalf of Isaac's children.

6. His prayer was answered. Although God's reply is missing

11. *Neof.*: omitted.
12. *Neof.*: "A heavenly voice."
13. *Neof.*: "The only two in my world."
14. *Neof.*: omitted.
15. *Neof.*: "The first time."
16. *Neof.*: "Your decree."
17. *Neof.*: omitted.
18. *Neof.*: "Listen to the voice of their prayer and answer them."

here, it was obviously inferred from Genesis xxii, vv. 17–18, as an old liturgical formula quoted in the *Mishnah*, shows: May He who answered Abraham on Mount Moriah, answer you, and may He listen to the voice of your cry this day![19]

In short, instead of reducing his role to that of a passive victim, as the Bible does, the Targum ascribes to Isaac an active and prominent part in the story of the *Akedah*.

Islamic Narrative of Akedah

To this dramaturgic recitation, I add the crucial elements of the Islamic narrative (from Sura 37.102):

- The son is not named. It could be Isaac, the son of Abraham and Sarah or Ishmael, the son of Abraham and Hagar.
- Abraham tells the son about the dream he has had.
- While Abraham prays for an heir, God gives him news of a coming son.
- In *hadith*, the purported sayings of the Prophet, Muhammad says that when Abraham is ready to sacrifice his son, the knife slips away three times.
- Finally, Abraham gets hold of himself and proceeds to sacrifice the son out of faithful obedience.
- The rescue replacement ram is carried to Abraham from paradise and the son is spared. (Abraham now resides as the loving heart of God to Earth in paradise, "the bosom of Abraham.")
- The Festival (or Feast) of Sacrifice, *Eid al-Adha*, the major festival in Islam, commemorates this pivotal moment in the faith. After the days of vision and days of knowledge comes the day of sacrifice—commemorating that the deed was enacted and must now be reenacted.
- In the journey to Mecca, the ram (or sheep, cattle, or camel) is sacrificed. To this day, the faithful carry this roast of sacrifice to neighbors (asking for forgiveness) and to the

---

19. *Ta'an.*, ii, 4.

poor. The meaning of the parable seeks to be the restoration of fractured fraternity and community, reconciliation with God and the accomplishment of justice and peace with the poor.

THE AKEDIC HISTORY OF GOD

The following reflections on the theological hermeneutics of the theme of *Akedah* offer insights on the history of God in the three faiths.[20]

Judaism

Judaism's *Akedah* is formative for all subsequent Abrahamic faith and for human history. Cutting through archaic and primordial religion, where abstract cosmic force and substance perdure in infinite stasis and superstition, Abraham and his offspring Israel meet, then introduce to history, a God who speaks and acts. This God goes out, cares, yearns, seeks, gives, and hopes. This God is by definition disturbing and disruptive. Despite the Genesis cosmology—crafted in the crisis of exile and claiming that divine word and will stills a restless disorder and draws cosmos from chaos—in truth, the creature is now put on edge, on guard. Humans now find themselves under observation and expectation. The God of creation, of the garden, the One who pries and intrudes, One who won't leave us alone.

Yahweh God, who presents himself as "I am" or "I will be," becomes known as demand and draw, requirement and acceptance, setting the world in directional purpose and enlisting faithful community in that endeavor. The sustaining goal for the world, as the rabbis taught, is *tikkun olam* (the healing of the world) or the "kingdom of God."

Abraham is *al-Khalil*, the friend of God. Like Jesus at the Emmaus rest stop, God sits down to meal with Abraham. Yet Karen Armstrong reminds us that "He inspires terror and insists upon distance."[21] Singular devotion is demanded even in that age when the plurality of deity is self-evident. "No other gods" makes sense only when there is an experienced pantheon. The attempt to make *Yahweh* the only God might seem plausible if times are good and the Deuteronomic blessings and relief of adversaries ensue. But this God is no "font from whom all blessings flow."

---

20. Vaux, *Jew, Christian, Muslim*, 58–73.
21. Armstrong, *A History of God*, 21.

This God puts folk to the test, takes them toward the unknown, sets in motion a spiritual journey that can best be called "an ordeal." Here the *Akedic* character of the nature of history and the history of God comes into focus. God has gone out to the world in loving risk. In freedom, humanity is invested with responsibility and destiny. Divine venture and human plight meet to precipitate crisis, well depicted by the electric finger-touch on the creation fresco of the Sistine ceiling. *Akedah* is inevitable within this potent crossfire. *Emmanuel* (God with us) requires holiness and compatibility. Estrangement demands price. Finding out who we are provokes us to examine where we have gone wrong, what we have become, and where we need to go.

The heart of the crisis, which requires costly reconciliation, is moral. God wills the fulfillment of life and the just ordering of interhuman associations and relationships with the world. Humans strive for self-aggrandizement and exploitation of others and the world. God wills that the creation be sustained and flourish. Man seeks to tear it apart and use it up in self-indulgence. A *dénouement* or *Götterdämmerung* is provoked. The options remain: God must be banished (Nietzsche), humanity destroyed, or costly rapport purchased. *Akedah* propounds this salvation story. Judaism effects this with rigorous covenant, chastening martyrial history, culminating in Holocaust, and exacting Diaspora. Apocalyptic Judaism and Christianity resolve the crisis in suffering messiology, Islam in Ishmael's travail, a perpetual sacrifice in the face of the world's violence—all *Akedah*.

In the liturgical and calendric history of Israel, we find a clue to the Hebraic theology of *Akedah*. The Abraham/Isaac tradition is celebrated not on Yom Kippur, the Day of Atonement, but on *Rosh Hashanah*, the celebration of the new year. According to the *Rosh Hashanah* liturgy, this is ". . . a day of remembrance, a day for blowing the *shofar* (ram's horn, Isaac's vicar), a holy convocation, a memorial for the departure from Egypt." This dating signifies that in the history and character of God, *Akedah* is not primarily a matter of sacrifice and expiation, but a matter of victory, resurrection, and new life.

For Judaism, *Akedah* is an historical legacy. This history or destiny of God's redemptive "Way" in the world is woven into *Akedah*. *Akedah* is a proto-martyrial and paradigmatic moment, a precedent of faith by whose sacrifice all subsequent generations will live. In the *Talmud* of Genesis *Rabah*, *midrash* on *Akedah* from the fourth or fifth century c.e., the event is spoken of as a "living memorial," something like the dynamic perpetuity of the "cross of Christ." It is not only an ancient example of faith, but an expression of faith with ongoing efficacy. The history of God, in other words, is redemptive history. The constitutive events of Israel's history, exodus, Sinai and exile, for example, not only signal the constant and ongoing character of God, but carry on a liberating chastening spirit among the faithful community. In *Rosh Hashanah*, the ram's horn of Isaac celebrates Sinai and the overture of law into the world. As Carol Delaney summarizes, the horn ". . . created on the sixth day of creation . . . is a clarion call of God's ongoing rule over creation and will sound again in the last days."[22] Weaving together etiology and eschatology in the history of God with the world further corroborates our thesis in reconciling salvation and social justice. *Akedah* signifies Passover and temple sacrifice as well as exodus, exile, and all aspects of historical deliverance. It parables the faith and work of God in the world.

Another aspect of the history of God in Hebrew history arises from this complementarity of salvation/sacrifice and liberation/justice. These themes focus on the controversial issue of messianic history and the question, "Who is the messiah?," one of the great "servant" texts of the exilic author Isaiah introduces the paradoxical vision of the servant as leper:

> He was despised and rejected by others;
> a man of suffering and acquainted with infirmity;
> and as one from whom others hide their faces
> he was despised, and we held him of no account.
>
> Surely he has borne our infirmities
> and carried our diseases;
> yet we accounted him stricken,
> struck down by God, and afflicted.
> But he was wounded for our transgressions,
> crushed for our iniquities . . . (Isa 53.3–5)

How does *yahid*, "the favored one," the servant, the beloved son (*agapetos*), become the "despised one"? Assuming that this is both a personal, proleptic text and a public text (referring to an individual, yes, but primarily to the corporate community—to the social history of the people), the history of God is a process that seeks to shape an individual and communal *Akedah*—a way of life.

22. Delaney, *Abraham on Trial*, 119.

The sheep that "before its shearer is silent" (Isa 53.7) is one who bears the iniquity of all persons who, like "sheep have gone astray" (v. 6). Resonating with this the calendric book of Jubilees, Judaism times *Akedah* at the moment when the Passover lambs are sacrificed in the temple. History, as *Heilsgeschichte* (holy history), is the story of God. For Hebrew writers, biblical and extra-biblical, that story involves risky outgoing, a covenant, a bearing of the burden caused by breach of that covenant and misspent freedom. The way of God follows through in justice and love, concluding in a gift of life and an ensuring redemption. In this saga, Judaism is the "light to the world."

The enigmatic history of the Jewish people raises troubling implications for the history of the God of Israel. In Deuteronomic biblical theology, God leads the faithful people to prosperity (Promised Land) and leads a faithless and unjust people into punishment and exile. The history of persecution, martyrdom, ghettoization, and Holocaust bring conflict and anguish in light of this heritage. "Why did the heavens not darken?" asks Arno Mayer, Princeton's historian of the European Holocaust, echoing the *Akedic* suicide at Mainz.[23] The silence, disengagement, even justice of God, becomes deeply problematic. To the mind of this privileged Christian observer of God's chosen people, one who agonizes over this persecutorial history and the Church's complicity and causality in it, I ask whether the *Akedic* history of God may in some way interpret that horror. Ironically, God's people Israel, along with the poor and despised of the world, may bear the messianic cross out through time.

To sum up this cursory overview of the history of God in Hebrew religion, God is a god of word, will, wisdom, and way. Primordial, Parmidean religion resists the notion of divine expression and historical activity, especially when that manifestation is concrete. Buddhism, for example, resists even the notion of the existence of God (which also may be a biblical belief). Abraham and the patriarchs, prophets, and priests dare to follow and meet Yahweh in concrete, disturbing, and communicative presence. Divine disclosure is concrete, direct command received by Abraham, Jacob, Moses, or the prophets.

Word is a prime quality of the history of the God of Israel. Without this, *Akedah* is hallucination. That God is good will, and not the peeved and petulant deity of the Greek gods or the tribal deities of forest and

---

23. See Mayer, *Why Did the Heavens Not Darken?*

Christianity

Christianity is founded in this *Akedic/yahidic* (beloved son-servant) tradition. Jesus sustains the heritage of Isaac. Ironically, the most a-historical sect of Judaism, Christianity creates the most palpable and problematic history. A decidedly apolitical itinerant Galilean rabbi-teacher becomes the occasion for the political transformation of movements called Jewish-, then Gentile-Christianity. These, in turn, transform the Western world and in recent centuries, global society. The *Akedah* for this movement becomes the way of suffering transformation or of triumphing catastrophe. In the spirit of Torah and Decalogue, the early Christian movement was called "The Way." "See how they love each other" was an early designation. It was an irenic, pacifist movement that eventually created an empire. Initially, the resistance to Roman power was less exaggerated in either establishment Judaism or even the apocalyptic Judaism that gave it birth. With its foundational constituency gathered from secularized workers, people of the land, and Jesus' own family circle of Davidite Galileans, the movement focused on simple Torah righteousness ("love of God and neighbor") and ethical piety. As it proceeded into Paul's Gentile mission and the apostolic conversion of the Roman Empire, the Christian community became a mystically-derived ("Christ in me"), Spirit-driven, evangelical movement. God had come near to his long exiled people, "those who walk in darkness have seen a great light." This intense experience and vision of new existence (*en Christou*) categorically displaced the more eclectic piety of the Hellenistic world in which one could be both Jew and Christian. It became a forceful worldly commitment that eventuated in the Constantinian Christian Empire.

This phenomenon of the fourth and fifth centuries preceded the rise of Islam by a handful of generations. Islam may in fact be caused by the neglect of Arabia in both Judaism and Christianity. In any case, radical and existential piety became state religion. All this would contribute to the *Akedic* history of the Christian God. In the frightful anti-Semitic and then anti-Islamic debacle from Constantine to the Crusades to the Holocaust, Abraham's call to kill the "beloved son" overcame the call to save and sustain. The forwarding groundwork of *Akedah* is given in discernment of the God of Israel who became "The God and Father of our Lord Jesus

Christ." In the primitive Christian community, the God story underwent a subtle, but Earth-changing, transformation. In Fitzmyer's *Romans*, for example, he argues that those caught up in the Jesus movement, especially the nascent Gentile Christian side of the movement, interpreted the messianic event—life, obedience, suffering, death, resurrection of Jesus—in *Akedic* terms, *i.e.*, in terms of vicarious sacrifice for the people of Israel and the world. No similar usage is found in the first-century Hebrew texts: ". . . That Isaac was to be sacrificed on behalf of Israel, or on behalf of anyone else, is never mentioned."[24]

In my thesis, the early Christian apostles and the apologists of the first three centuries learned *Akedah* from Israel, through the mediation of Hebrew Christians—like James the brother and Mary the mother of Jesus—and from the Jerusalem congregation.

They in turn gave theological history an *Akedic* twist as Pauline, Petrine, Lukan, Markan, even Johannine schools, slowly accented existential consciousness. "Christ-in-you" mysticism, spirited enthusiasm, along with a decided turn against performance of the "Way" ensued. Experience, not performance, became central to salvation. The sacrifice quality of *Akedah* often took hold without the ethical component. To me, this is the danger, as salvational Christianity stripped of Jewish ethics led to the cultural accommodation of the Christianized/Roman Empire. Before long, Holy War, then Crusade, was being waged against not only Islam, but also against Diaspora Israel.

Two fundamental concepts derived from Judaism, but distinctively different, shaped the Christian God-story. The first is the concept—inimical to Judaism, at least in its triumphalist caste—that Jesus is the crucified messiah and that indeed God is "the crucified God."[25] This rendition of the story of God was drawn from Jewish messianic literature about the son, the servant, the savior (Messiah) in texts such as Psalm 2, 22, 89, 110, Isaiah 42 and 53. But these texts were measured and interpreted by the experience of the life and teaching, but more the suffering, death, and resurrection of Jesus. This lens into the Christ-event shaped both the Jewish and the Christian God-story. It is not far from the mark to say, from what we know today of faith and ethics from the first century b.c.e. through to the Christian era, that Judaism forms Christianity and Christianity forms

---

24. Fitzmyer, *Romans: Anchor Bible*, 531–32.
25. See Moltmann, *The Crucified God*.

Judaism. This reciprocity and mutual formation, with all its gifts of grandeur and danger, focuses in *Akedah*.

The second concept involves the logic and necessity in this very concept of the crucified messiah. In the tale of the will of God for the world, Jesus must live, suffer, die, and be raised for the efficacy of his destiny and for the "Way" of God to be accomplished. There is no resurrection without the death and no death without the resurrection. Pain and deliverance is reality concomitant with creation and freedom. This paradoxical confounding of Jewish messianic logic is buttressed by a plethora of New Testament texts that seek to fathom the Jesus experience both pre- and post-resurrection and to refute heretical tendencies to disjoin cross and crown.

From this theology arises the more normative *Akedic* history of God in Christianity as the "Lamb of God" heritage that leads Quakers and Mennonites, for example, to call the war of God in history the "war of the lamb." In John Howard Yoder's classic description, the "war of the lamb" is the powerful witness of martyrdom.[26] Here, Christians like Dietrich Bonhoeffer take up the cross and follow the Lord, living out the Gospel of God in keeping the commandments, enacting social justice in the love of God and care for the poor. This provokes the vengeful ire of the world inciting persecution "for righteousness' sake" (Matt 5.10). The war of the lamb is thus "filling up the suffering of Christ" (1 Pet 1.1) as *Akedah* is reenacted as the ongoing merciful sacrifice of the Son of God for the sins of the world. In this tradition, paschal mystery perpetually reenacts the grace of *Akedah*, Passover, the temple slaughter of the lambs, the crucifixion, and the white robes of the martyrs. The composite offering of body and blood, life and death, Eucharistically enlivens the church and world. The blood of God mingles in the tragedy of the world, even in the gnarled ruins of the World Trade Center.

The summary of the Christian story of God is to show us One who so suffered, One compassionate . . . for God is love.

Islam

I know so little about Islam. It has taken me many years to esteem her as a sister faith. I am still not well impressed with Qur'an as scripture, and I decry the antics of fundamentalist militants as much as I do the acts

---

26. See Yoder, *The Politics of Jesus*.

of Jewish religious belligerents or Christian crusaders. But I find myself looking more carefully these days at Islam for two reasons. First, in the aftermath of the events of September 11th, the whole world is prompted to better understand Islam. Second, in recent history, Muslims have acted more faithfully for the poor. In Africa and throughout the Middle East, Muslims are the champions of the oppressed. All too often Jews and Christians defend the privileged. That to me is an *Akedic* sign. The third attraction has come as I ponder *Akedah*. This later-day sister Abraham faith seems to fathom most completely and acutely the Abraham/Isaac sacrifice. At the ending of *hajj*, or *Eid al-Adha* (the Feast of Sacrifice), Muslims the world over bend the neck in prayer, recalling Isaac's contrite obedience. At this season, Muslim families sacrifice the lamb, analogously in faith, submit the carcass to the flame, then share the roast with the poor. What is the history of God (Allah) in Islam that supplies *Akedah*? Carol Delaney observes:

> ... Because Islam is conceptualized as a return or recall to the one true original religion given in the beginning to Abraham, his story may be more actively present in Islam than in either Judaism or Christianity.[27]

Abraham is a *bar mitzvah*, a son of the "Way" of God, prophesied to be an idol buster (iconoclast) so much that King Nimrod of Babylon orders all the first-born sons slaughtered. In that recurrent imagery, Abraham survives because his mother hides him in a cave. (Those who visit the rock cave in Bethlehem purporting to be the "stable" of Jesus' birth recall the force of this image.)

The connection between command, obedience, and transgression in *Akedah* is profound in Islam. The iconoclast strictly adheres to the structure of the first three commandments, where "no other gods," "no false idols" and no defamation of "the Name" are strictly enjoined. In my view, this connection between command, prevalent idolatry and blasphemy, injustice and evoked sacrifice is the essence of *Akedah*. Abraham is called to sacrifice Isaac (or Ishmael) as adherence to "first-fruits law" (Exod 22.28–29). It is also to test Abraham's loyalty ("no other gods") and his subordination of all other values, even his prized *agapetos*, the long awaited, only beloved son. Isaac also is a penitential and vicarious sacrifice. He is offered on behalf of the sin of the people and for the per-

---

27. Delaney, 184.

petuation of the people (the seed of Abraham). The rich tapestry of the act is expression of Torah faithfulness.

Muhammad rebuilds the *Ka'ba*, the temple of God, with the black stone (the staying hand of God?) as a recounting of *Akedah*. Henceforth the *hajj*, the journey of the faithful, will reenact the journey (and trial) of Abraham. This pilgrimage now becomes the paradigm for the meaning of God and our life.

The essence of the Muslim history of God is that of restoration. In human disobedience, the world has gone wrong and despoiled creation. Only an expression of human righteousness can recover the primeval harmony of God with his creature. In Judaism, Torah restores this concourse and congress.

> ... make straight in the desert a highway for our God. (Isa 40.3)

Jesus, the Son of God, effects the atonement and incarnates that way for Christendom. In Islam, in the spirit of law and Gospel (*Injil* and *Taurut*), Abraham becomes the prototype and representative of faithful and righteous humanity having accomplished rapprochement.

AKEDAH AND THE HUMAN CONDITION

How does *Akedah* inform the human condition, especially pain, disease, and suffering? Are social justice and individual responsibility, for example, a cause in human travail? If so, the phenomenon of human experience may corroborate the *Akedah* thesis. The prevalence of disease, suicide, poverty, and famine point to a deeper fracture within human flesh and within the body of humanity. This wound cries out against the powers of evil toward the power of God for the grace of deliverance. The human oblation is felt on Earth from the dawn of creation.

> The whole creation groans in the travail ...
> We groan within ourselves as we
> Wait for the redemption of our body ...
> We are killed all the day long ... regarded
> As sheep for the slaughter ... (Rom 8)

Human disease, even death, is a specter that we seek to do something about. The stigmata of the Fall or the Four Horses of the Apocalypse—war, disease, famine, death (Rev 6)—become not so much enigmas to which we submit, but entities to be construed as enemies, resisted in the arduous and apocalyptic contention of good and evil. Famine, writes Nobel Laureate Amartya Sen, is caused by poverty.

Three conclusions can be offered to verify the corroboration, which the human condition displays toward and receives from *Akedah*. They concern: a) the preeminence of life over death; b) the positive rendition of suffering and death; and c) the affirmation of sacrificial justice and caring love as the enduring essence of redemption.

- *Preeminence of life over death.* A fundamental premise of *Akedah* is that life has the final word over death. The final word at Moriah is not sacrifice and death, but rescue and resurrection. Life is a preeminent value in the Semitic theistic anthropology that emerges with the shadowy *hajj* of Abraham from *Haran*. The wandering faithful band bound in hope—which we call the *Habiru*—give to the world the assertion that the prime interpretative value in the God-loved world is *l'chaim*—life. A global health and well-being, therefore, is not a desirable dream or a worthy ambition, but an imperative, fundamental human right, a required condition that makes anything less, blasphemous.

- *Positive rendition of suffering and death.* Part of the materialistic and acquisitive ethos that has been fashioned in this land, which ought to be animated by Judeo, Christian, and Islamic values, is the biblical association of anxiety, acquisitiveness, and fear of death. Accepting mortality is the correlate of the love of life. Abrahamic trust in the reliable promise of God ("your seed . . .") and Christic trust in that father who is "able far beyond our imagination," fathoms that strength is hidden in weakness, that in death we are in life.

- *Justice and caring love as the enduring essence of redemption.* Sacrificial justice, rather than futile personal justification, is the *Akedic* purpose of life. Abraham gave over his only-beloved son, as did the God and Father of Jesus—Messiah for the remedy of sin and the healing of the world (*tikkun olam*). This self-abnegating justice in concern for others is the ultimate corroboration of *Akedah*.

The story of Abraham and Isaac has emerged in biblical history as the dominant parable for the way God deals with people and the way human experience is interpreted within the divine purview. The experiences of life and death, health and suffering, are analogies or parables between the story of God and the human story. *Akedah* mediates each reality to the other. *Akedah* is a normative parable that speaks to questions such as:

- What is happening in human life?
- Ought it to be this way?
- What has gone wrong?
- Why has it become this way?
- What is needed to make it right?
- How do we get there?
- How are we taken there?

AN INTERFAITH THEOLOGY OF AKEDAH

The striking continuity, commonality, and complementarity that I have begun to note among the three filial faiths of Abraham starts to compose what I would call a common theology. In the U.S., we like to call ours a Judeo-Christian nation. In the age of President Obama, we are becoming a Judeo-Christian-Muslim-secularist country. We are one people, one nation—red and blue—conservative and liberal, gay and straight, men and women, rich and poor. On a global scale, we seek to create "slum-dog millionaires"—one world where rich and poor, Americans and Africans, healthy and sick, well-to-do and down-and-out live in sacrificial sharing—*Akedah*. This is our rightful response to the God of Abraham—God who is Abraham's father and therefore ours. The father of Itzak, Ishmael, and Ieusus—this God asks that we live as a commonwealth, giving and sharing one to the other.

Our lives all intertwine. "We're all in the same boat," says one commentator on the present house-foreclosure crisis, "if our neighbor faces bankruptcy or foreclosure, we lose value on our own home." In Herman Melville's *Moby Dick*, he cites the Parable of the Monkey Rope. It is an *Akedic* metaphor, for *Akedah* is about binding, roping, and cutting . . . the ligatures of connection, care, and trust.

> ... You have seen Italian organ-boys holding a dancing ape by a long cord. Just so, from the ship's steep side, did I hold Queequeg down there in the sea, by what is technically called in the fishery a monkey-rope, attached to a strong strip of canvas belted 'round his waist.
>
> It was a humorously perilous business for both of us. For, before we proceed further, it must be said that the monkey-rope was fast at both ends, fast to Queequeg's broad canvas belt, and fast to my narrow leather one. So that, for better or worse, we two, for the time, were wedded; and should poor Queequeg sink to rise no more, then both usage and honor demanded that instead of cutting the cord, it should drag me down in his wake. So, then, an elongated Siamese ligature united us. Queequeg was my own inseparable twin brother; nor could I any way get rid of the dangerous liabilities which the hempen bond entailed.
>
> So strongly and metaphorically did I conceive of my situation then, that while earnestly watching his motions, I seemed distinctly to perceive that my own individuality was now merged in a joint stock company of two; that my freed will had received a mortal wound; and that another's mistake or misfortune might plunge innocent me into unmerited disaster and death. Therefore, I saw that here was a sort of interregnum in Providence; for its even-handed equity never could have so gross an injustice. And yet still further pondering—when I jerked him now and then from between the whale and ship, what would threaten to jam him— still further pondering, I saw, I saw that this situation of mine was the precise situation of every mortal that breathes; only in most cases, he, one way or the other, has this Siamese connection with a plurality of other mortals. If you banner breaks, you snap; if your apothecary by mistake sends you poison in your pills, you die.[28]

Melville's depiction of the human condition of inextricable reciprocity and shared destiny is both descriptive and normative truth. We are by natural condition intertwined with each other. If the flies gather on your neighbor's raw garbage, they fly across onto your child's tram. If your neighbor has a welcoming light in the parlor window, your safety is enhanced.

---

28. Melville, *Moby Dick*, 439.

AKEDIC EXISTENCE

But beyond this descriptive truth of mutual self-interest, there is a deeper normative truth: "Those who speak truth to power . . . will pay for it . . ." Martin Luther King, Jr. took the old Quaker phrase as his motto. Bonhoeffer echoed the wisdom in saying, "When Christ calls a man, he bids him come and die."[29] King's speech, "I've Been to the Mountaintop"[30] announces this deeper wisdom: "For those who want to save their life will lose it, and those who lose their life for my sake will find it." (Matt 16.25) It realizes the *Akedic* mystery, "Blessed are those who are persecuted for righteousness' sake, for theirs is the kingdom of heaven" (Matt 5.10).

The characteristics of *Akedic* existence arise on close reading of Kierkegaard's *Fear and Trembling*, in his portrayal of the *Akedah* of Abraham and Isaac.

- The command to obey in faith sends shudders through the soul.
- Breaking commands sends one on a journey into the unknown.
- The innocent mother's child is carried along unknowingly into that crisis.
- The "hero" or "poet" rescues the wanderer from moral oblivion.
- The hero is moral guide—the subject and object of one's love.
- Through the "hero" (Abraham), we know of eternal consciousness constituting the sacred human bond.
- Human heroism is measured by the greatness of one's love.
- "Divine madness" is highest human passion (the paroxysm of faith).
- "This world is in bondage to law of indifference while in world of spirit . . . only he that works gets the bread, he who was in anguish finds repose, he who descends the underworld rescues the beloved, only he who draws the knife gets Isaac."[31]

---

29. Bonhoeffer, *The Cost of Discipleship*, 44.

30. Martin Luther King, Jr., "I've Been to the Mountaintop," speech delivered April 3, 1968 to Mason Temple (Church of God in Christ Headquarters) in Memphis.

31. Kierkegaard, *Fear and Trembling*, 57.

- The life of responsibility is one of "labor, heavy laden . . . fear and dread."
- Moral authenticity is being condemned a "would-be killer" before the God who commands the mandatory sacrifice as "first-fruits offering."
- Authentic humanness must confront "divine madness."
- The "sword of God slays and saves."
- God tempts (allows adversary to tempt), yet God is love.
- God must be loved with "all one's soul," *i.e.*, even unto death.
- Loving God in faith reflects glory on God (*summum bonum*).
- Infinite resignation leads to "suspending the ethical."
- "Though he slay me, yet will I love him." (Job 13.15)
- "He resigned everything infinitely, and then grasped everything again by virtue of the absurd."[32]
- Knight finds right in self, not in external law (Luther).
- Self is receptor of spirit—will of God.
- In the finite world, the only thing that can save one is the absurd grasped through faith. The encasement and enslavement of finitude finds release in God known in contradiction to the world.
- The pathway to this release of life is command obedience through faith.
- Resignation (renunciation) is the eternal consciousness (love of God in faith [obedience]).
- Irony and humor (the absurd) inhere in faith.
- Temptation (*Anfechtung*, *Fristelse*) is assertion of particularity against universal.
- Yet in faith particulars (individuals) transcend the universal and touch the absolute.

32. Ibid., 70.

- Abraham's act is absurd (*skandalon*), like the cross of Christ.
- It is beyond reason, logic, goodness, even justice.
- Human duty to God is absolute; therefore ethics is relative (commandments 1, 2, 3).
- The relational call of God (word, will, command) is the ultimate good.
- The will of God is a solitary path.
- Distress and dread is the paradox of faith.[33]

For he who loved himself became great in himself, and he who loved others became great through his devotion, but he who loved God became greater than all.[34]

---

33. Vaux, *Jew, Christian, Muslim*, 96–98.
34. Kierkegaard, 50.

II

Ethics

The Common Good—Torah, the Law of Christ, Taurut

FAITH AND ETHICS—STARTING POINTS

Ethics in Context

STANLEY HAUERWAS BEGINS *THE PEACEABLE KINGDOM* WITH A REMINDER that all ethical thought is contextual and must be viewed within its specific historical setting:

> All ethical reflection occurs relative to a particular time and place. Not only do ethical problems change from one time to the next, but the very nature and structure of ethics is determined by the particularities of a community's history and convictions. From this perspective the notion of 'ethics' is misleading, since it seems to suggest that 'ethics' is an identifiable discipline that is constant across history.[1]

The study of ethics can be useful for addressing general questions related to fairness, justice, rights, obligations, virtues, and benefits to society, but responses to questions of ethics also vary from one community to another (and from one time to another) and may well carry different meanings. As people in different times and places have sought to deter-

---

1. Hauerwas, *The Peaceable Kingdom*, 1.

mine what kind of individuals, institutions, and societies they must be, their understandings about moral life have reflected their culture and their values. In the modern world of globalization, then, we must increasingly accept cultural diversity and the different ethics and moral rules that comprise various cultures.

A community's ethics emerges from the worldview through which it experiences and interprets reality. In U.S. culture, for example, what many consider a moral vacuum emerges from a broader worldview that espouses autonomy, self-containment, efficiency, competitiveness, and self-advancement, a worldview that separates us from our history and our communities. Success for individuals is characterized by self-reliance, competence, detachment, and the ability to appear in control at all times. This cultural ethos discourages individuals from committing to social causes or engaging in authentic service, and the result is a loss of not only moral character, but also a sense of meaning—as we become estranged "from what character ethicists call *the good*, or the *telos*, or the larger human purpose of life."[2]

But ethics requires humans to commit to a greater good. A sense of morality and ethical principles allows us, compels us even, to question the authority of the world in which we live—especially if that authority is in conflict with our ethical norms and imperatives—and then act accordingly: "Worldview (basic convictions) helps shape character, and character overflows into action."[3]

The Nature of Ethics

Using philosophical categories, Christian ethicist George Forell offers a useful overview of various approaches to ethics and systems of moral thought.[4] His analysis of these various types of ethical systems reveals some of the dangers inherent in grounding ethics in one universal principle.

Universalistic Hedonism

From the standpoint of universalistic hedonism, ethics derives from the principle of "the greatest good for the greatest number," a notion that fa-

---

2. Stassen & Gushee, *Kingdom Ethics*, 56–63.
3. Ibid., 63.
4. Forell, *Ethics of Decisions*, 21–34. These categorizations are found primarily in Christian ethics, although they could conceivably ground any faith tradition.

vors the organization of society—the *public* good—over the needs and preferences of the individual—the *private* good. Although this ethic accrues obvious benefits for the greater good of the society, and even takes into account the needs of people in the future, it proves difficult to establish or define "the greatest good" and is open to a wide range of highly subjective and potentially damaging interpretations. Nazism and communism are the most extreme examples of this ethic, which has been used to justify "cleansing" or "purifying" the race for the ultimate good of future generations.

Supernatural Hedonism
An ethics that advocates right action now in exchange for pleasure or reward later is an ethic of supernatural hedonism. The expectation of pleasure is a form of hedonism—living only for personal comfort or well-being. Even the promise of a future reward or punishment in heaven or hell, as in some Christian philosophies, reflects an attempt to take control of God's goodness and privilege one's own happiness as the ultimate good. Hedonists then use God for their own ends, to achieve happiness. Those guided by this type of ethic choose what is good and right only as a "subtle form of self-seeking, of gaining eternal pleasure and avoiding eternal pain."[5]

Naturalism
Finding an objective and universal standard for ethics—knowing what is right and good for all—can derive from naturalism, an ethic that uses nature as a standard. Humans are considered the end product of evolution, and according to the law of survival of the fittest, are meant to endure and thrive. This means that seeking the survival of the fittest is good, and anything perceived as a deterrent to survival is bad or unethical. The danger here is that survival of the fittest has generally meant survival of the *strongest*. But evolution can be cruel, and using this ethic as a guideline for moral behavior results in a failure to protect the weak and vulnerable. Based on the premise that it is "unnatural" to interfere with the evolutionary process, it promotes the survival of those whom nature intends to weed out. The negative implications of this ethic are many, the most obvious being eugenics, the logical extension of biological naturalism, most evident in 20th-century America and in Nazi Germany.

5. Forell, *Ethics of Decisions*, 23.

Naturalism in Economics (*laissez-faire* economics)

The naturalism ethic also can inform economic principles. *Laissez-faire* economics is a form of naturalistic ethics. If in society in general, the fit (strongest) should survive, in economics so too should the strong prevail in the struggle for survival. Out of this ethic comes the justification for avoiding price regulation, wage control, social security, and healthcare benefits—actions that would interfere with the law of natural economics. Proponents of naturalistic economics would view affirmative action and other movements to provide economic equity improper and in conflict with nature. This interference is perceived as threatening to the freedom of the economically strong/dominant. But what economic naturalists do not acknowledge is the impact of racial discrimination and other forms of economic oppression in diminishing the freedom of certain individuals.

Relativism

Any attempt to identify and define a universal ethical standard is complicated at best. Standards based on pleasure, the common good, or nature can be interpreted in a variety of ways. Ethical relativists argue the impossibility of finding an objective and universal standard for deciding right from wrong. Since every situation is different, what may be right and good in one context or instance may not be in another. Relativists conclude that no ethical choice is *inherently* better than another, and that each individual must identify the ethical standards by which to live. Without any objective standard, there results as many different ethics as there are individuals.

Prudential Ethics

Prudential ethics, like supernatural hedonism, is geared toward results in the future, and proponents of this approach make decisions based on what the future may bring into being. Every ethical choice of action can be justified by its result, so the end is what is deemed good or bad—as opposed to the action itself. Once again, the interpretation of what is considered good is a problem. In Nazi Germany, for example, the creation of a superior "master" race was considered a good end to enough individuals to justify genocide. In addition, the good itself may never come to fruition.

Aesthetic Ethics

An opposite approach promotes living in the here and now, rather than waiting for a future goal to which prudential ethicists aspire. This ethic suggests that life has no real meaning and suggests that trying to find a meaning and purpose in the future is futile. This guideline promotes learning to live now and enjoy one's life, and not worrying about the future. Aesthetic ethicists strive to use senses and emotions to "give meaning to life and to transform meaningless into beauty."

How Faith Informs and Shapes Ethics

In secular communities, moral laws and principles emerge out of consensus—eventually becoming public law—and these become the foundation for ethical behavior. But the agreement of the community, or even its best thinkers, does not constitute an unconditional and final authority for moral or public law. Secular philosophy or morality forged from an amalgam of sources is not sufficient as a foundation for a sustainable or workable public ethic.[6] Nineteenth-century Reform Rabbi Isaac Mayer Wise pointed out that in history, revelation has been the only dependable authority for ethics: "In the early days of humanity, definitions of morality were accepted as facts of superhuman reason, as revelations, as messages of inspired men. This gave them recognizable authority."[7]

Theological and faith traditions also give rise to moral and ethical substance and styles. For the three Abrahamic traditions, revelation continues to be the dependable authority Rabbi Wise speaks of. For Jews, Christians, and Muslims, ethical thought focuses not on the question of *What is right and what is wrong?* but *What is right and wrong according to God?* Starting from the sure knowledge that God embodies all that is good and right in life, Jews, Christians, and Muslims seek to understand how to make the goodness of God real in their lives, how to live in accord with God's goodness, and how to become God-like. Followers of all three faiths attempt to move beyond the expectations of tradition or culture—to discern and accept God's will as the ultimate moral good, "Thus says the Lord: 'Stand at the crossroads, and look, and ask for the ancient paths, where the good way lies; and walk in it, and find rest for your souls.'" (Jer

---

6. Vaux, *Jew, Christian, Muslim*, 113.
7. Kravitz and Olitzky, *Pirke Avot*, 95–96.

6.16) Abraham's children find rest in learning, listening for, and being led by God's ethical guidance.[8]

The ethical guidelines embedded in each tradition have weight historically, but they also have authority today. The architects of these traditions—the great teachers, leaders, and prophets of the past—left us guides and resources for making ethical decisions. Although they lived in different contexts and could not possibly have foreseen the moral challenges we face today, they left sure guidance for future generations in their strong conviction that the final and definitive authority will always be God.[9]

In Judaism, ethical monotheism is the belief that there is one God, that all morality for all of humanity comes from this God and that God's ultimate requirement is that people treat each other decently and humanely. Everything emerges from this one principle. Similarly, Christianity fosters in individuals a vital and personal relationship with God through faith in Christ, and it is this relationship that allows followers to become who God intended them to be. Their external actions—in personal interactions, families, work, churches, cultures, and communities—are a reflection of who they are, who they have become through faith in Christ.[10] The distinctiveness of ethics in Islam depends primarily in its submission to Allah in all things—guiding believers' relations with God, self, the universe, and society.

The Individual in Community

In the fourth and fifth centuries, as Christianity emerged out of Judaism and other religious sects and movements as a dominant cultural force, it brought with it a change in sensibilities. Christians gradually developed new convictions about morality and ethical behavior, exploring questions related to what is right and good, the goal and meaning of human behavior, and Christian formation of the human being. Emerging from this context were new institutions that sought to foster the formation of human character and provide guidance of the soul. This, then, was one of the major changes that came about as Christianity flourished—the role of faith as an institution of morality and ethical behavior.

8. Forell, 49; Hollinger, *Choosing the Good*, 13–15.
9. Johnson, *Patterns of Ethics in America Today*, 19–20.
10. Hollinger, 11–12.

According to Aristides, what characterized Christianity were its moral beliefs about God and humanity and the implications for behaviors and practices. He saw Christians collectively as a common *ethos* (similar to a nation), joined together by common beliefs. Christians had their own code of behavior and attempted to live by this code in their daily lives: ". . . becoming a Christian meant something like the experience of an immigrant who leaves his or her native land and then assimilates into the culture of a new, adopted homeland."[11]

What is instructive about the formation of Christianity as an institution of morality is the ability of community to foster morality in the individual. Aristotle, one of the first philosophers to study the importance of community in the development of moral character, argued that people did not learn to be good through reason—but by learning, practicing, and forming good habits. The best way to develop character is to live and work within "a moral and educative community." This can be summed up by a common phrase in Greek moral philosophy: "Habit makes character."[12]

Moral intuition and character—the instinctive discernment of right from wrong, fair from unfair—are not given qualities, something we all possess, but are developed through relationship in community. Integral to a community's culture is a code of ethics and moral behaviors. Individuals "do not become moral agents except in the relationships, the transactions, the habits, and reinforcements, the special uses of language and gesture that together constitute life in community."[13]

Judaism, Christianity, and Islam all are faiths grounded in a strong understanding and appreciation of community. Religious communities, in particular, foster ethical behavior and right conduct by urging believers to envision a world where ethical behavior is the norm.[14]

SOURCES OF ETHICAL PRINCIPLES

In all three Abrahamic faiths, God sent word to humans (law and prophets) to remind them of their moral responsibility. The Torah, for Jews, is believed to have been given to Moses on Mount Sinai after the exodus from slavery in Egypt; Christians have the gospels of Christ; and Muslims

11. Meeks, *The Origins of Christian Morality*, 12.
12. Ibid., 7.
13. Ibid., 8–10.
14. Ibid., 2, 7–12.

have the Qur'an and the Prophet's teachings. In each faith tradition, there are several spheres of moral knowledge—beginning with religious teachings in the form of written scripture, subsequent interpretations of those scriptures, and translations of the teachings into practical and ethical guidelines for daily life.

Judaism: Torah and Tanakh

Written Scripture: Tanakh
In Judaism, believers look first to written scripture for answers to questions about ethical behavior. Torah—the Hebrew word for "teaching"—most commonly refers to the Five books of Moses (the first five books of the Bible or the Pentateuch)—*Bresheit* (Genesis), *Shemot* (Exodus), *Vayicra* (Leviticus), *Bamidbar* (Numbers), and *Devarim* (Deuteronomy). But Torah also refers to the complete Hebrew scriptures—*Tanakh* is more often used to describe the entirety of Hebrew scripture, which includes the Torah, *Nevi'im* (prophets), and *Ketuvim* (writings).

Included in the Torah are a variety of guidelines: cultic instructions, ritual prescriptions, statutes and ordinances, and laws and requirements, but the most significant expression of ethical guidelines is the Decalogue—set forth in Deuteronomy and Exodus. For Judaism (and Christianity and Islam as well), the Decalogue serves to guide ethical decisions across all areas of human life. Extending far beyond the Jewish tradition, the Decalogue has become the "moral charter of world civilization . . . the centerpiece of ethical theology of Judeo-Christian culture." Inherent in the Decalogue is an ethic that calls for monotheistic loyalty, filial and parental love, and respect for God's creation—it is the binding agreement that comes from the covenant relationship of the people with God.[15]

Jewish theologian and ethicist Byron L. Sherwin cites a rabbinic tradition that distinguishes the first set of tablets Moses received from the second, suggesting that the first set included teachings from the spiritual realm. It was a perfect Torah, Torah as it was meant to be, a Torah God intended for a whole and perfect world. This tradition sees Moses breaking the first set of tablets not out of anger but out of his understanding—after seeing the people worshipping the Golden Calf—that the world was imperfect and not yet whole. The first Torah, written by "the hand of God" for a redeemed people was not the proper law for a corrupt and unre-

---

15. Vaux, *Jew, Christian, Muslim*, 117, 120, 139, 141.

deemed world. The second set of tablets Moses receives address issues relevant to sin and human experience in an imperfect world—violence, war, crime, deception, and murder.[16]

Oral Torah: the Talmud

For Orthodox Jews, God revealed the Torah to Moses, and it was passed down over the years as an oral tradition and developed by later generations of scholars. In the second century, Rabbi Judah the Prince—who feared, after the death of many teachers in the Jewish revolts, that the law would be lost—gathered and recorded the teachings in written form as the *Mishnah*. Additional interpretations of the *Mishnah*—known as the *gemara*—were added between the second and fifth centuries, and together these two commentaries became known as the *Talmud*.[17] These commentaries and interpretations are a systematic presentation of rules of conduct and moral and spiritual teaching developed by scholars in the academy and in the law courts, and they reflect a consensus of thinking in the Jewish community over many generations. Unlike the Hebrew Bible itself, the *Mishnah* is ordered topically to make it easy to identify everything the Torah teaches on a specific subject. Associated with the development of the *Mishnah* and *Talmud* is first-century rabbinic teacher Hillel, who is best known for articulating the "ethic of reciprocity" or the "Golden Rule" of Jewish ethics—"What is hateful unto you, do not do to your neighbor." Another major figure in the Jewish ethical tradition is second-century sage and scholar Akiba ben Yossef, who was a major contributor to the *Mishnah*.

Two levels of authority or law in the *Talmud*: the *halakhah* ("the way to be taken" or "the path one walks"), questions that relate to Jewish practice and carry the power of law and are defensible in Jewish courts; and the *aggadah* ("tales" or "lore"), which are not laws but stories, legends and folktales that address historical or ethical issues.

The term "Torah" then, while used most commonly to describe the Five Books of Moses or the complete Hebrew Bible in written form,

---

16. Sherwin, *Jewish Ethics for the Twenty-First Century*, 128–29.

17. Two *Talmuds* emerged during this period. One was developed by scholars in Israel sometime in the fourth century who combined their commentary (or *gemara*) with *Mishnah*. This commentary was written in Aramaic and became known as the Jerusalem (Palestinian) *Talmud*. The other was the Babylonian *Talmud*, created by scholars about 500 c.e. in Jewish communities in Babylonia, and it is the more comprehensive and commonly referenced of the two.

also refers to the entire corpus of Jewish teachings and law in its oral (*Talmudic*) form. While the written Torah is the most authoritative source for Judaism, the oral law explores the mystery of scripture on a deeper level, interpreting the teachings for the entire Jewish community and offering moral guidelines for the daily activities of life. Not only has the *Talmud* interpreted and deepened Jewish understanding of the Law, but also it has preserved the power and continuity of Judaism over centuries. It now comprises the comprehensive and authoritative expression of Judaism today.

Another important rabbinic text emerging from the *Mishnah* that informs ethics in Judaism is the *Pirkei Avot*, also called "Ethics of the Fathers." The only component of the oral law that addresses ethical and moral questions, the *Avot* is a collection of 1,000 years of teachings and sayings about how to live fully and ethically.

Social and Personal Obligations: Mitzvot
Also in the Torah (Five Books of Moses) are the *Mitzvot*, 613 statements or principles of ethics contained in the Biblical law. These are called collectively the Law of Moses, the Mosaic Law, or simply the Law. Most well-known is Maimonides' enumeration, which sets forth either positive requirements to perform a certain act or negative commandments to refrain from doing something. Although there has been debate over this tradition, even today many Jews refer to the total system of law in the Torah as the 613 commandments. Intended to cover every aspect of human experience, the *Mitzvot* translate the basic elements of morality and faith into daily life and behaviors. The *tzitzit* (knotted fringes) of the *tallit* (prayer shawl) correspond to the 613 commandments, reminding wearers of all Torah laws.

Christianity: The Law of Christ

Foundation: the Old Testament
Built on the foundations of Judaism, Christianity is consistent with the basic morality set forth in Jewish teaching. The Decalogue especially assumed great importance in first-century Judaism and in the ethical thought of John the Baptist, Jesus, and Paul. In his Sermon on the Mount, Jesus reminds us that he came not to destroy the law but to fulfill it, so when it comes to ethics he might even be considered a reformer of the

Hebrew tradition. While the Jewish tradition emphasized the *letter* of the law, Jesus expanded on it and forced his followers to listen to the *spirit* of the law. Jesus' teaching, while fully consistent with Jewish law, was not a call to do away with the existing teachings but to go beyond the law to account for our lives before God.

Most Christians consider the Decalogue a moral law applicable to our lives today—the commandments offer a broad understanding of humans' relationships with God and with each other—and many consider the teachings of Proverbs important for shaping character. In addition, many other Old Testament texts are important resources for Christians in forming character—the prophets, for example, in urging us to honesty, righteousness, and justice.

For texts that are troubling, some Christians believe that God's self-disclosure is appropriate to people's understanding of his will and plan. Many also consider the relationship of the Old Testament to the New Testament as a function of progressive revelation, the ongoing unfolding of God's plan that reaches its culmination in the death, resurrection, and ascension of Christ. God's full plan becomes clear through Christ and the Holy Spirit; as a result, many Christians read the Old Testament with the "fuller" New Testament in mind.[18]

Christ's way: the New Testament

The gospel of Jesus Christ is the foundation of Christian ethics. Jesus did not present an entirely new system of ethics, but offered the world "the law of Christ." His creative reinterpretation of the law gets to the very heart of Judaism's ethical thinking, which was *paidagogos* (tutor) before he came.[19] The original Hebrew law and the Gospels have been combined into one system. And the cornerstone of the Gospels—and Christian ethics—is Jesus' new spirit of love. The deeper meaning and reality of the new spirit of love Jesus taught was moral duty found only in obedient love of God. By holding faith in God as the highest ideal, Christians would naturally seek to do the will of God. All morality for Jesus could be summed up in the commandment to love God and love one's neighbor as oneself: "faithfulness to the Commandments involves not only nominal strictness to these good rules but also a disposition toward God's way as

---

18. Hollinger, 157–64.
19. Vaux, *Jew, Christian, Muslim*, 129, 131.

one is freed from lesser loyalties. The heart given to God is the foundation of ethics."[20]

Christianity also moves beyond obedience to the law of the covenant by allowing believers to share in the authority realized in Christ. Through the new moral order brought about by Christ—and with the assistance of the Holy Spirit—believers are allowed to make moral decisions creatively. Rather than being a challenge to God's authority, this is "a restoration of Adam's lordship in the natural order, the lordship by which he calls things by their names."[21]

The New Testament proffers ethical principles that have meaning and broader application beyond their immediate context. When Jesus summarizes the Old Testament law, "You shall love the Lord your God with all your heart, and with all your soul, and with all your mind" and "You shall love your neighbor as yourself" (Matt 22.37, 39), he is offering a timeless principle that has broad application both then and now.[22]

For Richard Longenecker, principles are the heart of New Testament ethics: "what we have in the New Testament is a declaration of the gospel and the ethical principles that derive from the gospel, and a description of how that proclamation and its principles were put into practice in various situations during the apostolic period."[23] Both principles and biblical paradigms implicitly contain ethical guidelines and point to an understanding of reality that embodies moral direction.

The Christian Bible, then, includes a variety of teaching for ethics—from specific laws in the Decalogue to general principles, stories, and paradigms that inform ethical choices. Christians interpret the individual parts in the context of the entire Bible, with special focus on the revelation of Christ and the witness of the apostles in the New Testament.[24]

Other Writings: Augustine, Aquinas, and Luther

Other important thinkers like Augustine contributed to the development of Christian ethics. Calling on earlier Greek thinkers to develop a philosophy of ethics, Augustine explored the question of motivation in Christian living. If a desire to gain a reward or avoid punishment in the

---

20. Ibid., 118.
21. O'Donovan, *Resurrection and Moral Order*, 24.
22. Hollinger, 167–73.
23. Ibid., 168.
24. Ibid., 169, 173.

hereafter is a primary motivation for loving God and neighbor, then it is not truly morality. Adhering to the moral law out of fear is not ethical behavior—the motivation for moral living, for Augustine, could only be the love of God. His *The City of God* also was foundational for Christian social ethics. In its depiction of human history as a dispute between the earthly city in which order comes through violence, and the heavenly city whose inhabitants worship and love God, *The City of God* contributed to Christian thinking about the distinction between right and wrong in societies.[25]

Aquinas, too, called for an ethic emerging from natural law, and he saw morality as coming from human nature and the behaviors most suited to it. For Aquinas, when one does what is right, that also is what is true to her or his nature: "God is not offended by us except by what we do against our own good." In his *Summa Theologica*, which outlines the connection between Christian theology and ethics, Aquinas understood the Christian moral nature as being founded on virtues that shape Christian life.[26]

In the Protestant tradition, Luther made significant contributions to ethical thought. Believing that there was no separate standard of goodness, Luther claimed that the good is simply whatever God commands us to do. His "three hierarchies" or "three estates"—the church, the home, and the state—were seen as structures given by God for the ordering of creation.[27]

Islam: The Holy Qur'an

In *Taurut*, Muslims believe that Allah sent messages to humanity through five Prophets: the *Suhuf* (Scrolls) revealed to the prophet Ibrahim (Abraham) and now lost; the *Taurut* (Torah) revealed to the Prophet Musa (Moses); the *Zabur* (Psalms) revealed to the Prophet Daud (David); the *Injil* (Gospels) revealed to the Prophet Isa (Jesus); and the *Qur'an* revealed to the Prophet Muhammad. For this reason, Islam assimilated much of the ethics of Judaism and Christianity. Muhammad came from the Arab center of Mecca and, although Semitic paganism was the dominant cult in the area, he was exposed to Jewish and Christian influences. As a result, the Qur'an reflects ethical precepts from the two other Abrahamic faiths.

---

25. Hauerwas, *The Hauerwas Reader*, 38–9.
26. Ibid., 40–1.
27. Saarinen, "Ethics in Luther's Theology: The Three Orders," 195–215.

Holy Scripture: Qur'an

Considered to be the sole source of God's word, the Qur'an is not a book of law but a work of moral admonition, a collection of 114 chapters called *suras* that detail for followers specific Islamic guidelines on ethics, rituals, and law. Much of the Qur'an deals with humankind's relationship to God, but there also are passages about prophecy and prophets and the importance of accepting Muhammad as a genuine Prophet and messenger of God. A large part of the Qur'an also deals with human relations, statements detailing the necessity for justice, fairness, goodness, kindness, and forgiveness. Because they are specific directives, they carry an authority and force that abstract rules do not.

According to the Qur'an, a new prophet emerged in the Judeo-Christian tradition and received a new revelation. Muhammad's understanding of the purpose of God's earlier revelation was to form the Jewish and Christian communities. The new revelation was a call not to overturn the old law but to restore it to its original meaning—and, of course, the formation of the Muslim community of believers.

It is God's voice alone that we hear in the Qur'an; no one else speaks. Many of the themes and images from the Hebrew Bible and the Gospels are found there, but in the Qur'an there is no narrative thread, only God's utterances. Much of the Qur'an is written in such a way that readers must have some basic understanding of the subject matter in order to understand its teachings. *Suras* in the early part of the Qur'an are similar to the Jewish prophets in warning of God's judgment and in exhorting humans to reform. The later ones offer detailed guidelines for practicing Muslims.

It is not a historical piece in the way of the Torah or the Christian gospels; instead the Qur'an is a revelation of God's will for humankind as told by God himself—through the Angel Gabriel to the Prophet Muhammad. Some narratives, however, can be traced to stories from the Hebrew Bible or from Christian Gospels. For example, there are several versions of the Ten Commandments throughout the Qur'an.

Most of the Qur'an's approach to moral behavior centers on belief in the one and only God, the creator of all beings—so that positive and negative moral qualities have to do not with good and evil or right and wrong but with belief or unbelief.[28]

---

28. Peters, *The Children of Abraham*, 35–9.

As with the Jewish tradition, Muslims have relied on the commentaries of religious authorities and learned scholars to help them interpret the Qur'an and to expand on its teachings—suggesting that the Qur'an is most likely not read literally. These commentaries express the thinking of scholars, mystics, and theologians across 1,400 years of the tradition and offer a view of morality in Islam and the way in which ethical precepts are applied in everyday life.[29]

Hadith: Sayings of the Prophet

While there is a significant ethical strand in the Qur'an, it does not constitute a complete expression of the moral and ethical ideal for Muslims. Perhaps as important as the Qur'an as a source for moral and ethical questions is a secondary form of revelation, the *hadith*—the collections of stories and sayings of the Prophet Muhammad that Muslims believe he received during a vision in 610 from the angel Gabriel (telling him "recite!"). These stories amplify and expand on the revelations in the Qur'an.

Included in the *hadith* are a summary of the moral obligations of a Muslim:

- Return any property belonging to others.
- Do not hurt anyone.
- Do not charge interest on money loaned to others.
- Husbands should treat their wives well, as they are partners together.
- Do not make friends with people of bad character.
- Do not commit adultery.

Much like the early stories of Christ's life, the words and deeds of the Prophet were passed on from one generation to the next through an oral tradition—these stories and sayings were popular with the first generations of Muhammad's followers, but were not gathered and recorded until 100 years after his death. Muslims believe that both the Qur'an and the *hadith* were spoken by the Prophet; while the Qur'an was recorded in writing and carefully preserved, the *hadith* was handed down orally. Like the *Mishnah* in Judaism, reliability of the *hadith* was evaluated based on the credibility of those who taught and transmitted them; a science re-

29. Brockopp, *Islamic Ethics of Life*, 3–4.

ferred to as "knowledge of men" kept biographical data on these teachers to assess their reliability. Similar to the way the veracity of early Christian writings is evaluated by how likely the writer was to have known Christ, the "knowledge of men" tradition is a kind of "apostolic succession" of teachings. Eventually, though, the *hadith* were recorded and became the primary resource for Muslim knowledge of Muhammad's teachings known as the *Sunnah* (exemplary practice) holy writings.

Muslims do not believe Muhammad was divine—the divine words were what was recorded in the Qur'an (the word of Allah)—Muslims believe he delivered God's own words; the Prophet's sayings were advice to the community, similar to the difference between the Gospels and Paul's writings.[30]

Shari'ah: the Way of Faith and Life

Out of the divine revelations given to the Prophet Muhammad—both in the Qur'an and *hadith*—a broader body of law has developed over time, prescribing both personal obligations and public responsibilities. Religious duties, *ibadat*, include the obligations to God commonly known as the Five Pillars of Islam: daily prayers (*salāt*); pilgrimage to Mecca (*hajj*); fasting during Ramadan (*sawm*); payment of alms for the poor (*zakāt*); and faith in the Oneness of God (*shahādah*).

Mu'amalat is the other category of law, and it involves relationships and interactions between individuals—including marriage, divorce, and inheritance laws.[31]

These books of Islamic law, called *Al-sharī'ah* (way of faith and life), are not a set body of rules but an ethical system to answer questions that arise within the Muslim community. It characterizes actions as being "required"; "recommended"; "indifferent"; "reprehensible"; and "forbidden." There is no one universally accepted law, rather *Sharī'ah* emerged out of four different schools of jurisprudence—special consideration was given to the founders of the four schools of law (in the eighth-ninth centuries) who were thought to have special wisdom and insight into the meaning of the Qur'an and the *hadith*—developed rules for using these written sources and handling internal contradictions. Theological and legal debates eventually resulted in an authoritative sanctioning of the decisions by the jurists, and were nobilized by some to be a system of divine

---

30. Ali and Leaman, *Islam: The Key Concepts*, 45.
31. Vaux, *Jew, Christian, Muslim*, 138.

commands—*'ilm* (indubitable knowledge). Using a rational method to interpret the written sources, the jurists applied them to the entire realm of human existence.

As with Judaism and Christianity, Islam also relies on later writings to inform ethics. Scholars and religious authorities over the centuries have expanded on written sources and added their own commentaries and interpretations. Not only do these writings help us better understand the beliefs of Islam, but also they reflect an ongoing expression of Muslim writing from scholars, mystics, and theologians for 1,400 years.[32]

ETHICS AND RELIGIOUS IDENTITY

Judaism: An Ethics of Responsibility

Rabbi Jonathan Sacks, chief rabbi of the U.K., identifies as Judaism's most distinctive idea its "ethics of responsibility," the belief that God—in giving humankind the gift of freedom—challenges us to use this gift to enrich and improve the lives of others, to create and foster freedom for those around us. God teaches us to do his will; we are to reach out and respond to the world just as he reaches out and responds to us.[33]

The message of the prophets, spoken on behalf of God, is clear: accept responsibility. All of the great prophets repeatedly call Israel to have a social conscience, to realize that all are responsible for making the world better for those living now and for those who come after. Failing to accept this responsibility is a failure to understand what God has called humans to do. The Hebrew Bible—in fact, life itself—is God's call to human responsibility.[34]

Human responsibility, however, means much more than blindly following the commands of the Hebrew Bible. Humans, having been given intellect and the ability to distinguish between good and evil, truth and falsehood, are called to study and immerse themselves in divine writings in order to understand for themselves what ethical behavior involves. One of the foundations of the tradition, especially when it comes to Jewish ethics, is the belief that God's way can be learned by reading and studying scripture. Central to Jewish identity, then, is the challenge of discerning what is right and good and acting on that understanding. This is God's call.

32. Ali and Leaman, 43–46.
33. Sacks, *To Heal a Fractured World*, 3.
34. Ibid., 28.

Ethical living in Judaism—living in the image of God—has three requirements: enriching God's word, mending God's world, and enhancing the divine image within each human being. Acting unethically diminishes God's word, world, and the divine image in each individual and, by extension, is an affront against God.[35]

Christianity: An Ethics of Love

Humans' ethical duty, as articulated in the life and teachings of Jesus, can be found in "obedient love," loving God with all one's heart, soul, and mind and loving one's neighbor as oneself. Choosing to do good means to choose a life of love, both the love of moral virtue that relates to one's character and the love of principle that relates to behavior. For Christians, love is not an abstract idea, but a path for choosing the good over and over in one's daily life. It is love in action that distinguishes Christian ethics.

This is a love fully grounded in God. As John tells us, "Beloved, let us love one another, because love is from God; everyone who loves is born of God and knows God" (1 John 4.7). The Christian understanding of love comes from the nature and actions of God, so God's goodness and love are the basis for human goodness.[36]

This love is not *eros*, a seeking of self-fulfillment or desires of the human heart and soul, and it does not mean loving others in order to get something in return, but rather it is *agape*, a spirit of love and concern that finds expression in good deeds and service to others, promoting the well-being of others. It involves mutuality and unselfish outpouring. This is no ordinary love, but a pouring out of one's very self for others. Jesus' life and teachings demonstrate this obedient love, from the beginning of his ministry to his death on the cross. This love extends even to strangers and enemies, as Jesus makes clear to the disciples in his Sermon on the Mount:[37]

> For if you love those who love you, what reward have you? Do not even the tax collectors do the same? And if you salute only your brethren, what more are you doing than others? Do not even the Gentiles do the same? You, therefore, must be perfect, as your heavenly Father is perfect. (Matt 5.46–48)

---

35. Sherwin, *Jewish Ethics*, 10.
36. Hollinger, 64–65.
37. Harkness, *Christian Ethics*, 54; Hollinger, 16–17.

Christian love for others—particularly enemies—should be as strong as the love for friends. Loving friends is not difficult and does not distinguish Christians from others, but loving enemies demonstrates the depth of the love Jesus speaks of.

Paul also speaks of the centrality of love, "the whole law is summed up in love" (Rom 13.10) and he names the overarching character of Christian ethics in terms of love, ". . . the only thing that counts is faith working through love" (Gal 5.6). For Paul, faith working through love is the way in which humans participate with God in creation—the way that was realized in Christ and made possible by the Holy Spirit.[38]

Augustine also connected Christianity with love. In *On the Morals of the Catholic Church*, he characterized Christian virtues as different forms of love for God. He outlined four virtues of Christianity, all different forms of love: *temperance*, love giving itself to the object of love; *fortitude*, love bearing all for the sake of the loved one; *justice*, love serving the object of love; and *prudence*, love distinguishing between what enhances or diminishes it. While the four virtues are forms of love for God, out of these four loves follow the obligation to love our neighbors.[39]

Islam: An Ethics of Character

Islamic ethics—*akhlāq*—often is defined as "good character." The Prophet Muhammad, when asked "Which Muslim has the perfect faith?" responded "One who has the best moral character." Islam has become a religion heavily focused on the building of individual character, and there is a strong relationship between strong faith and good character. It is believed that a person is not able to attain perfect faith without also having good character. One's behaviors and actions—specifically good deeds—are critical to being a Muslim. Because most people act instinctively out of their basic character, when it comes to behaving morally, having a strong character is as important as rules. Sura 5:105 warns Muslims, "Believers, guard your own souls. The person who has gone astray cannot hurt you if you are rightly guided."

The Five Pillars of Islam, in fact, direct believers toward building character and developing high morals and ethical standards. It is believed that a person who follows Allah's commands and performs good deeds

---

38. O'Donovan, 26.

39. Hauerwas, *The Hauerwas Reader*, 38; "The Christian Definition of the Four Virtues," Christian Classics Ethereal Library.

will automatically develop good character. All of the pillars instill in believers a sense of discipline, self-control, piety, humility, and caring for others:

- Oneness of God (*tawheed*)—believing in Allah as one God and submitting to the commands of Allah unconditionally teaches humility, generosity, piety, and righteousness.
- Daily prayers (*salah*)—praying five times a day protects believers from sin, unlawful deeds, disbelief, and evil actions.
- Charity (*zakat*)—observing charity establishes kindness and love, reduces the love of material wealth, and increases a desire to help others in need.
- Fasting (*sawm*)—fasting builds self-control and abstinence from worldly desires, and teaches empathy for others who do not have enough to eat.
- Pilgrimage to mecca (*hajj*)—pilgrimage builds self-control, humility, modesty, brotherhood, kindness, and caring.[40]

THEMES COMMON TO JUDAISM, CHRISTIANITY, AND ISLAM

Created in God's Image

Judaism

Even before the Decalogue, Judaism establishes a foundation for ethical behavior.[41] Three times the Torah tells us that humans are created in God's image: "And God created the human being in His image, in the image of God He created him: male and female He created them" (Gen 1.27). According to the classical rabbis of the *Mishnah*, the *Talmud*, and *midrash*, being made in God's image is a reflection of God's love for humans.[42]

---

40. "Islamic Ethics," Wikipedia.

41. All three Abrahamic faiths have a principle of ethical monotheism, the belief that there is one God who created us and from whom all ethical standards emerge. If God is good, and God created humans, then he created us to carry out his will and designs on Earth.

42. Talmudic rabbis taught that God not only reveals the Torah but also observes its

Awareness of the divine image within. The rabbis claimed, not only are humans created in the image of God, but they have been given the gift of knowing that they are. Man's *awareness* of the divine image within humans is an even greater sign of God's love for us: "Beloved is man, for he was created in the image of God; but it was by a special love that it was made known to him that he was created in the image of God, as the Torah says, 'For in the image of God He made man.'" Jewish *midrash* suggests that, when angels are near humans, they say, "Make way for the image of God."[43]

Imitation of God. In Judaism, being created in the image of God means imitating God, acting as God acts, choosing as God chooses—to clothe the naked, feed the poor, help the sick, comfort the lonely, to do acts of compassion, righteousness, and holiness.[44] Maimonides includes imitation of God as one of the commandments, and cites Jeremiah in his claim that God wants us to emulate him:

> This is what the Lord says:
> 'Let not the wise man boast of his wisdom
> or the strong man boast of his strength
> or the rich man boast of his riches,
> but let him who boasts boast about this:
> that he understands and knows Me,
> that I am the Lord, *who exercises kindness,
> justice and righteousness on Earth,*
> for in these I delight,'
> declares the Lord (Jer 9.23–24).

Maimonides suggests that God wants us to imitate him in this exercise of kindness, justice, and righteousness. This passage sums up the ultimate purpose of Judaism, "to honour the image of God in other people, and thus turn the world into a home for the divine presence."[45] *Imago Dei* becomes *imitatio Dei*, as humans learn to walk in God's ways.

---

commandments, with one exception. The Torah prohibits making an image of God, yet God did so in creating human beings. See Sherwin, *Jewish Ethics for the Twenty-First Century*, 1.

43. Sherwin, 1.
44. Ibid., 2–3.
45. Sacks, 4.

Other interpretations of the divine image. But throughout classical Jewish literature, there are other interpretations of what it means to be made in God's image. The Torah itself relates the *imago Dei* to the human capacity to make ethical choices, to distinguish good from evil, and to discern right from wrong. Other interpretations relate the divine image to the human:

- ability to speak;
- ability to love as God loves;
- ability to participate in God's spiritual nature;
- ability to create;
- awareness of beauty, truth, and goodness;
- capacity for love, caring, and compassion;
- free will to choose what is good and right.[46]

Human reason. Maimonides argued that the divine image rests in our ability to think and reason. Because God is an intellectual being, rational faculty is the unique characteristic humans share with God. For Maimonides, ethical action calls for use of the mind and human reason, specifically discerning between truth and falsehood, good and evil acts. This is what distinguishes humans from all other created beings.[47]

Partners in the work of creation. Judaism also is characterized by a belief that humans—being made in God's image—are intended to be partners with God in the work of creation. God has given humans stewardship over other creatures, giving them a role in co-caring for the rest of creation. While humans can work in partnership with God to enhance God's world, only God is capable of redeeming the world, which is yet unredeemed. The partnership between God and humans—founded in the divine-human covenant—ultimately can lead to redemption of the world that God and humans desire.[48]

---

46. Dorff, *To Do the Right and the Good*, 5–7; Johnson, 12–13.
47. Sherwin, 1–3.
48. Ibid., 130.

Christianity

The same scripture passages that inform Judaism's view of *imago Dei* shape the Christian worldview as well. "Then God said, 'Let us make man in our image, after our likeness.'" (Gen 1.26) In God's estimation, humans are unique in that God created them in his own image. And it is this divine image that distinguishes humans from everything in the created order. And we can only understand human beings in the context of the Creator in whose image they were made.

Stewardship and partnership. As in Judaism, Christians see part of the image of God in humans entailing stewardship over all of creation—with a role in caring and co-creating with God.[49] For Christians, God's actions are the norm for our own actions. We are to reflect God's faithfulness in our man-made covenants and agreements; we are to follow God's truthfulness in our relationships and dealings with others; we are to emulate God's justice in dealing with the poor and oppressed; and we are to forgive as God forgives us.[50]

God in human history. But what is unique in Christianity and significant to Christian ethics, is the incarnation of Jesus, a visible expression of God's very self in human history. Jesus is the "image of the invisible God, the firstborn of all creation" (Col 1.15), and he sets the standard for Christian ethical behavior and character, the clearest articulation in all of history for what it means to live a life of moral virtue. Believers are called to follow the way he set forth and to reflect his image. By the same token, the Holy Spirit helps Christians discern ethical and moral behavior. So Christian ethics, in addition to accepting the divine commands of God set forth in Hebrew scripture, also incorporates the teachings of Jesus and the work of the Holy Spirit in a Trinitarian ethic.[51]

Relationality and interdependence. Some theologians consider relationality a unique attribute related to being made in God's image. Since creation is a gift of God, and humans have a relationship to other living beings, we have a responsibility to oversee the rest of creation with care and justice. Just as the three persons of the Trinity are related in the Godhead,

---

49. Forell, 66–68; Hollinger, 72.
50. Hollinger, 67–68.
51. Ibid.

individuals also have the capacity for relationship—in our relations with other humans and other beings.

Part of the image of humans involves the mutuality Christians see among the Father, Son, and the Holy Spirit. The true nature of human beings is not in individualism or autonomy but in interdependence and mutuality with others. It is through Christ that Christians come to fully understand and realize their relationship with God, with creation, and with others.[52]

Islam

Islam conceives the divine image in a slightly different way from Judaism and Christianity. For Muslims, God is beyond any image, so even human beings cannot be said to be made in God's image.

God's representatives. In Islamic thought, human beings have been made as God's viceregents, or representatives, on Earth: "Behold thy Lord said to the angels: 'I will create a vicegerent on Earth.' They said, 'Wilt thou place therein one who will make mischief therein and shed blood?—whilst we do celebrate Thy praises and glorify Thy holy name?' He said, 'I know what you know not.'" (Sura 2.30) As representatives on Earth, humans are to represent God as caretakers of creation and, in submission to God, are called to choose justice.

Trust for creation. According to Sura 33:72 in the Qur'an, God first offered the "trust" for creation to the heavens, to the Earth, and to the mountains. They were afraid, and it was only humans who were willing to accept this trust. Morality and responsibility toward creation are central to Islam. But moral choice is not a given for Muslims, because humans are always tempted to evil. In spite of this, however, humans have the moral and intellectual capability to choose good and avoid evil—and this capability comes from being made in the image of God. This morality is a uniquely human attribute, the one that makes humans most like God.[53]

---

52. Ibid., 72.
53. Schweiker, Johnson, and Jung, *Humanity Before God*, 8.

Sanctity of Human Life

Judaism

Human worth, in Judaism, derives from the fact that humans are created in God's image. Each individual human being is sacred, created in God's image and bearing the divine life that was imprinted into him. This concept underlies all of Jewish ethics. Because humans are formed in the image of God, no part of man's nature is intrinsically sinful or evil. Rabbis in the classical Jewish tradition used the Biblical story of creation to emphasize the inherent equality and dignity of all individuals—and the innate sanctity of human life.[54]

God the ultimate source of worth. Based on the belief that God is good—and that God has created all of humankind in God's very image—Judaism embraces the conviction that all humans derive their worth and sacredness from the ultimate source of worth and meaning. Because of this legacy of inherent dignity, worth, and meaning, humans are called to cherish life, never take it for granted, and to live it the way God intended life to be lived. By virtue of the fact that God is involved with human life, concerned with their well-being, and intimately connected in a covenant partnership, is proof that God sees humans as "sufficiently godlike."[55]

Freedom to turn from God. American Jewish philosopher Eugene Borowitz claims that humans have unprecedented value, because God has given them freedom of choice, which includes the freedom to turn away from God, the ultimate source of their worth and value. Although God wants humans to obey his commandments, they have the choice to turn away from God in alienation. But God treats all with mercy; any sinner who genuinely is in *teshuvah* (turning back or repentance) will be forgiven and granted mercy. God's mercy is a sign of how much he values human beings, showing us that no one has the right to strip another of their inherent dignity and worth—these are inalienable gifts from God that can never be lost.[56]

---

54. Johnson, 7–8, 23.

55. Borowitz, "The Torah, Written and Oral, and Human Rights: Foundations and Deficiencies," 25–33.

56. Ibid., 26–27.

Christianity

Being made in God's image also implies for Christians an inherent dignity and worth in all human beings. This inherent dignity and worth cannot be taken away and forms the foundation of ethical behavior—treating others with respect and consideration. "Whoever sheds the blood of a human, by a human shall that person's blood be shed; for in his own image God made humankind." (Gen 9.6) Christians are called to protect and care for all of God's creation; life belongs to God and it is humans' responsibility to safeguard and preserve it. Because Christ died at the hands of his enemies, we are charged with responsibility for our neighbor's and even our enemies' lives. The Christian commitment to protect life relates to the hope that we will live in a new age in which all will be equal. Because God values our lives, we must value life.[57]

Islam

In Islam, human worth—and the sanctity of human life—are revealed and expressed both in life and in death.

Inherent dignity and worth. In Judaism and Christianity, the inherent dignity and worth of every human being emerges from the belief that each is formed in the image of God. And while Islam also upholds the sacredness and ultimate value of humanity, human life in the Muslim tradition is grounded in the belief in the human person as the viceregent of God. In this role, human beings enjoy a special relationship with God and are entrusted to be God's representative on Earth. Human life is a promise and a trust from God, so the humanity of all individuals is to be respected. The Qur'an repeatedly enjoins Muslims to respect the sanctity of life: "Do not kill the person that God has made sacred, except by right." (Sura 17.33)

The sanctity of life in Islam also is revealed in death. God, the author of life and death, transforms death into a larger picture that reflects God's plan for humankind. God remains intimately involved with human beings—from the beginning of life, through death and resurrection: "God gives you life then makes you die, then He shall gather you to the Day of Resurrection, wherein there is no doubt, but most do not know." (Sura 45.26) An individual's life accrues meaning at the moment of death, as he or she passes from the transitional moment of life into God's much larger vision.[58]

---

57. Hauerwas, *The Hauerwas Reader*, 134.
58. Brockopp, *Islamic Ethics of Life*, 179–80.

Saving an entire world. In all three traditions, there is a belief that one human is worth an entire world. Judaism details this most clearly: if you kill one individual, you are destroying all of his or her potential offspring and descendants. Conversely, saving one person "saves an entire world." From this perspective, human value comes from being the possible father or mother of future generations. *Mishnah* teaches that the human race was created through one individual person, so that every human must say, "For my sake was the world created." Jewish *midrash* also points out that, when coins are minted the image on each one is exactly the same, yet God made each human being distinctive and unique. What this proves is that anything unique is more valuable, demanding a higher price, than something common and plentiful. The fact that every individual is unique assigns value and worth to every human life. This belief is echoed in Christianity and Islam as well. Jesus heals one blind man, one leper, one lame person—and he heals all of humankind in that act. In the Qur'an, each individual human life equivalent to that of the entire community—and should be treated with care, respect, and reverence.[59]

Responsibility for Justice and Charity

Judaism
The emphasis in Judaism on the inherent sanctity and worth of humanity leads to teachings about human rights and justice. Because human beings are equal before God, every individual is entitled to freedom, respect, justice, peace, and access to security—all the rights one needs to become fully human. We must treat each other with mercy and justice—just as God treats us. And, because every human is made in God's image, each is deserving of love and care.[60]

Centrality of justice. The notion of justice in Torah law was a departure from earlier Babylonian statutes that did not treat all equally. In the Code of Hammurabi, for example, penalties were different for different classes of people—commoners or aristocrats. For example, if an individual killed the son of an aristocrat, that individual's son would be put to death as punishment, but if the same individual killed the son of a commoner, the punishment would be much less severe—a fine or brief imprisonment.

---

59. Johnson, 7–8.
60. Johnson, 8; Borowitz, 27.

Torah law was more just in two ways: it imposed punishments only on those who committed the crimes themselves, and punishments were the same regardless of the victim's status. Under Torah law, justice must apply to everyone equally, "You and the stranger shall be alike before the Lord... the same rule shall apply to you and to the stranger who resides among you." (Num 15.15–16) Even God is called to justice in Judaism; in a key passage in Genesis, when God decides to destroy Sodom, Abraham challenges God to do what is just, "Shall not the judge of all the Earth act with justice?"[61] (Gen 18.25)

Rabbi Sacks suggests that one of the greatest contributions of Judaism to society is the belief that a people is judged by how well justice prevails—and justice is at the very heart of Judaism.[62] Deuteronomy 16.20 makes clear an important mandate in Judaism, "Justice, justice, you shall pursue." While other commandments in Hebrew scripture are important and expected to be followed when called for, Jews are obliged not only to make sure justice prevails in situations of injustice, but also to seek ways to *promote* justice in the world.

Retributive and distributive justice. So important is the notion of justice in Judaism that it delineates two different types of justice. When God says of Abraham, "I have chosen him so that he will instruct his children and his household after him to keep the way of the Lord by doing what is right and just" (Gen 18.19), the Jewish tradition defines the "way of the Lord" by two distinctive forms of justice, *mishpat* and *tzedakah*. *Mishpat* is retributive or procedural justice, the settling of disputes through the use of law, weighing evidence and hearing both sides of a conflict. But Torah requires more than procedural justice; it calls for *tzedakah* or distributive justice. While there must be justice in applying and carrying out the law, more important is the way in which people live, receiving wealth as God's blessing and distributing it fairly to all who are entitled.[63]

God the owner. The concept of human rights originally came into being in connection with owning property, and one of the functions of government was to protect an individual's claim to property acquired legally. And although the Jewish tradition has long valued property rights, an

---

61. Telushkin, *A Code of Jewish Ethics, Volume 2*, 407.
62. Sacks, *Faith in the Future*, 43.
63. Sacks, *To Heal a Fractured World*, 33.

even stronger value is the belief that God ultimately owns all of creation. From an economic perspective, God is owner of everything (*baal, koneh*); politically speaking, God is the king (*melekh*); and in all aspects of life, God is the creator (*bore', yotzer*). The notion of human rights as we understand it today, then, is not a component of classic Jewish doctrine. In exploring the foundations of human rights in the Torah, Borowitz suggests that "there is almost a hint of blasphemy in the assertion that individuals might have property or even personal rights that in any way could be like God's or, more heretically, allow one to challenge God's absolute status."[64] As the Psalmist tells us, "The Earth is the Lord's and all that is in it." (Ps 24.1)

Because God is the ultimate owner of land, no one has the right to own it or sell it on a permanent basis. The Torah makes provisions for inequalities that exist in society, with the goal being not so much to distribute wealth, material goods, and land equally, but to create "a level playing field for each generation" so that any wealth acquired in one generation is not passed on to the next generation.[65] No one should forget their debt and gratitude to God, who is responsible for all wealth and blessings—becoming too attached or having too much wealth and possessions can foster complacency. Financial wealth is not considered bad in and of itself; in fact, there is a Hebrew term for money, *damim*, which also means "blood." Money sustains life just as blood does. Maimonides taught that wealth was a tool that could be used for good or for harm and that ultimately should be used for "moral and spiritual ends."[66]

Loans and interest. Judaism also prohibits charging interest or profiting from another's misfortune; both Leviticus and Deuteronomy offer clear mandates on this issue: "If one of your countrymen becomes poor and is unable to support himself among you, help him . . . Do not take interest of any kind from him . . . You must not lend him money at interest or sell him food at a profit." (Lev 25.35–38) and "Do not charge your brother interest, whether on money or food or anything else that may earn interest." (Deut 19.19)[67]

---

64. Borowitz, 25.
65. Wilson, *Economics, Ethics and Religion*, 29–33.
66. Sherwin, *How To Be a Jew*, 124.
67. Ibid., 29–33.

Righteous acts of charity. The concept of *tzedakah* in Judaism combines two closely-related concepts—justice and charity. While justice traditionally involves fairness when someone is entitled to something, charity generally means giving when one is not necessarily entitled. Because everything ultimately is owned by God, Judaism distinguishes *possession* and *ownership*. Someone may possess a plot of land, but God owns it: "The land must not be sold permanently because the land is Mine; you are merely strangers and temporary residents in relation to Me." (Lev 25.23) Individuals are only stewards or trustees of material things given by God, so what some might regard as charity is, in Judaism, required by law.[68]

Maimonides expands on the notion of *tzedakah*—righteous acts of charity—by enumerating eight ways of giving leading from the least to the most virtuous:

- One gives but reluctantly.
- One gives less than is appropriate, but with a giving heart.
- One gives after being asked.
- One gives before being asked.
- One gives in such a way that the donor does not know the identity of the recipient.
- One gives in such a way that the recipient does not know the identity of the donor.
- One gives in such a way that neither donor nor recipient knows the identity of the other.

From this perspective, the highest form of charity does not involve a gift of material goods or funds, but helping an individual restore strength and self-sufficiency (through employing or setting the person up in business), so that he or she maintains self-respect.[69]

Love of neighbor. Although the Torah assigns no special meaning to the verse, "You shall love your neighbor as yourself, I am the Lord" (Lev 19.18), classical Jewish sources have given it preeminent importance. Rabbi Akiva in the second century declared the mandate to love your neighbor as yourself "the major principle of the Torah." One hundred

---

68. Sacks, *To Heal a Fractured World*, 32.
69. Kravitz and Olitzky, 30.

years earlier, when asked by a student to "teach me the whole Torah while I stand on one foot," Rabbi Hillel gave his now-famous response: "What is hateful unto you, do not do to your neighbor. This is the whole Torah! All the rest is commentary. Now, go and study." This "Golden Rule" summarizes how Jews should behave, prompting them to evaluate carefully their actions toward others.[70]

Care for strangers and the vulnerable. This care and compassion extends to strangers and "aliens" as well. Although Judaism has a long-standing history of distinguishing Jews from Gentiles and upholding very specific laws about relations between the two groups. Borowitz gives a more nuanced perspective on the theme of the alien in Torah. It is his argument that Torah—and the history of the Jews—point to an attitude of human interaction and equality, a "Jewish ground for a universal declaration of human rights."[71] He quotes the law as set forth in Exodus 23.9—"you must not oppress the stranger, for you know the heart of the strangers having yourselves been strangers in the land of Egypt"—and Leviticus 19.33—"The stranger who resides with you shall be to you as one of the homeborn. You shall love him as yourself, for you were strangers in the land of Egypt."[72]

The Torah also demands concern the powerless in society: the widow and orphan, the deaf and blind. God advocates on behalf of the powerless, and he models care and decency for those who are vulnerable and weak. While oppression of the Jews over the course of history has prompted them to draw ethical boundaries closer to home, as anti-Semitism has decreased, Jewish thought has increasingly embraced a principle of "inalienable individual human dignity."[73]

Sharing with community. In the Jewish tradition, life and God's creation are only good when shared. Judaism places a heavy emphasis on community, and ethical action is considered "the happiness we make by sharing."[74] This sharing is not duty or even sacrifice, because it benefits the giver more than the receiver. Individual striving for personal fulfillment is

---

70. Telushkin, 9.
71. Borowitz, 28–29.
72. Ibid., 29.
73. Ibid., 29–30.
74. Sacks, *To Heal a Fractured World*, 5.

not the source of meaning in life; rather, we find meaning in being part of a community, in giving to help others and in doing what one can to make the world a better place. What is called for instead is humanness and humanity. Ethical acts for Jews, then, are an offering rather than a duty. The concept of *Mitzvah*, in fact, is about obligation to the community with the goal being to create "a community of service to God." So that serving others and serving God are one and the same.[75]

Christianity

Justice is a prevailing theme and central value of Christianity as well. Christians live within the tradition of God's covenant with Abraham, including the requirements of the Decalogue (Exod 20), most of which define relationships between human beings. For Christians and Jews, these requirements detail the kind of justice and righteous living God expects from all people. Other passages, such as Micah 6.8, also offer ethical guidelines for Jews and Christians, helping them further understand the meaning of justice and righteousness.

Jesus as the model for justice. For Christians, however, justice and righteousness are fully understood through the life and mission of Jesus. He embodies the covenant agreements outlined in the law, but to them he adds new insights about a justice based on love, the kind he describes in his Sermon on the Mount (Matt 5.1–11).[76]

Responsibility to the poor. As in Judaism, justice in the Christian tradition extends to economic matters and responsibility to the poor, which is an important theme of Luke. In the parable of Lazarus in Luke's gospel, Christ shows concern for the rich and the poor and, in speaking to the Pharisee, the tax collector, and the rich ruler, says, "Sell everything you have and give to the poor, and you will have treasure in heaven." (Luke 18.22) In Christianity, spiritual fulfillment must always come first and while the Gospels are not prescriptive about distributing wealth, there is a message that the needs of all must be met—and that it is the duty of

---

75. Ibid., 6.

76. Some Jewish ethicists consider Christian ethics to be based on charity or philanthropy, helping others out of Christian love. In Judaism, ethics is based on social obligation, not a spontaneous feeling. Critics argue that, while love is a valuable principle, it is not as dependable as *zedakah* (righteousness and charity), which requires Jews to help the needy regardless of their feelings for them. See Sherwin, *Jewish Ethics*, 132–33 and *How To Be a Jew*, 213–15.

Christians to make sure this happens. In the early chapters of Luke, there is a subtle suggestion that poverty itself is a virtue—a condition that may bring special favor from God.

Although all believers are equal in God's eyes, the Gospels acknowledge that we live in a world with poverty and material inequality. In writing to the Corinthians, Paul mentions church members' generosity: "Out of their most severe trial, their overflowing joy and their extreme poverty welled up in rich generosity. For I testify that they gave as much as they were able, and even beyond their ability." (2 Cor 8.2-3) Paul does not go as far as Luke does in suggesting that poverty is virtuous, suggesting only that each give "according to what one has, not according to what he does not have. Our desire is not that others should be relieved while you are hard pressed, but that there might be equality." (2 Cor 8.12-14) We are left with the message that those who have power over and access to resources have a responsibility to those who do not. As in Judaism, the focus is on obligation to the well-being of the community, but not specifically on collective ownership or equitable distribution.[77]

Caution for the wealthy. In Luke, we hear Christ's caution about putting wealth and possessions above everything else: "Watch out! Be on your guard against all kinds of greed; a man's life does not consist in the abundance of his possessions." (Luke 12.15) Christ teaches that faith in God must be first, and that wealth has the capacity to distract us from the love and worship of God. The accumulation of material wealth can lead to worship of idols: "No servant can serve two masters. Either he will hate the one and despise the other, or he will be devoted to the one and despise the other. You cannot serve both God and Money." (Luke 16.13) It is not the goods themselves that are condemned, but the way people use them. The famous gospel message, "How hard it is for the rich to enter the kingdom of God! Indeed it is easier for a camel to go through the eye of a needle than for a rich man to enter the kingdom of God" (Luke 18.24-25), is a reminder of how easy it is for the wealthy to fall into greed.[78]

Justice as compassion. Christians, like Jews, are called to seek justice on God's behalf. But Christ models for his followers a challenging of authorities when they are in conflict with the justice God demands. Because righ-

---

77. Wilson, 71–74.
78. Ibid., 68–71.

teousness is a gift from God, it is God's vision ultimately that will prevail. In the parable of the sheep and the goats, the king reminds us of God's justice: "Just as you did not do it to one of the least of these, you did not do it to me." (Matt 25.40) Justice, in the new vision Christ inaugurates, is the political form of compassion, the social form of love. This is a new ethic for relations between God's people, a "compassionate justice grounded in God as compassionate."[79]

Love of neighbor. Like the Golden Rule in Judaism, Jesus offers a generalized principle to guide followers' intent and behaviors, "Therefore all things whatsoever you desire that men should do to you, do you even so to them. For this is the Law and the prophets." (Matt 7:12) Christians, like Jews, are called not only to love their neighbors but also to care for strangers and even enemies. Just like the Hebrew Bible makes it clear that people must treat their enemies fairly: "If you see your enemy's donkey lying down under its burden and would refrain from raising it, you must nevertheless raise it with him" (Exod 23.5) and "If your enemy is hungry, give him bread to eat. And if he is thirsty, give him water to drink" (Prov 25.21), so does Christianity call for loving one's enemy: "But I tell you: Love your enemies and pray for those who persecute you." (Matt 5.44).[80] This enemy-love is central the Gospels. Because God in Christ has shown love to the entire world—to the point of dying for the sake of everyone—Christians are to show love to their enemies. What this means is not conceding to domination, but refusing to participate in the destruction of any human created in God's image.[81]

As Reinhold Niebuhr points out, Christian ethics must maintain a balance and tension among three parameters: love, power, and justice. When these parameters are out of balance, so too are morality and ethics. All three are needed for a strong ethical system.[82]

Islam

Like its sibling faiths, Islam also emphasizes responsibility for justice and charity.

---

79. Borg, *Jesus*, 185–86.

80. Telushkin, 17.

81. Vaux, Syllabus for Christian Moral Theology class, Garrett-Evangelical Theological Seminary, Fall 2008.

82. Ibid.

Command to do justice. Justice is a key concept throughout the Qur'an and an important obligation for every Muslim: "My Lord has commanded justice." (Sura 7.29) In Muslim thinking, justice is closely tied to concepts of equity, equality, and honesty. A great deal of the Qur'an deals with human relations, emphasizing particularly the command to do justice. Because the tradition assumes that there will always be inequality among humans, justice does not necessarily mean equality but fair and equitable treatment. Moral actions, for Muslims, are those that bring justice, making sure all are treated fairly and compensating for loss or deficiencies some may experience. Muslims see the Prophet Muhammad as the standard for morality and justice, a "beautiful example" (Sura 33.21) for followers to imitate.

Distributive justice. All Muslims must be able to live with dignity, but there is no commandment for redistribution of wealth. Instead, believers are expected to give alms as part of serving God. Having wealth is considered a sign of God's bounty, a way to serve God and should be accompanied by generosity: "Your riches and your children may be but a trial: but in the presence of God is the highest reward. So fear God as much as ye can; listen and obey; and spend in charity for the benefit of your own soul and those saved from the covetousness of their own souls . . . If you loan to God a beautiful loan, he will double it to your credit." (Sura 65.15–17) God's abundance is for all to share, although they may not share equally.

Usury and interest. As in Judaism, Islam forbids Muslims *riba*—exploitative interest charged by a lender to a borrower: "If the debtor is in a difficulty, grant him time till it is easy for him to repay," (Sura 2.280) and constitutes hoarding of wealth by the rich. Forgiving a loan is especially worthy.[83] Abusing wealth—gifts given by God—distracts humans from focusing on higher values and is considered "a pittance of this world" and a "delusion of this world." Muslims are expected to contribute to the moral health of society as a whole.

Golden rule of Islam. According to Islamic tradition, Muhammad is believed to have said, "None among you is a believer until he wishes (loves) for his brothers and sisters what he wishes (loves) for himself." Scholars interpret "brother" to mean any human being, whether Muslim or of another faith tradition.

---

83. Wilson, 122–25; Ali and Leaman, 67, 82.

Care for the poor. Charity is one of the pillars of the Muslim faith and a cornerstone of Qur'anic teaching. Believers are commanded to "Give orphans their property, do not replace [their] good things with bad, and do not consume their property with your own—a serious crime." (Sura 4.2) The Qur'an strongly emphasizes socioeconomic justice, helping the poor and the vulnerable and admonishing the wealthy not to hoard material goods: "Whatever gains God has turned over to His Messenger from the inhabitants of the villages that belong to God, the Messenger, kinsfolk, orphans, the needy, the traveler in need—this is so that they do not just circulate among those of you who are rich—so accept whatever the Messenger gives you, and abstain from whatever he forbids you." (Sura 59.7) Those who are wealthy should use their riches to practice generosity and charity: "They ask you what they should spend. Say: 'Whatever bounty (*khayr*) you give is for the parents, the near of kin, the orphans, the needy and the wayfarer. And whatever good (*khayr*) you do, God is completely aware of it.'" (Sura 2.211)[84]

Importance of community. The bond of community is very strong in Islam. Throughout the Qur'an, Muslims are described as "brothers" (Sura 49.10), who when bonded together are as impregnable as a building reinforced with lead (Sura 61.4). Especially important is the concept of *Ummah* in the Qur'an, which means "ideal community" and is compared to a mother who shows love and compassion for all her children, particularly those who are weak or vulnerable. Through these verses, Muslims are called to care for and provide sustenance for the poor, and are even required to lay down their lives for the well-being of the *Ummah*, the Muslim community.[85]

Justice for enemies. Like Judaism and Christianity, Islam calls believe to treat even their enemies fairly: "Let the enmity of a people [towards you] not determine you upon an unjust course; be fair, it is closer to *taqwā*. (Suras 5.8, 5.2)

---

84. Ali and Leaman, 81–82.
85. Wilson, 46–57.

Sin and Ethical Choice

In each of the three Abrahamic traditions, the theology of sin informs and shapes ethical precepts. For Jews, Christians, and Muslims, sin involves taking matters into our own hands, attempting to rely solely on our own strength and will to solve problems and accomplish goals.[86]

Judaism defines sin as violating God's commandments and law. But because humans are created in God's image—and have been given reason, intelligence, and the ability to discern good from evil—they have the ability to make ethical choices for themselves: "If you do well, will you not be accepted? And if you do not do well, sin is lurking at the door; its desire is for you, but you must master it.'" (Gen 4.7) Sin in Judaism is an action, not an inevitable state of being. In the Jewish worldview, God expects humans to sin, but responds with justice and mercy: "Depart from evil, and do good; so you shall abide for ever." (Ps 37.27) God also gives humans freedom and he gives them power, the power to choose and to make mistakes. But God does not expect human perfection: "There is none on Earth so righteous as to do only good and never sin" (Eccl 7.20), humans sin, and God forgives. All God wants from humans is that they do the best they can.[87]

In the Christian worldview, each human—although made in God's image—is born with original sin they cannot escape through their own efforts. Although believers are to model themselves and their ethical behaviors after Jesus, forgiveness is not contingent on performing acts of justice or charity. Because of the Fall, believers are alienated from God, from others, from themselves, and from nature—and not able to resist falling into sin. Pride and self-centeredness, the "basic sin of being centered in ourselves rather than in God, is at the bottom of all other sins."[88] Every sin Christians commit today, then, is an expression and manifestation of original sin, of human efforts to out-wit God and ignore the fact that God is the true center of human lives. Without God's help, Christians are not able to choose good on their own.[89]

Islam, like Judaism, has no doctrine of original sin and, therefore, no need for divine redemption. Humans do sin, and a common theme in the Qur'an is the idea of man's willfulness, ingratitude, and insolence toward God. God is aware of human sin and addresses it through prophethood and revelation. Humans can be forgiven through repentance during their lives

---

86. Vaux, Syllabus for Christian Moral Theology class.
87. Sacks, *To Heal a Fractured World*, 12.
88. Forell, 74.
89. Dorff, *To Do the Right and the Good*, 12–13, 75–78.

and through loving God and following the Prophet: "Say: If you love God, follow me; God will love you and forgive you your sins." (Sura 3.31)[90]

Mending the World

Judaism

Mitzvah and care for the community are key tenets in Judaism, but they are just the beginning: Jews are called to do more than just improve life for themselves and for their communities.

Tikkun olam. In Judaism, ethical obligations extend to *tikkun olam* (mending, improving, or repairing the world).[91] The world needs healing, but humans must not leave this process entirely up to God; God has assigned human beings as partners in the task of mending the world. As caretakers and stewards of the gift God has given, humans are to do what they can to make a difference, to repair the broken places and bring justice and compassion into the world. According to Judaism, the purpose of humankind is to see the image of God in others and "to mend the fractures of the world, a day at a time, an act at a time, for as long as it takes to make it a place of justice and compassion where the lonely are not alone, the poor not without help; where the cry of the vulnerable is heeded and those who are wronged are heard."[92]

Resisting evil. Judaism teaches that there is real evil in the world and that humans have the moral duty and obligation to resist and overcome it—by force, if necessary (although force is not the only way). There is no room in Judaism for resignation or withdrawal: whenever one can do something to confront evil, he has a moral obligation to do it. Humans have

---

90. Ali and Leaman, 40.

91. Sixteenth-century Rabbi Luria set forth the doctrine known as *tzimtzum* (contraction, self-effacement, withdrawal), which suggests that God withdrew into himself to create a space for the world. This first action of God was self-effacement, and it is only when God is hidden that the world can exist. But because God could not create a universe without his presence, he sent rays of light into the world. The light was too powerful to be contained, so the containers broke and scattered rays of light throughout the world. Ever since, the world has been fractured, with "broken vessels," and it is the task of humankind to gather the broken pieces and fragments of light and return them to their proper place. For more, see Sacks, *To Heal a Fractured World*, 74–75.

92. Sacks, *To Heal a Fractured World*, 5.

the power to lessen physical pain and suffering, reduce the occurrence of disease and tragedy, eliminate poverty and war, and eradicate social ills. Jews must never accept as inevitable the problems they see around them. Throughout the Hebrew scripture, Jews are commanded to fight evil: "And thou shalt eradicate the evil from your midst." (Deut 13.5) Judaism consistently teaches that Jews must not only love what is good; they also must hate what is evil: "Ye that love God, hate evil." (Amos 5.15) In Judaism, faith is not acceptance of the world as it is, or acceptance of ourselves as we are; instead it is protest that calls Jews to be "God's question-mark against the conventional wisdom of the age, to build, to change, to 'mend' the world until it becomes a place worthy of the divine presence because we have learned to honor the image of God that is humankind."[93]

Individuals working for the whole. Tikkun olam is progressive development, happening one day at a time and one act at a time, as Jews live in mutual obligation with the community. It is accomplished through the immediacy of daily *Mitzvah* and emerges out a vision of a future world. Each person is challenged by God to contribute his or her unique gifts and capabilities, fulfilling the task only he or she is able to fulfill.[94] Each individual addresses a specific area in need of mending, supporting and building on actions that came before. As each of us works to create a new world of justice, "we place our small piece in a mosaic that will finally provide a new pattern—a new religious and social order."[95]

Christianity

Although the language is different, the Judaic notion of "mending the world" remains throughout Christian thought.

Kingdom of God. In Christianity, the healing of the world is characterized as God's kingdom coming to Earth. Central to Jesus' mission and ministry was his message that "The time is fulfilled, and the kingdom of God has come near . . ." (Mark 1.15). What this refers to is God's kingdom here on Earth, a transformed reality in which there is justice and peace and abundance for everyone. The kingdom of God refers to the way the world would be if God were king, and reflects God's dream, will, and hope for the world. This is a world in which all belong equally, and all will

---

93. Johnson, 14–15; Sacks, *To Heal a Fractured World*, 27–28.
94. Sacks, *To Heal a Fractured World*, 72.
95. Kravitz and Olitzky, 110.

share in God's abundance. Christ is the ultimate transformer of this new reality, but we, too have a role in healing or mending the sinfulness of the world.[96]

Opposing evil. Jesus teaches his followers to drive out evil: "He called his twelve disciples to him and gave them authority to drive out evil spirits and to heal every disease and sickness." (Matt 10.1) So, too, are Christians called to oppose evil when they encounter it. In the 20th century, Bonhoeffer stated this most clearly when he said, "The demand for responsible action in history is a demand no Christian can ignore. We are, accordingly, faced with the following dilemma: when assaulted by evil, we must oppose it directly. We have no other option. The failure to act is simply to condone evil."[97] Even Jesus' statements that appear to advocate passive acceptance of wrongdoing—such as "But if anyone strikes you on the right cheek, turn the other also" (Matt 5.39)—are actually very clear examples of non-violent resistance.[98]

Body of Christ. Similar to the Jewish tradition, in which individual members are expected to do their part in healing the world, so too are Christians called to contribute their God-given gifts for the well-being of the community and the world. As Paul reminds us, "Now you are the body of Christ and individually members of it" (1 Cor 12.27) and "For just as the body is one and has many members, and all the members of the body, though many, are one body, so it is with Christ." (1 Cor 12.12). Christians working together become Christ's body in the world, each doing his part to make God's kingdom, God's dream for the world, a reality. Some theologians refer to this as "participatory eschatology," the notion that Jesus calls us directly to participate in bringing God's kingdom to Earth, especially in sayings such as "But strive first for the kingdom of God and his righteousness, and all these things will be given to you as well." (Matt 6.33) God does not bring about this change solely, nor do we: in the words of St. Augustine, "God without us *will* not; and we without God *cannot.*"[99]

---

96. Borg, 187–89, 251–52.
97. Bonhoeffer, *Ethics*, Internet Encyclopedia of Philosophy.
98. Borg, 247–48.
99. Ibid., 259–60.

Islam

Muslims are strongly encouraged to forbid evil, create a just world, and cooperate with others to bring about an improved earthly reality.

Forbidding evil. Muslims are ordered by the Qur'an to "command right and forbid wrong" as "the believers, both men and women, support each other; they order what is right and forbid what is wrong . . ." (Sura 9.71). In addition, a common *hadith* (Prophet's saying) summarizes the command to forbid evil: "Whosoever sees a wrong, let him change it with his hand. If he is not able, then [let him condemn it] with his tongue. If he is not able, then [let him hate it] with his heart, and that is the weakest faith." The principle of doing good and forbidding evil is a key concept in Islam—Muslims are required not only to refrain from evil but also to prevent others from doing evil, to prevent evil from taking place around them.[100]

Creating a just world. The Qur'an also exhorts believers to work to establish political order, an equal and just moral and social world order designed to "reform the Earth" and eliminate "corruption on the Earth."[101]

Cooperation among communities. Similar to the Jewish concept of Jews working together to mend the world, and Christians working together as the body of Christ, is the Qur'anic vision of cooperation between communities who have the same goals: "O People of the Book! Come [let us join] on a platform that may be common between us—that we serve naught except God" (Sura 3.64) The Qur'an is not calling for an ecumenical religious community, but instead is inviting cooperation among communities to work together to build a new kind of ethico-social world.[102]

Faith and Works

Judaism

In Judaism, the focus on law (works) is balanced with an equal emphasis on belief in God (faith). In *God in Search of Man*, Abraham Heschel addresses the relationship between faith and works in Judaism:

---

100. Ali and Leaman, 20–21.
101. Ibid., 20–21.
102. Ibid., 20–21.

> The dichotomy of faith and works which presented such an important problem in Christian theology was never a problem in Judaism. To us, the basic problem is neither *what is the right action?* nor *what is the right intention?* The basic problem is: what is right living? And life is indivisible. The inner sphere is never isolated from outward activities ... It would be a device of conceit, if not presumption, to insist that purity of heart is the exclusive test of piety. Perfect purity is something we rarely know how to obtain of how to retain. No one can claim to have purged all the dross from his finest desire. The self is finite, but selfishness is infinite. God asks for the heart, but the heart is oppressed with uncertainty is its own twilight. God asks for faith, and the heart is not sure of its own faith. It is good that there is a dawn of decision for the night of the heart; deeds to objectify faith, definite forms to verify belief.[103]

Faith in a world to come. The liturgy of Judaism attests to a strong belief in the world to come, the period of time that begins when earthly existence ceases to be. Prayers such as "God revives the dead with great compassion" in the traditional liturgy, and "God plants eternal life in our midst" in the Reform tradition, signal a hope in a Messianic Era. Implicit in this idea is the promise of divine retribution and resurrection. The concept of Resurrection for each Jew suggested that sins would be punished and wrongs righted. Even in modern liturgy, there exist statements about resurrection, a hope that lives on in modern Judaism. This hope has existed from ancient times; Maimonides found it a cardinal principle. Although not as strong a link as in Christianity, there is in Judaism a connection between faith, works, and being resurrected in the world to come.[104]

Working to bring shalom. In the Jewish tradition, the phrase *shalom*—most commonly interpreted as "peace"—more accurately might be translated as "wholeness" or "completeness." Although the term is used in variety of ways, it has come to mean social and personal perfection, an expression of salvation. The deeper meaning of *shalom* can be seen as it applies to God—as the one who holds together opposites in creative tension: "God is called the 'maker of *shalom*,' who creates both good and evil, light and darkness, war and peace and combines them into a single reality."[105] In

---

103. Heschel, *God in Search of Man*, 296–97.
104. Kravitz and Olitzky, 13–14.
105. Breslauer, *A New Jewish Ethics*, 107–8.

imitating God, humanity (both individuals and society) has a responsibility to hold within itself seemingly opposites ideas: affirming complexity and conflict while at the same time embracing diversity, inclusion, and the possibility of pluralism. This is an ecumenical ideal, and each individual has the responsibility to bring it about.[106]

Christianity

The apostle Paul's focus on justification, which suggests that Christian works are not as important as Christian faith, has been interpreted as denying the importance of ethical conduct: "For we hold that a person is justified by faith apart from works prescribed by the law." (Rom 3.28) Faith, for Paul, is not belief in certain tenets or creeds, nor is it simply trust or fidelity to Christ. According to Paul, "faith is, in effect, finding our true life within the life of Christ."[107] Through Christ, we can find and know God's peace; we have been justified because he has prepared the way for us.

But at other times, Paul argues for the importance of both the internal (faith) and the external (works) aspects of our Christian lives: "For by grace you have been saved through faith, and this is not your own doing; it is the gift of God—not the result of works, so that no one may boast. For we are what he has made us, created in Christ Jesus for good works, which God prepared beforehand to be our way of life." (Eph 2.8–10) Although we cannot earn God's grace through good works, we can respond to this faith formed in love with good works—and these works are an important sign of our faithfulness. While it is impossible to do any good works outside of faith, works can be an expression of genuine faith. But God's internal working of grace within us will always be present in anything we do, and particularly in the ethical choices we make.[108]

Islam

Faith and works are both requirements for Muslims: "To those who believe and do acts of righteousness give the good news that they will go to paradise." (Sura 2.23) Piety and submission to God, along with moral deeds, are equally important in determining one's fate in the afterlife.

---

106. Ibid., 107–8.
107. Hauerwas, *The Hauerwas Reader*, 139.
108. Hollinger, 12–13.

Importance of belief. There is, in Islam, a heavy emphasis on belief; the Arabic term "Islam" means total submission of one's desires to God. In fact, the final measure of a Muslim is belief in the one and only God, and followers are divided strictly into categories of believers and unbelievers.

Good deeds. But, at the same time, good deeds and an individual's character are just as important as piety and submission to God. The Five Pillars of Islam—belief in the oneness of God, daily prayers, charity, fasting, and pilgrimage—are all designed to teach and instill the character attributes of discipline, self-control, piousness, humility, humbleness, modesty, high morals, caring and love. The pillars help Muslims attain moral perfection both internally and externally, and it is believed that believers who follow God's commands and perform good deeds achieves good character.

Salvation. In Islam, the present life is considered merely a pastime: "The present life is nothing but show and frivolity, but the Final Abode is surely better for the pious." (Sura 6.32) A successful outcome of this world is the promise of paradise, another reality in which believers will be rewarded. God created the world, and God will be the final judge. When the Day of Judgment comes, all humans will be "reckoned" for their worth and will have to account for their deeds; those who have sinned will be punished and those who have been righteous and have submitted to God will be rewarded. One of the reasons the Prophet was sent, Muslims believe, was to warn humankind of the day of reckoning to come.[109]

Submission and Humility Before God

Judaism

A Hasidic saying sums up the concept of humility in Judaism: "A person should always carry two pieces of paper in his or her pockets. On one should be written, 'For me the world was created,' and on the other, 'I am but dust and ashes.'"[110] Jews are called to have humility before God and before other humans—remembering their inherent worth and that of every other human. Genuine humility requires a willingness to deny oneself and to be open to hearing and following God's will, even when (especially

---

109. Peters, 42.
110. Kravitz and Olitzky, 43.

when) it contradicts one's own ideas or desires. Abraham's willingness to sacrifice Isaac is the supreme example of submission, obedience, and humility before God. In that single choice to follow God's command, Abraham put aside hubris (the attempt to be more than human), knowing that it is impossible to understand God's justice unless we ourselves are gods. The call of humility is to be the finite beings God created us to be—with limited knowledge, life-spans, and horizons but still made in the very image of God: "We may be no more than an image, a faint reflection, of God himself, but we are no less."[111]

Christianity

Christ teaches that humility—before God and others—is a prime virtue. In the Sermon on the Mount, Jesus proclaims, "Blessed are the meek, for they shall inherit the Earth." (Matt 5.5). And, in another famous passage in Matthew, we hear Jesus say that "So the last will be first, and the first will be last." (Matt 20.16). Over and over, Christians are taught to show humility by putting others before themselves: "Do nothing from selfishness or conceit, but in humility count others better than yourselves." (Phil 2.3)

Humility also involves refraining from boasting. "Come now, you who say, 'Today or tomorrow we will go into such and such a town and spend a year there and trade and get gain;' whereas you do not know about tomorrow. What is your life? For you are a mist that appears for a little time and then vanishes. Instead you ought to say, 'If the Lord wills, we shall live and we shall do this or that.' As it is, you boast in your arrogance. All such boasting is evil." (Jas 4.13–16)

Throughout the Gospels, we hear Christ's message that humility is his way—not self-effacing or false humility, but the humility that comes from acknowledging that we are nothing before God and that God is the author and ultimate source of everything.

Islam

The idea of submission is at the very heart of Islam: "Say: Lo! my worship and my sacrifice and my living and my dying are all for Allah, Lord of the Worlds." (Sura 6.163) The term "Islam" itself is translated as "submission" and comes from the word *aslama*, which means "to surrender" or "resign oneself." Total and unconditional surrender of one's desires to the will of God is thought to bring personal peace, and the greeting *salaam alaykum* (peace be with you) reflects the connection between peace and surrender. Muslims understand the Prophet Muhammad as a facilitator of this submission to Allah. One of

---

111. Sacks, *To Heal a Fractured World*, 26–27.

the pillars of Islam is Unity, the principle that unites all of humankind in submission to Allah. All Muslims have a moral responsibility to surrender to God's will, to recognize that Allah is Creator over all of creation, and to follow Islam (Sura 7.172). Although submission to Allah during this life brings fulfillment, the true rewards will be in the hereafter.[112]

Muslims also are enjoined to be humble before God: "Do not be disdainful of other people, nor walk in arrogance in the Earth. God does not love any person who boasts arrogantly. Be moderate in your pace and lower your voices. The most unpleasant of voices is the ass's." (Sura 31.18–19) Muslims believe that the humble, self-effacing person ultimately garners more respect and prosperity than the person who is boastful and powerful. Humility also entails acknowledging that an individual cannot count his achievements or possessions as his own, but as gifts of God, to whom is due all gratitude.

AN APPLIED INTERFAITH ETHIC

The three Abrahamic faiths are powerful forces animating our world today. If we continue to think of them as separate and competing traditions with different goals and values, we are sure to create a future of conflict and hostility. As the world becomes more globalized, we become more aware of both the differences and commonalities of our faith traditions.

Although slightly different in focus, in reality, the ethical systems of Judaism, Christianity, and Islam share a common foundation. They also intersect along several key parameters: the belief that all humans are created in the image of God, honoring the sanctity of human life, a responsibility for justice and charity, a commitment and a call to "mend the world," and a belief that both faith in God and good works are our human duty. These common threads—the common good—can serve as a starting point for an interfaith ethic that will respect, safeguard, and enhance human life in an increasingly complex world.

The ethic of these communities of faith, along with the belief structure underlying those values and virtues, arise from scripture first and foremost. These are "peoples of the book": the activities of interfaith scriptural study now command our attention.

---

112. Naqvi, *Ethics and Economics*, 48–9; Peters, *The Children of Abraham*, 41–42.

III

Scripture

The Common Word—Interactive Interfaith Reading

SEARCH FOR A COMMON WORD

SØREN KIERKEGAARD, THE MAJOR THEOLOGICAL INFLUENCE ON KARL Barth, convinced him that scripture alone could renew human life, in person and communion, from cultural evil toward grace and goodness. Toward the end of his life, Karl Barth (1886–1968) was invited to the Vatican to address the Secretariat on Christian unity. After his expected comments lauding the ecumenical dialogue of Catholics with the varieties of Orthodox and Protestant faiths, he surprised the commission by asking about the relations of Christians, in general, with the "Jewish people." This particular concern of Barth and of protégé Dietrich Bonhoeffer might be expected from the two great prophetic challengers of the Nazified Catholic and Protestant Church in Germany—both resisters to the Holocaust.

Barth's query sets the stage for any valid discussion of our search for a common word in scripture among the Abrahamic faiths. Just as the parallel and comparative consideration of Torah, *lex Christi*, and Qur'an focused the section on ethics, this section seeks to put the scriptures of the three faiths—*Tanakh, halakhah,* and *midrashim*; the Christian Bible; and Qur'an and *hadith*—on the table together where they can be seen in their progression, synergy, difference, and particularity and universality. In this section, I:

- take note of historical influences, synergies, and dissonances;
- forge an ecumenical hermeneutic for tri-tradition study of scripture;
- identify crucial "chains" of correlated scriptures; and
- consider the processes for interfaith reading.

HEBREW SCRIPTURE

The three faiths—Judaism, Christianity, and Islam—have emerged in human history in sequence and thus possess a strong, unbreakable connection. In the metaphor of the Sufis and William Perkins of Cambridge University, we are linked by a "golden chain."[1]

In affirming this close link, which becomes clear through a process known as Scriptural Reasoning[2] and the consideration of *midrashic* sequences in sacred texts, I do not foresee some *gemischt* amalgam or a least-common-denominator syncretism, but the awareness that each faith possesses a radically true and integral divine dispensation linked to the others in historical association. Limitations of space allow only an enumeration of these interlacing theological common threads.

Judaism as Parental Faith

Judaism appeared among the family of Semitic tribes and nations in the ancient Near East when the great peoples and empires of the region—the far East (China and India) and West (Greece)—were far more impressive. Amid the great empires of Egypt, Assyria, and Persia, Israel was a small player on the stage of history. It was into the empires of Greece and Rome that Christianity appeared within the bosom of Judaism. Together,

---

1. William Perkins (1558–1602) was a 16th-century theologian most known for his guide to the Puritan understanding of soteriology. He depicted a believer's conversion experience as a "golden chain" leading from unbelief to complete obedience. See http://www.apuritansmind.com/WilliamPerkins/PerkinsGoldenChainChart.htm.

2. Scriptural Reasoning is the practice of reading the sacred texts of various religious traditions—primarily Jewish, Christian, and Muslim texts—in communal, interfaith groups for the purpose of discovering common themes, allowing for open communication, and establishing new relationships. Visit the Scriptural Reasoning Web site at http://www.scripturalreasoning.org/index.php.

rabbinic Judaism and nascent Christianity began a process of robust universalist and unitary monotheism. Cosmopolitan and comfortable Rome, tolerant of the plethora of diverse cults and religions, was shocked by this bold new reality when the Apostle Paul proclaimed that One God and Father—the Lord of history—now reigned over the *oikumene*, the whole inhabited Earth. The preceding deities and cults had offered their indispensable preparation, now the whole world—(*olam*, Hebrew, *ulam*, Aramaic/ Arabic) was the realm of the One God and Savior—the Lord of Nations.

Israel's God, theology, and way of life would assume a dominant influence in the world through its irascible offspring: Christianity and Islam. While Judaism claims fewer than 20 million adherents worldwide, it exerts a vast influence on the stage of history and culture. Judaism's law is universally codified, its ethics globally emulated, and its God worshipped to the distant coasts. At nearly 2 billion constituents each, Christianity and Islam together constitute more than half of the world's population.

How did Christianity convey and perpetrate the Name (presence and power) of the God of Israel? Simultaneous to the Roman destruction of the Jerusalem Temple (circa 66 c.e.), Paul announced that the cross and resurrection of Jesus Christ proceeded into the world as the home and temple of God. Israel now clung to a synagogic Diaspora with an episodic yearning for return to Zion. Israel's future became interwoven with Christianity for good and for great evil (Crusades, Inquisition, and Holocaust). In both of these traditions, synagogue and scripture, the worshipping community, and the Bible became the Lord's conveyance.

In a most vital form of Christianity—Jewish Christianity—the faith conferred on people the theology, ethic, way, wisdom, and worship of Israel. This convergence was not supercessionism, but the respectful conveyance of the salient, generative power of Judaism. The Kingship, Lordship, and Logos wisdom of Jesus in world history, however, remained enigmatic. It may well be further clarified by the mystery of messianic history embodied in ongoing Judaism and global Islam. As John Howard Yoder and Jack Miles show, Jesus' kingship—much to the dismay of the insurgent onward Christian soldiers—was that of the Lamb (Rev 22:1), as the nations became "the kingdoms of our Lord and of His Christ." This displacement, even in the seemingly endless age of empires, was to be eschatological and ethical, not political. Purveying the silent and salient Name and Wisdom of the God of Abraham and the saving, righteous inheritance embedded in the "seed of Abraham" surely involved the religious history of Israel, Christianity, and Islam.

The Legacy of Judaism

The theological connections of Judaism and Christianity were much discussed in first-century scholarship. Some of the elements of Hebraic faith that Christianity entirely adopted or adapted are:

- the creation of the world ex nihilo;
- the construal of history as salvation history;
- the advent and destiny of the Messiah;
- the *Akedic* structure of redemption; and
- Yahweh's "Day of the Lord" as the consummation of nature and history.

Creation

Greek philosophy and Hindu cosmogony conceived the world as an eternal, Parmidean process with patterns recurring and fluctuations flowing cyclically and rhythmically. Judaism, through Christianity and Islam, introduced the dimensions of space and time, nature and history now marked by concrete and linear reality as divine allocation and allotment. That the creation proceeded from nihil point through purposive expansion, elaboration, and eventual expiration became a secular, scientific datum—derived from faith.

That there is a creator and consummator of this world and all worlds is a common belief of Jews, Christians, and Muslims—proof of their fraternal theology.

Salvation History

Cosmic history may be ameliorative, *tikkun olam*, and restorative of paradise. It also may be entropic and apocalyptic—a kind of stage for the pilgrimage of creation, as Augustine and Bunyan conceive, ending in the view of most cosmologists today, in cosmic conflagration or deep freeze. Modest good sense keeps open the question of John Polkinghorne's *The End of the World and the Ends of God*.[3] Abrahamic peoples all proclaimed a pathway of meaning in nature and history wherein "God is working

3. See Polkinghorne and Welker, *The End of the World and the Ends of God*.

his purpose out as year proceeds to year." Providence verging toward predestination is a conviction of fundamentalist, Orthodox, and liberal faith. A deep and abiding faith that "God watches out over his own," ever troubling to unionists and co-federalists in their opposing trenches, is deep-seated in the three faiths.

Messiah

The concept of messiah, the anointed One—agent of divine purpose, sent messenger and prophet—pervades the three faiths, both uniting and dividing. The King resides in the Adamic, Abrahamic, Mosaic, and Davidic line. Son of God and Son of Man[4] are promising, yet deeply problematic notions. Demi-god and demi-man are offensive to all. True God and true human ring with authenticity in each facet of the heritage.

While writers like Peter Ochs and Khalil Gibran explore *perichoretic* Godhead within Jewish and Muslim parameters, most in those traditions find the Trinity at best perplexing and at worst polytheistic. Two responses seem relevant: While Jesus himself seems reticent to invoke divinity ("Why do you call me good?"), scholarship today (such as that of Larry W. Hurtado, head of the Divinity School at the University of Edinburgh) sees a sublimely high Christology—King and Lord—fully in keeping with the enveloping Judaic thought world. It now appears that Judaism had a full concept of Messiah, *Logos*, Word, Son, and Wisdom until the final mutual excommunication in the fourth century.[5]

From the Christian side, we realize that Trinitarianism is highly colored by a Greek metaphysics somewhat at variance with Semitic thought. Modern theology from Moltmann and Ford, Derrida and Levinas, Soskice and Pickstock to Ruether and Webster, show that biblically and Hebraically-tenored Christology is safely and solidly monotheistic and intellectually coherent. Somehow, sometime, in some way, I believe Messiah, Divine Wisdom—*hikmah* and *Sophia*—will complete Israel, fulfill Christianity, and consummate Islam. Such embrace will finally realize the whole family of God.

---

4. The Greek word *anthropos*—often translated as "mankind"— means "human being" or "person" (as opposed to "*andros*," the Greek word for "man"). The phrase "son of man" is more accurately translated as "son of the human being."

5. See Boyarin, *Border Lines*.

The Akedah

My recent research[6] convinces me of the central theological substance of the three faiths in the *Akedah*—Abraham's sacrifice of the beloved son. Here is the matrix of the redemption/resurrection motif fundamental to each tradition. In Judaism, it informs Passover, exodus, *Rosh Hashanah*, even tribulation.[7] When Jon Levenson lived in Skokie and taught at the University of Chicago, he wrote, in our library in Evanston, the masterwork of this literature, *The Death and Resurrection of the Beloved Son*. Paul Matthews Van Buren (the great scholar of Jewish-Christian relations) and Donald Juul (New Testament professor) further illumine this motif in the Christian faith.[8] Think of Romans 8:32—"who did not withhold His only son, but gave him up for us all, will not he freely give us all things in him." Think of John 3:16—"God loved the world so that he gave His only son" (monogenos/agapetos). The temptation, baptism, and transfiguration of Jesus, as well, are thoroughly *Akedic* texts.

The theme is felt perhaps most profoundly in Islam. In the *Eid al-Adha*, we find the travail of the two mothers and two sons, the crisis of historical tribulation, the matrix of temptation, the anguish of Islam's elymosenary mission to the poor, whose wretched residence sweeps the central swath around the Earth. All the while, as Max Weber foresaw, Judaism and Christianity prefer comfortable, prosperous, middle-class existence.

Akedah is to me the irrefutable evidence that we are brothers and sisters at the very essence of faith and value. We are therefore to put on the new humanity—where there is neither Jew nor Greek, slave or free, but God who is One is all in all.

At the root of Christian scripture is the Bible of the Jews. When Philip Yancey writes of the Bible Jesus read and Paul the Apostle alludes to sacred writ, they speak of Hebrew scripture.[9] Both Jews and Paul likely knew of sacred writings (scrolls or parchment folios) that included texts in Hebrew, the Septuagint (an entire Hebrew Bible in Greek) and certain sacred writings in Aramaic—the vernacular Hebrew of the Greco-Roman world—what could be seen as a cognate language of Arabic.

---

6. See Vaux, *Jew, Christian, Muslim* and *An Abrahamic Theology for Science*.

7. See Spiegel, *The Last Trial*.

8. See Levenson, *The Death and Resurrection of the Beloved Son*; Van Buren, *According to the Scriptures*; and Juul, *Messianic Exegesis*.

9. See Yancey, *The Bible Jesus Read*.

As the Christian era dawned and the two news faiths emerged, rabbinic Judaism and early Christianity, Jewish scripture existed in an entire Hebrew text—the Tanakh—which we know from the Qumran community evidence in the Dead Sea Scrolls. Jesus read the Tanakh scroll in the Capernaum Synagogue (Luke 4.16–30), and Paul studied the same, we may believe, with Gamaliel (Acts 5.34). Both, we may conjecture, read (heard) LXX (Septuagint), which was widely known in the great Greco-Roman metropoliti of Nazareth (Sepphoris) and Antioch.

Yahweh's Day of the Lord
Eschatology is a common culminating scriptural motif. The climax of world history will be a cataclysm (paroxysm) of judgment and grace, when all humanity and creation will be called to account for its use of life and freedom. Here the prevalent mistakes of life on Earth will be rectified: the poor will be vindicated and blessed and, in surprising, topsy-turvy disclosure (quite unlike the "left-behind" fantasies), the tables will be turned, and God's good way for this world and eternity will become clear.

CHRISTIAN SCRIPTURE

Christian scriptural canon was not settled for centuries. The Marcion, Manichean, and other Gnostic challenges sought to excise the Hebrew Bible and much gospel material in favor of dualistic, spiritualistic, and unbiblical perspectives and these nearly prevailed. Hundreds of gospels, psalms, acts, and apocalypses abounded. In my own view, corroboration of Torah-focused, Decalogic, prophetic, and Abrahamic (*Akedic*) horizons is useful in determining what is authentically spiritual. For Christians, *midrashic* corroboration back to Judaism and forward into Islam is helpful and supportive to understanding. Jewish Christianity (James, Thomas, pseudo-Clementine, etc. materials) counterbalance Gnostic, spiritualistic, and hyper-apocalyptic approaches, grounding Christian scripture in Semitic prequel and sequel literature with more thoroughgoing worldly and ethical substance.

Christian scripture, through a rich tapestry of Hebrew texts—from Daniel to Proverbs to 4 Maccabees and new covenant materials from John to James—is grounded in an Abrahamic and Mosaic prophetic and Christic (messianic/*Logos*) ethos. Though first-hand apostolic witness became the criterion of the canon, interfaith scriptural study best fathoms the *midrashic* chain. "Thus saith the Lord" becomes the overriding authority.

I learned this when I first read Jaroslav Pelikan's *Mary Through the Centuries*, in which his textual foundations ran from the Samuel stories through the gospels (Annunciation and Magnificat) through to the Qur'an (e.g., Sura 19).[10]

MUSLIM SCRIPTURE

Touching on the *Eid al-Adha* (the Feast of Sacrifice) and the *Akedah* (perhaps the pivotal theological axis of Islam with its Isaac/Ishmael fulcrum) reminds me of the relative ignorance of Islam portrayed thus far in this essay.

Stanley Fish has bitingly attacked my oversight in a 2007 essay in the *New York Times*. Addressing the irony of ignored truth claims in our world of profuse religiosity (yet absent theology), he reflects that this mischievous yet essential "one true God" stuff is being obfuscated by silly debates of whether America is a Christian, Judeo-Christian, or a none-of-the-above culture. Governor Fordice (who prefers the "Christian" to the "Judeo-Christian" designation) will not join the "multiculturalist appreciators of everything." Fish demurs: "Once it's Judeo-Christian, it will soon be Judeo-Islamic Christian and then Judeo-Islamic-Native American Christian and then . . ."[11]

Not enamored with Alasdair MacIntyre's provincialism as is fellow post-modernist Fish, I prefer to struggle on into the difficult twilight of the theological horizon of "One God," inter-Abrahamic Scriptural Reasoning. Not only truth and goodness, but survival itself, I believe, may hang on this quest.

This by way of prefacing my admittedly novice treatment of Islam's relationship to its forerunners Judaism and Christianity. The three Abrahamic faiths, I propose, consummately see the One and unified God as the finisher of faith (perhaps through faith-tradition pathways), the One who, at the end of all things, will be "all in all." In that *pleroma* (fullness) or *parousia* (paradise in Aramaic/Arabic), what we saw only dimly will be seen in clarity, what we have known in part will then be fully known. (1 Cor 13.12).

The pathway and connectivity between Judaism, Christianity, and Islam is complicated, but essential to the establishment of my thesis. I first note the historical continuity.

---

10. See Pelikan, *Mary Through the Centuries*.
11. Fish, "Religion Without Truth."

Historical Links

Many see the origins of Islam in the Jewish/Christian community identified with James, Jesus' brother, his mother and family, and the community called *Ebionim* (the poor ones). After the flight to Pella amid the Roman-Jewish wars, most of the poor faithful were killed in the first Jewish holocaust at the hands of Rome, where "blood flowed down the temple steps like water" (Josephus). Just as the original Semites emigrated from Arabia to Mesopotamia, now from the Mesopotamian cities of Edessa, Antioch, and Pella, a Judeo-Christian remnant may have gravitated south where they would lay the foundations of Islam.

By the seventh century, a form of Christianity was found in Arabia, in Jaba—now modern Yemen. In Muhammad's lifetime, the influence of Syria, Mesopotamia, and Persia was felt in Arabia. Christianity in Abyssinia and Diaspora Judaism in the same region would prepare the soil for the growth of Islam.

The link seems to be Jewish Christianity east and south of Jordan, the Monophysite church of Syria, the Agoa tribe of the mountain peoples of Syria (who still spoke Aramaic), and the Christianized kingdom of Axum, Abyssinia, now Eretria and Ethiopia. Here Muhammad sought refuge in the fifth year of his call, 615 c.e. In this sanctuary and in the revealing pre-Islamic poetry of the region, most Arabists feel, lie the origins of Islam.[12]

Theologically and ethically, Islam seemed, at its outset, to be a reform movement within Christianity. "Why did you wander from your Christian and Jewish origins?" these proto-Muslims were asked by their protector king in Abyssinia:

> 'We were a barbarous nation,' they admitted, 'worshipping idols, killing our own people, devouring the weak. Then God sent us an apostle, one of our own.' He summoned us to God, to believe in his unity, to worship him and abandon stones and idols. He commanded us to speak the truth, to be faithful to our trusts, to observe our duties to kinsfolk and neighbors, to refrain from forbidden things and bloodshed, from consuming the property of orphans and widows.'[13]

---

12. See Trimingham, *Islam in Ethiopia.*
13. Van Leeuwen, *Christianity in World History*, 217.

The Decalogical form of this confession shows that the thread of connection, a virtual life-giving ligature between (Judeo) Christianity and Islam, can be found in the conveyance of Word, Will, and Wisdom of God epitomized in Torah, Decalogue, and *Akedah*—the cardinal Abrahamic, Mosaic, Prophetic, and Christic substance. If this and the former convergence with Judaism are correct, then Christians will want to abandon their supercessionist posture toward Judaism, seeing the only "good Jew" as a "Jew for Jesus." We also can put aside the view that Islam is a Godless, violent, pagan religion whose people are the proper objects of conversion. Muslims are already "for Jesus," I have discovered. We may even wish to view the prophet Muhammad as one in the succession of Amos or Paul—prophets called in the history of God to restore faith and righteousness—the meaning of Torah, Decalogue, and *Akedah* (*Logos*).

To begin to land this plane, which I hope has left you a bit anxious and out of breath but in the end hopeful and ready to go to work, let me say that each faith must continue to fill out its particular evangelizing and proselytizing vocation. My friend, Tariq Ramadan, at the university at the other end of the long rowing course (Oxford), once told me "listen to my story, and I'll ask you to tell me about Jesus." Jews ought to advocate and share with the world Yahweh's way, Torah, Decalogue, prophetic justice, and shalom. Don't give up, we need you. Without you, we Christians and Muslims will lose our way. As Stanley Hauerwas said in his customarily raucous way, Jews should give Christians reasons to become Jews, and Christians give Jews reasons to receive Christ. Christians and Muslims need to be continually renewed and refreshed by the Law and the Prophets—*Tanakh*.

Christians need to share Jesus Christ with the world. He sustains the way of Israel bringing salvation and peace. He is savior and Lord for the people of the world.

Muslims need to share their distinctive inheritance and mission—the rigor and intensity of synthetic faith and life, the heart for the poor, which is the heart of God.

The Need for Interfaith Scriptural Reasoning

Muslim tradition speaks of "peoples of the Book" (*Ahl al-Kitāb*), Jewish and Christian scriptures: *Taurut* (Torah), *Zabur* (Psalms), and *Injil* (four Gospels). Jews also use this phrase (*Am Hasefer*) as self-referential—embracing their sacred corpus of Torah, *Tanakh*, as well as *Mishnah* and

Talmud. Muslims use a similar primary and secondary canonical standard when they combine Qur'an, the direct divine revelation to Muhammad from the angel Gabriel in the Medina and Mecca recitations, and the *hadith*, a more interpretative sequel. Qur'an is direct, literal word of God (*verbum Dei*), perhaps similar to the Decalogue in strictest Judaism and in Christianity where God actually spoke and inscribed (in stone) *vox Dei*.

Some of Christian tradition is typical of the Puritan John Wesley, who in the 18th century studied at Oxford, learning Hebrew and Old Testament, Greek and New Testament and Arabic and Qur'an. This is an exception. In the broader tradition, suspicion and mutual rejection prevails. Jews have repudiated Christian sacred text as idolatrous and polytheistic until very recently when, for example, Jesus' Sermon on the Mount was included in the sacred body of Jewish literature (Reform Judaism). Christians (from Marcion on) have often rejected Jewish texts as crude and violent. Both of these bodies most generally have repudiated the Qur'an as pagan and blasphemous.

Only today—in a world of Christianity repentant of its complicity in the Holocaust and in the post-September-11th Israeli-Palestine-anti-terrorist atmosphere—has an interfaith fascination and interaction developed. Today, interfaith Scriptural Reasoning is cautiously being explored in Americo-Israel and Eurabia in particular—the dominant Judeo-Christian strongholds and cleansed de-Judaized Europe where Islam flourishes—but also throughout the Muslim, African, and Asian worlds. When Muslim-Christian encounters begin in earnest in Pakistan and India, Nigeria and Kenya, Indonesia and Beijing, we will know we have seen the dawn of a new day in a new world.

A NEW HERMENEUTIC

Scriptural research today is done in comparative and historical continuity models with a heavy accent on sociocultural analysis. Any visit to AAR (American Academy of Religion, which includes world scholars) and SBL (Society of Biblical Literature), which is international as well, shows the coming frontier of comparative, interfaith biblical-scriptural research and teaching.

Outlines of the new hermeneutic become clear as we look at the approaches of the three leaders of the Cambridge interfaith center: David F. Ford, Peter Ochs, and Timothy Winter. In many hours of collaboration with these colleagues, I have seen the following convictions and commitments.

David F. Ford: Faith in Action

The Regius Professor of Divinity at Cambridge (and my mentor in the Interfaith Scriptural Reasoning section of CARTS) is the brains and inspiration behind interfaith work in the university, the theological academy, and broader faith communities. We all take strength for our endeavors from his leadership. One of the world's leading theologians, David worked with his distinguished (now deceased) father-in-law, Daniel Hardy in the mid 90s to form Scriptural Reasoning groups (laboratories); Scriptural Reasoning theory committees (to shape theoretical concepts and strategies), *in situ* centers (St. Ethelburga's Centre for Reconciliation and Peace in the financial district of London), and pioneering endeavors such as the pan-Islamic "Common Word" initiative.[14] Educated in his native Ireland, Cambridge, Yale, and Tübingen, David is a biblical scholar, a theological pioneer, a lectionary preacher, and a scholar of wisdom.[15] On campus, he can be seen riding his bicycle into Trinity College, and in his back-pack are his Greek New Testament, Hebrew Bible, Septuagint, and a copy of the Qur'an.

For David Ford, Scriptural Reasoning is a medium for faith active in life. A liturgical person, David is committed to faith as enacted in Decalogue, prophetic confrontation, and building of the world in grace and love, justice and peace. Joining hearts and mind—even hands—across the oft-troubled rivulets running among the three faiths, David sees Scriptural Reasoning as construction of bridges across faith traditions where we "lay me down" in sharing/absorbing/redeeming reciprocity.

Fords' conceptual motivation is not to achieve division-ending consensus or amalgamation, but friendship, trust, mutual respect and "back-to-the-books" authenticity within one's own tradition. If a transcending point of reference can be reached, if suspicion can painfully and slowly be examined, and if prejudices and stereotypes can be challenged, scripture's own salience from all sources can be allowed to shine forth.

---

14. "A Common Word," the work of Muslim scholars, clerics, and intellectuals, identifies the common ground between Islam and Christianity. The complete document is available on the Web site of A Common Word, http://www.acommonword.com/.

15. See Ford, *Theology*.

Ford's approach takes two directions. First, in a new hermeneutics, he seeks to bring the best insights of biblical exegesis and interpretation to bear on interfaith conversation. The divinity faculty at Cambridge is a treasure store of biblical scholars and conferences, where probes are always under way to glean from the plethora of new work on Hebrew, Christian, and Muslim scripture the insights made possible by recent archeological, historical, and cultural research. In a fall 2007 sabbatical I attended, for example, there were dozens of classes and seminars on "Jewish Christianity," drawing on discoveries rising from research on Ebionism, pseudepigraphal texts, Dead-Sea-Scrolls work, *Nag Hammadi* manuscripts and the recent trove of scholarship of Jews', Christians', and Muslims' heretofore unexamined (and often erroneous) ideas.

Ford also accents confessional emphasis where Anglican and Methodist, Catholic and Orthodox Christianity, Reform and Orthodox Judaism, and *Shiah* and *Sunni* Islam seek renewal and scriptural return and rigor within their parochial circles.

Peter Ochs: Embrace of Interfaith Perspectives

Peter Ochs, founder of the movement of Scriptural Reasoning and professor of Jewish Studies at University of Virginia, is a prophetic, pastoral soul. In a Scriptural Reasoning workshop on "care for the poor," he noted how texts in Judaism and derivatively in Christian and Muslim traditions emphasize how we are not to impoverish the poor by charging interest on loans. The biblical heritage is the very antithesis of popular banking culture, which either amplifies interest rates or positively "gouges" the poor with sub-prime (exorbitantly accelerating) loans.

I still remember the funeral mass for Daniel W. Hardy in the old Cambridge St. Benet's Chapel. Rabbi Peter was the homilist. He offered rabbinic solace from the Gospel of John. He spoke personally to Dan's family and daughter, to David and to each of the grandchildren. He found personal encouragement for each heart-broken survivor, each in their very particular situation. Scripture alone speaks from God to the human heart.

Peter's unique emphasis in the Scriptural Reasoning endeavor is an uncanny and winsome openness, kindness, and enthusiastic embrace of interfaith perspectives. He bears out Buber's dictum that Judaism's mission and destiny on Earth is to establish justice and peace.

Educated at Yale and Jewish Theological Seminary, Peter's work has focused on modern Judaism and cultural issues. An early book[16] pointed toward his interest in Scriptural Reasoning and pioneered the neo-Barthian movement of reconnaissance of textual concentration throughout progressive world faiths—a movement animated by the example, for many decades, of Orthodox Judaism in the *yeshiva* and Qur'anic study in the *madrassas*. In another work with John Howard Yoder, Ochs traced the "parting of the ways of Judaism and Christianity."[17]

He now superintends the Web site for the Society for Scriptural Reasoning at AVA with his doctoral assistant Jacob Goodson, my former student at Garrett. In a helpful instructional essay, he lays out a body of rules for Scriptural Reasoning, which also discloses his own fears and hopes for the movement. The outline and first paragraphs of introduction are most illuminating from this pastoral-prophet.

The Rules of Scriptural Reasoning[18]

Dear SSR Colleagues,

Shalom. After four years of shared scriptural interpretation at our annual gatherings, we decided this year to stop what we do, for a moment, and reflect on how we are doing what we do "*Naaseh v'nishmah*," the angels say when God commands: "we do first, and then we seek understanding." So, the Rabbinic sages in *b. Talmud Shabbat* describe the precedence of action over reflection in what we might call one functional epistemology of Scriptural Reasoning. There is no measure, ratio, logos, or rule of merely human reasoning adequate to encompass or predict the rule of practice and thinking that will be displayed in divine speech. So we wait, like the angels, receiving the speech, imitating it through out actions and, only then, come to ask ourselves, "What is it we are doing after all? What rules of life have been engendered in us?"

"Why ask at all?" we might inquire. We ask because we are not angels, being at the same time smarter and more sinful. Out of our sinfulness, imperfection, and error the "imaginings of our hearts being bad from our very youth" (Gen 8.21) comes both our inability to enact precisely what God has

---

16. See Ochs, *The Return to Scripture in Judaism and Christianity*.
17. See Yoder, Cartwright, and Ochs, *The Jewish-Christian Schism Revisited*.
18. Ochs, Introduction to "The Rules of Scriptural Reasoning."

asked and our need for intelligence, as a means of getting out of the trouble we perpetually put ourselves in. Intelligence, or what Michael Wyschogrod calls our "quality of brightness," is the capacity to reflect on our actions and discern in them traces of the divine will. These traces serve as a mirror in whose reflection we may criticize our actions that have not been in accordance with God's word. After critical reflection, they also function as a guide that may direct our actions in greater fidelity to that word in the future. Unless God were to exhaust himself with continual criticism and re-revelation on our behalf, we have no choice but to appeal to our intelligence to help perform God's work. While there is no choice in the matter, this is still another source of *tsores* (trouble) for us. In fact, the SSR appears to have arisen specifically in response to the great failing of Intelligence in the modern world. The shared sense of this Society is that the dominant paradigms of reason both in the university and in our seminaries are deeply flawed. We believe that these paradigms have tempted not only the academy, but also an alarmingly significant part of our religious communities, to reverse the terms of the angels' pledge: we will understand things first on our own terms and only then see how the words of the Creator, Revealer, and Redeemer apply. This type of Copernican revolution, while rightly elevating our limited potential for good, ultimately leads to something bad: vicious dialectic of totalitarian versus nihilistic reasoning. In other words, the modern practice of Intelligence transforms the activity of reflection into the object of reflection. Reflection, however, is not itself an object. Aristotle's reflecting-on-reflection god may think otherwise, but that is the point: either we are not gods or Aristotle's god is not God. When we identify the rule of our actions with the activity of reflecting on reflection, we inherit a world of our own making: totality or nothing.

Members of the SSR tend to view the disasters of Western society in the 20th century as consequences of this awful dialectic. While acknowledging and moving within and beyond modern thought, the purpose of SR is to recover the practice of listening for the speech of God that both preceded and still provides the terms for modern thinking. The goal is, as much as is possible and appropriate, to reenact traditional Jewish, Christian, and Muslim practices of scriptural reading and interpretation in order to reconstitute modern Intelligence as practice of reflecting on the rules of Scriptural Reasoning.

Timothy Winter (Abdal Hakim Murad):
Two Ways of Reading Scripture

The Islamic Mullah at Cambridge and lecturer in Islamic Studies on the faculty of divinity brings yet another perspective on Scriptural Reasoning. Like Ford and Ochs, Winter is a passionate scholar deeply involved in life. In an essay that appears in *The Promise of Scriptural Reasoning*,[19] he argues that academically situated Scriptural Reasoning has a unique role. Learned reflection serves the broader practice of scriptural faithfulness, the personal study in family discipline, and congregational and confessional active deliberation among the faithful. Winter finds the Jewish-Muslim encounter especially fruitful, given the profound affinity (and difference) of these two movements. Winter, like his Oxford counterpart Tariq Ramadan, is fascinated with the presence of Islamic study in the universities of Western Europe and North America.

Muslim studies have often been performed by Christian or Jewish scholars who tend to overlay their observations on Islam with the biases of Hegelian higher criticism or those of "Orientalism."[20] Lacking the profound respect and reverent study of Christian thinkers like Kenneth Cragg or David Burrell—who spent long years in the study of Arabic, Qur'an, and Islam—these more pedestrian scholars can only offer distorted pictures of Islam as ridiculous of those that dominate the bipolar Manichean of the American consciousness.

Winter identifies the two ways of reading scriptures—the outside and inside. Scriptures of Hebrew, Christian, and Muslim traditions often taunt us with two seemingly opposite ways in which they can be viewed. "Take your son . . . and offer him" vs. "Do not lay your hand on the boy. . . ." (Gen 22.2, 12) and "Celebrate the drowning of the Egyptians" vs. "What are you doing, they are also my people" (Exodus and *Rabbah*, the *midrash* to Exodus). Winter draws on Islamic hermeneutics to speak to a modus of "what is apparent" and what is surprising. In my teaching, I often speak of what "we want scripture to say" and what, "by God," it really says.

In a trenchant demotion, Jacques Derrida would not privilege any communication—writing or speech—with ultimacy or normativity. All

---

19. Winter, "Qur'anic Reasoning as an Academic Practice."

20. Orientalism refers to the academic study of the "orient," which includes Islam, the Middle East, and the Far East—as opposed to the "occident," made up of England, France, and the U.S.

human words remain human words. The words bear only those human mysteries and meanings.

Winter's view is resonant, but different. Scripture is valid and vibrant in its own right. He finds "plain sense" interpretive wisdom in the Qur'an and *hadith*. Although he dismisses the "shaping" importance of precursor movements of the Muslim scriptural ethos—the influence of the warring movement of Jewish Christianity; the mediating wisdom of pre-Islamic Arabic poetry; and the concurrence and influence of Jewish and Christian scripture and devotion—he affirms the innate and inherent power of Islamic scripture to illuminate and inspire faithful textual mediation of God's very being and will and human submission to that truth and goodness.

In this spirit, Winter affirms the Abrahamic pan-scriptural validity and complementarity of Afdal al-Din Kashani (d. 1213):

> [God] adorned the mark of these three sending-downs for three communities: The folk of the Torah, the Gospel, and the Qur'an. Despite all the prophets, He said that only these three levels of sending-down should be kept standing. Thus He says, "O Folk of the Book! You are not upon anything until you uphold the Torah (*Taurut*) and Gospel (*Injil*) and what was sent down to you from your Lord." (Qur'an, Sura 5.68)[21]

This standpoint is the strongest assertion of Scriptural Reasoning and the broader enterprise of interfaith exploration and action.

To conclude this hermeneutical point: the epitome of human capacity, while living on Earth from and toward eternity, living in time and history from and toward infinity, is sacrificial love toward others in God. This is the rational gist of secret revelation conveyed from the bosom of Abraham in the parable of *Akedah*—dying for God. Abraham, with Hagar and Sarah, Ishmael and Isaac, resides with Moses and Elijah in eternity with messiah wisdom (John 8.40ff.). From there, He conveys into the world that metaphor and parable of ultimate reality. Géza Vermès summarizes the biblical verdict: "Abraham (in *Akedah*) proved his perfect love, and his example became the corner stone of the whole Jewish theology of the love of God."[22]

---

21. Chittick, *The Heart of Islamic Philosophy*, 228.
22. Vermès, *Scripture and Tradition in Judaism*, 193.

CURRENT EMPHASIS ON SCRIPTURAL REASONING

This corresponds with the papers presented at the very moving presidential inauguration of Iain Torrance as the new president of Princeton Theological Seminary—my alma mater. Signaling firmly that this historically scripture-grounded institution will be moving even more firmly in this direction, the theological workshop and the installation itself were a "clinic" in Scriptural Reasoning:

- David F. Ford spoke of reading scripture with intensity in academic, ecclesial, interfaith, and divine ways.

- Aref Ali Nayed, a visiting fellow with me at CARTS (and head of Jordan's Royal Islamic Strategic Studies Centre), showed how our fundamental human activity—reading, with the attendant activities of recitation, hermeneutics, interpretation, and appropriated action—was the deepest and most authentic liturgy of Church (synagogue and *masjid*), academy and society. Schleiermacher's *hermeneutica sacra* (to be distinguished from general or secular hermeneutics) allows one to read the very "voice of God" with others, not only in vivid and motivating ways, but in ways that open *aya/ayat* (the "operative signs"/"signs of the times" from God's self)—directional currents that flow into the "sea of the divine life."

- Peter Ochs used the wonderful biblical image of tents—like Abraham's opened to all sides all the while invoking the God of Israel, new each morning with fresh sharing (manna) for our sustenance for the day. Scriptural reading and reasoning for Jews is always seen through the tears of the *Shoah*—a constituting, seminal, one might say biblical, event. The eyes of genocide also become the eyes with which other communities read their scriptures—the Armenian Christians, the Palestinian Muslims, Sudanese and Rwandan Christians, and Muslims are obvious examples. For Jews, the Holocaust is now woven into the hermeneutical, rabbinic tradition. Ochs' gracious, what our colleague Janice Soskice calls his "evangelical temper," has graced the Scriptural Reasoning movement with moods of hospitality and expectant discovery.

To summarize the Scriptural Reasoning methodology: it begins with the assumption that most people in the world are people of faith already involved in the daily liturgy of searching the scriptures. Rulers and leaders of all walks of life—those who daily influence the common good in government, law, business, science and health—are also mostly people of faith, certainly sharing the subliminal piety and morality of the religious traditions. Whether their acceptance of scriptural authority is authentic or feigned, it is part of their world. The Abrahamic portion of the world's populace—estimated from half to two-thirds—gives special credence to the mode of Scriptural Reasoning, at least as a starting place.

The atmosphere for convened Scriptural Reasoning round tables—though cordial and respectful—is filled with suspicion caused by undertones of past history and overtones of provincial perceptions. The Crusades and counter-Crusades—the defeat of the Serbs in Kosovo in 1389—can be felt as yesterday occurrences. Medieval glory in Judaism and Islam—when Scriptural Reasoning was not only in vogue but was the assumed manner of exegesis, especially in *Al-Andalus*—has turned to a mood of remorse and humiliation especially in post-Ottoman *Dar al-Islam*. Such historical memories, often involving deceased friends or sacrifices of family members in the remote past—Auschwitz, Armenia and Jenin—are often moments of outpouring of fury, deep sympathy, apology, even forgiveness, wonderful ways to begin receptive study of holy texts.

The Scriptural Reasoning process also can be obfuscated from the outset by overtones of the transcendental sensations that rise to the surface when matters touching on blood, soil, home, and nation are at stake. It is a direct line of development from serving and sacrificing for one's own, to laying down one's life for one's friends (including one's fellow warriors), to offering one's life in martyrdom for one's God. When these sensibilities and sensitivities are taken into consideration, a productive and surprisingly creative process can ensue. In order for the Scriptural Reasoning covenant to unfold from confrontation to conversation to collaboration, David Ford commends the following maxims or game rules:

- Acknowledge the sacredness of scriptures to each group—for God's sake.
- Don't seek consensus.
- Don't shun argument through courtesy/seek truth.

- Draw on shared resources, *e.g.*, "pragmatists" from each faith.
- Allow time to read and reread.
- Seek the same goal: God's purpose of peace towards all.
- Foster hospitality, friendship, house, and tent.

To these procedural principles, I would add a set of "substantial" goals:

- Even though the purpose of Scriptural Reasoning is theological grappling and ethical action, we should engage scholars of the respective scriptures to clarify "chains" of texts that have *midrashic* connection, *i.e.*, texts that intentionally derive from ancestors and drive toward followers.

- Work with philosophers and critical theologians in each tradition to propose a "normativity" particular to each tradition, *e.g.*, why and how should Christianity refer to its precursor texts from the Hebrew tradition, and what is the Qur'an's connection with "the peoples of the Book?" This would seem to involve some very difficult work in the history of religion and in comparative religion to discern, then declare, what is the understood dispensation of each of the fraternal faiths in the providence of God and in the historical unfolding of cognate faiths. Several case studies of Scriptural Reasoning serve to illustrate the wisdom this dialogue has to proffer public deliberations, especially about the theme of this essay.

Scriptural Reasoning Case Study

Blasphemy, the Divine Name,
and the Death Penalty for Religious Conversion

One of the scriptural chains I often use at Scriptural Reasoning roundtables is what I call the blasphemy chain. The blasphemy chain hinges on the New Testament passage "People will be forgiven for their sins and whatever blasphemies they utter; but whoever blasphemes against the Holy Spirit can never have forgiveness . . ." (Mark 3:28–29) This text echoes the great Torah injunction: "You shall not make wrongful use of the Name of the Lord your God . . ." (Deut 5:11).

The Qur'anic *midrash* on this chain could be 16:106 (one of the critical *kufr*/unbelief/ lapsed belief or/apostasy texts), which concerns the issue of one who comes to disbelieve after believing, or a blasphemy text that concerns speech derogatory to God—rejecting revealed truth (*tahdhib*) and giving over to the lie or false belief (*iftira*).

This particular chain of Scriptural Reasoning has recently received attention from Muslim and Jewish/Christian political and military officials of Afghanistan and Anglo-America in the war on terrorism conflict in Kabul. It was resolved, as is so often the case, not by Scriptural Reasoning, but by high-level diplomatic pressure and threats. Abdul Rahman, who had converted to Christianity from Islam 15 years ago while working with a Christian agency aiding refugees, was accused of breaking the first commandments when he recently sought custody of his children and his family reported the conversion/ apostasy. The first two commandments, belief and proper confession, are strenuously kept in Islam and their negative sanctions, apostasy and blasphemy, can become matters of *Sharī'ah* (the body of public religio-societal law), even bringing the death penalty, a punishment arising from the Hebrew Torah. While Western interpreters of Qur'an say belief is never compulsory and that the great mercy and forgiveness of Allah pertains, these liberal interpreters contend that "freedom of religion" must hold political sway (at least countries under the control of American occupation, military strength, and foreign aid). More fundamentalist forms of Islam and the nations they influence, demur. The case was eventually resolved, as was the *Sharī'ah* case in Nigeria in which a pregnant woman was given the death penalty of stoning for adultery, for reasons of mental incompetence—which is another way of bowing to Anglo-Euro-American pressure. My somewhat cynical inference here is merely another argument for the importance of Scriptural Reasoning in public life.

The deep theological issue behind these textual disputes, and preliminary to any political resolution, is the theoretical issue of whether Jews, Christians, and Muslims worship the same God. Though such a question is ultimately irresolvable in terms of reason—despite the noble, centuries-long struggle on the matter from sages of the three Abrahamic faiths—it requires reaching a provisional working standpoint in order to ground some public policy regarding toleration and the role of the state in adjudicating matters of belief and unbelief.

Scriptural Reasoning Case Study
Akedah, Sacrifice, the Beloved Son, Martyrdom and Dying for the Faith

Another exercise we have often undertaken in our community during these agonizing years of terrorist and suicide attacks on the one side, and full scale invasion and occupation on the other, is the most salient chain of texts that showing the inescapable connection and interdependence among the three Abrahamic faiths. This is the *Akedah*, Abraham and the sacrifice of Isaac—that arches across from Genesis 22 through most of Jewish scripture into Hebrews 11.8–19 (with many New Testament cross-references such as John 3.16)—where that faithful obedience is extolled. It then evolves into Sura 37 of the Qur'an, which deals with the Isaac/Ishmael issue and Muslim themes of *jihad*, suffering, and martyrdom. This chain forms a bridge that is ultimately decisive on interconnection among the three fraternal faiths and their witness in the world.

In recent years, it also has become clear that these texts are fundamental to the exercise of terrorist and suicidal acts and authorized militaristic policies that often invoke the name of the God of those faiths within the very interfaith conflicts of our time—conflicts that often have fratricidal overtones, such as Israel/ Palestine, Afghanistan, Iraq, the events of September 11th, and the bombings of U.S. embassies in Tanzania on August 7, 1998.

Genesis 22.1–13[23]

¹And it came to pass after these things, that God did prove Abraham, and said unto him: 'Abraham'; and he said: 'Here am I.' ²And He said: 'Take now thy son, thine only son, whom thou lovest, even Isaac, and get thee into the land of Moriah; and offer him there for a burnt-offering upon one of the mountains which I will tell thee of.' ³And Abraham rose early in the morning, and saddled his ass, and took two of his young men with him, and Isaac his son; and he cleaved the wood for the burnt-offering, and rose up, and went unto the place of which God had told him. ⁴On the third day Abraham lifted up his eyes, and saw the place afar off. ⁵And Abraham said unto his young men: 'Abide ye here with the ass, and I and the lad will go yonder; and we will worship, and come back to you.'

---

23. Hebrew Bible translations by Mechon Mamre, http://www.mechon-mamre.org/p/pt/pto.htm.

⁶And Abraham took the wood of the burnt-offering, and laid it upon Isaac his son; and he took in his hand the fire and the knife; and they went both of them together.

⁷And Isaac spoke unto Abraham his father, and said: 'My father.' And he said: 'Here am I, my son.' And he said: 'Behold the fire and the wood; but where is the lamb for a burnt-offering?' ⁸And Abraham said: 'God will provide Himself the lamb for a burnt-offering, my son.' So they went both of them together. ⁹And they came to the place which God had told him of; and Abraham built the altar there, and laid the wood in order, and bound Isaac his son, and laid him on the altar, upon the wood. ¹⁰And Abraham stretched forth his hand, and took the knife to slay his son. ¹¹And the angel of the LORD called unto him out of heaven, and said: 'Abraham, Abraham.' And he said: 'Here am I.' ¹²And he said: 'Lay not thy hand upon the lad, neither do thou any thing unto him; for now I know that thou art a God-fearing man, seeing thou hast not withheld thy son, thine only son, from Me.' ¹³And Abraham lifted up his eyes, and looked, and behold behind him a ram caught in the thicket by his horns. And Abraham went and took the ram, and offered him up for a burnt-offering in the stead of his son.

JOHN 3.16[24]

¹⁶'For God so loved the world that he gave his only Son, so that everyone who believes in him may not perish but may have eternal life.'

HEBREWS 11.8–19

⁸By faith Abraham obeyed when he was called to set out for a place that he was to receive as an inheritance; and he set out, not knowing where he was going. ⁹By faith he stayed for a time in the land he had been promised, as in a foreign land, living in tents, as did Isaac and Jacob, who were heirs with him of the same promise. ¹⁰For he looked forward to the city that has foundations, whose architect and builder is God. ¹¹By faith he received power of procreation, even though he was too old—and Sarah herself was barren—because he considered him faithful who had promised. ¹²Therefore from one person, and this one as good as dead, descendants were born, 'as many as the stars of heaven and as the innumerable grains of sand

---

24. Christian Gospel citations from New Revised Standard Version.

by the seashore.' [13]All of these died in faith without having received the promises, but from a distance they saw and greeted them.

They confessed that they were strangers and foreigners on the Earth, [14]for people who speak in this way make it clear that they are seeking a homeland. [15]If they had been thinking of the land that they had left behind, they would have had opportunity to return. [16]But as it is, they desire a better country, that is, a heavenly one. Therefore God is not ashamed to be called their God; indeed, he has prepared a city for them. [17]By faith Abraham, when put to the test, offered up Isaac. He who had received the promises was ready to offer up his only son, [18]of whom he had been told, 'It is through Isaac that descendants shall be named after you.' [19]He considered the fact that God is able even to raise someone from the dead—and figuratively speaking, he did receive him back.

Sura 37.100–108[25]

100. "O my Lord! Grant me a righteous (son)!"
101. So We gave him the good news of a boy ready to suffer and forbear.
102. Then, when (the son) reached (the age of) (serious) work with him, he said: "O my son! I see in vision that I offer thee in sacrifice: Now see what is thy view!" (The son) said: "O my father! Do as thou art commanded: thou will find me, if Allah so wills one practising Patience and Constancy!"
103. So when they had both submitted their wills (to Allah, and he had laid him prostrate on his forehead (for sacrifice),
104. We called out to him "O Abraham!
105. "Thou hast already fulfilled the vision!" thus indeed do We reward those who do right.
106. For this was obviously a trial,
107. And We ransomed him with a momentous sacrifice:
108. And We left (this blessing) for him among generations (to come) in later times.

---

25. Qur'an translations by Yusuf Ali, http://www.islam101.com/quran/yusufAli/QURAN/3.htm.

These salient scriptures, and their interpretation, have indeed been fertilized and cross-fertilized by one and the other faiths. In *According to the Scriptures*, Van Buren has shown how the Hebrew *Tanakh* texts of the "beloved son" and the "royal son" passages in the Psalms became the interpretive matrix as the early Christians sought to fathom and explain the redeeming life, death, resurrection, ascension, and living-Spirit-presence of Jesus.[26] As I have shown in *Jew, Christian, Muslim*, during and after the formative era of the Christian movement, these three faiths interpenetrated and influenced each other in creative ways. Judaism, as it proceeded into the rabbinic era, influenced Christian exegesis, and in turn was influenced by that exegesis. Islam was profoundly shaped by these two "peoples of the Book" and likewise shaped its two parental faiths. It is no historical accident that the Apostle's Creed was finally given orthodox authority in 800 c.e. under Charlemagne, against the threat of Islam rising from the East and the South.

The theme "beloved son," subsuming sacrifice, martyrdom, dying in battle or in confession of the faith, is epitomized by this chain of texts. All three faiths have deep hermeneutical traditions that decipher the theme "dying for God."[27]

A brilliant essay[28] by Yvonne Sherwood, lecturer in Old Testament/ *Tanakh* and Judaism at Glasgow, has offered penetrating insight into the manifestation of these texts into public action through circuitous hermeneutical maneuvers. In her essay, Sherwood begins with the letter found in two locations on September 11th—in unchecked luggage at Logan airport and in the wreckage of American Airlines Flight #98. The suicide note found here spoke of a "sacred drama" then unfolding in this day of "big states'" contesting power (an apocalyptic metaphor). The letter used words like *taxis, jihad, bags, knives, tools, weapons*—words that seemed to convey a narrative and normative pattern and agenda that the events were simply following—suggesting the same detailed preparations Abraham took that morning before Sarah and her trembling son.

The letter texts of the pilot/martyrs continue with the telling words: "If God grants (*manna*) any one of you a slaughter—a *dhabaha* (to kill, sacrifice, cleave, split, or cut open an animal)—you should perform it as

26. See Van Buren, *According to the Scriptures*.
27. See Boyarin, *Dying for God*.
28. Sherwood, "Binding–Unbinding: Divided Responses of Judaism, Christianity, and Islam to the 'Sacrifice' of Abraham's Beloved Son," 821–61.

an offering on behalf of your father and mother." The words were steeped in Abraham's offering of Isaac at Mount Moriah—the sacred center of the three Abrahamic faiths. As throats were slit on United Airlines Flight #93 that fateful autumn day, this metaphor became their delirious frenzy.

Judah Goldin has suggested in his preface to the classic *Akedah* interpretation—Shalom Spiegel's *The Last Trial*—that the sacrifice of the beloved son is at the very nerve center of Judaism, Christianity, and Islam.[29] The metaphor also takes on renewed currency and energy in the wars on terrorism and in other periods of fratricidal conflict among the Abrahamic faiths—Crusades, Holocaust, and the panorama of violence that has ensued since 1948 in the Middle East. Indeed, in the late 20th and early 21st centuries, Abrahamic-*Akedic*-animated fratricide threatens to take on global proportions, bearing profound stigmata even in Africa and Asia.

Since the events of September 11th, the New York City Police Department has hired thousands of agents to undertake terrorist surveillance around the world—in Europe, Africa, and Asia. In an attempt to prevent and mute this fear of "Arab/*Akedic* (sacrificial)" violence, the U.S. now terrorizes the world with "homeland security" (*Heimat*) policies—laying waste to Palestine, Afghanistan, and Iraq in our own evangelical Anglo-American and Israeli *Akedic* fury. We can no longer discern the pursued from the pursuer, the terrified from the terrorist. And the world now stands aghast at the seeming unending violence: a Pakistani youth is shot in the chest as hundreds of London strike forces search his flat for a rumored (but non-existent) chemical weapon. We can hardly miss the religious, Abrahamic overtones in the violence—ironically, the same ethos that has given the world its sense of justice and peace.

The budgets of every nation in the world are already stretched to the breaking point by military/police/security expenditures, so that most social welfare and humanitarian measures (especially aid for the world's poor and sick)—measures that alone can really combat terrorism—are set aside. In a profound irony, the only way now to avert domestic crises such as hurricane Katrina—crises that all of the world's environmental scientists say we are bringing on ourselves through neglect and misplaced priorities—is to turn them over to the military and homeland security, giving a contorted new meaning to the phrase a "theology of the land."

---

29. See Spiegel, *The Last Trial*.

HOW CAN SCRIPTURAL REASONING INFORM PUBLIC ACTION?

What are the central points each faith tradition might offer in Scriptural Reasoning trialogue pointing towards public action? How are these salient *Akedic* texts instructive wisdom for the apocalyptic crises facing our world?

Judaism

Sherwood's essay reflects on how Judaism has reacted historically and politically to the Abraham text. I begin with an experience at Cambridge in the summer of 2006. In a gathering of the world's leading scholars on Scriptural Reasoning—led by founder Peter Ochs and Cambridge Regius Professor David Ford—we enjoyed a day of excellent presentations from the leadership at St. Ethelburga's Centre for Reconciliation and Peace in London and their Scriptural Reasoning tent. The old Roman Catholic church—bombed to rubble in an attack by the IRA—has built a modest new structure on the very ashes and wreckage of the old church, a phoenix-like attestation to the power of forgiveness and resurrection. Earlier this summer, Prince Charles and Scriptural Reasoning leaders spoke at the dedication of Abraham's tent that now sits on the site, a beacon in the midst of the cavernous financial center.

My thoughts ran to the moving setting of Coventry Cathedral, a new edifice built on the remaining shell of the ancient cathedral destroyed in the World-War-II bombing, and the inaugural event in which the premiere of Benjamin Britten's *War Requiem* was offered. In this monumental musical masterpiece based on the WWI poetry of Wilfred Owen, the *Akedic* song about Abraham's Sacrifice of Isaac was sung by a German soldier portrayed by baritone Dietrich Fischer-Dieskau and a British soldier portrayed by Peter Pears, the English tenor. In a shrill octave-arched duet, they sang of Abraham's anguished offering and concluded that God (or warring humankind) continues to madly offer his beloved son, and all the seed of Europe, one by one.

The Scriptural Reasoning commitment in Abraham's tents around the world is to sit down reverentially with our brother and sister believers in the Abrahamic covenant and discover the great commonalities we share and the urgent tasks of justice and peace that together we must assert against the warring madness and persistent injustice of our political and economic order. We seek to bring light and life to a world now obsessed with darkness and death. I was struck at the Cambridge meetings with the natural affinity of our Jewish and Muslim associates. In ancient Semitic peoples, the common culture—the Aramaic language and grammar and the common secular/sacred synthesis—binds them together. It sometimes seems to me that Christianity is an awkward, oft-troubling interloper between these two siblings. But they also are warring siblings—Cain and Abel, Isaac and Ishmael, Jacob and Esau.

Two brothers are seemingly destined to struggle endlessly in the bosom of father Abraham, and their mothers Sarah and Hagar are the pastoral and wilderness mothers yearning forever for their civilized and bewildered sons. The *midrashim* on Genesis (Rabbah 55:7B and Sanhedrin 87B) has the moving interrogation that, as Kierkegaard rightly claimed, makes humanity tremble:

God: Take your son.	Abraham: I have two sons.
Your only one.	Each is the only one to his mother.
The one you love.	I love them both.

Embattled and endangered sons is the theme of Jon Levenson's book, *The Death and Resurrection of the Beloved Son*. It is also the theme of Paul's Letter to the Galatians (4:21–31), which reflects the turmoil in first-century Judaism and Christianity. The *Judaioi* claim the second half of the biblical salutation ". . . the glory of my people Israel" and the *Goyim* the first ". . . light to the Gentiles" (*c.f.*, Isa 60, Rom 2). Galatians speaks of the validity of the two covenants that would seem to embrace the three Abrahamic peoples: the covenant of Sinai and of Jerusalem, one of law, one of grace, one of freedom, the other of slavery (we might ask which is the covenant of "obedient love?"). In any case, it is the self-claim and the other-recognition of each Abrahamic faith that today, through Scriptural Reasoning, each of the other branches of Abraham's tree belongs to one or the other authentic covenant. While a surface reading might imply that Paul is repudiating one claim and authenticating another, recent scholarship, Scriptural Reasoning, and inter-Abrahamic research resoundingly affirms the thesis of tripartite covenantal validity.

For Jews, the *Akedah* represents the covenant of sacred place and time. The high and holy architecture of this paternal faith of the world's peoples—Sinai, Torah, Mount Zion, the Temple—all focus in this sacred Abrahamic symbol. Passover and Exodus, *Yom Kippur* and *Rosh Hashanah* all fill out the paradigm. The sacrifice of atonement in which the lamb is offered (Exod 12:3–13), the Dali-esque extension of Abraham's cosmic offering of knife and fire out into all time and space (effecting atonement first on the Jerusalem pedestal and trough, then throughout world history as God's vicar people), God's suffering servant, His messiah—redeeming the world by bearing human sin—achieve forgiveness, atonement and redemption.

The complexities arise with our Greco-Latin mathematics, philosophy, and theology. These thought forms make it difficult for us to appreciate Semitic ontologies and temporalities. In *Radical Monotheism*, H. Richard Niebuhr argues that "to be a self is to have a God (Luther), to have a God is to have a history, and to have one God is to have one history."[30] Here is the rub. When the four Saudi hijackers cried out *"Allah Akbar"* as they seized United Airlines Flight #93 out of Newark Airport and turned it around over Cleveland back toward the East Coast, and when the other passengers, with death impending, cried out the *Kaddish* and the "help me, Jesus," they invoked the same "Merciful One"—One who surely grieves over all of their anguish.

The Abraham pericopes, when pondered in Scriptural Reasoning, disclose a *particular* "your seed" and a *universal* "as the stars of the sky and the sands of the seas" double destiny. In corroborative scriptures, in Christianity and Islam and in kindred Hebrew texts (*e.g.*, in Ezekiel 37, the creative tension set in the "Way of God" is that Israel's obedient destiny is to bear fruit that will branch out), we may infer that the Christian and Muslim dispensations are given to bring healing and messianic justice to the world all from the fertile ground of the foundational and enduring covenant with Moses and Israel. Israel must survive in the world in order to effect this universal redemption.

Christianity

Christian readings of Genesis 22 and its cognate *midrashim* (for example, Heb 11:8–19 and John 3:16) examined in the setting of Scriptural Reasoning begin with several of the exegetical and hermeneutical insights of Hebrew scripture study.

1. The sacrificial theme is followed through to its lethal conclusion as Jesus the "lamb of God" is offered for the sin

---

30. See Niebuhr, *Radical Monotheism and Western Culture*.

of the world. In rabbinic interpretation, this obedient follow-through is found in *Talmud* and *Mishnah* as Isaac insists, "tie my hands tighter so that when I wish to escape this fate I will not."[31]

2. Another theme in Hebraic *Akedic* interpretation that influences both Christianity and Islam is that both Father Abraham and Father God go silent after this episode. This observation reminds me of the profound insight of Jack Miles in his *God: A Biography*, in which he claims that after Job, God does not speak again.[32] *Midrash Rabbah* claims that after Genesis 22, God goes silent. The hush that descends is ominous and portentious—the glimpse of a foreboding future is felt. Israel's travail, exile, Diaspora, Crusades, Holocaust, and beleaguered homecoming speak only of the numbing silence of God. And so the crucifixion of Jesus on Jerusalem's Mount Golgotha. We recall William Billings' simple "New England Triptych":

> When Jesus wept, the falling tear in mercy flowed beyond all bound;
> when Jesus mourned, a trembling fear seized all the guilty world around.

3. A final motif of scriptural consideration of *Akedah*—especially in *midrash*, Christian commentary, and *hadith*—is the presence of Satan trying to be the "good guy" dissuading Abraham from offering the son. All *Akedic* material casts the story in temptation format: ". . . and God tested Abraham." The sacrifice must be costly—from Abraham and Isaac to Jephtha's daughter to Agamemnon and Iphenigea. Since God "himself tempts no one" (Jas 1:13), it must be the devil.

In Christian textuality, Christ/Messiah must die in order for sins to be removed and for atonement to be efficacious. In Peter's great confession at Caesarea Philippi that Jesus is *Christos* (Mark 8.29), it becomes clear that Jesus' work is to go to Jerusalem and not be deterred by Satan's great fear

---

31. See Spiegel, *The Last Trial*.
32. See Miles, *God*.

of his impending undoing. Here the Genesis 22 material is conflated, so that God, the son, and the ram are one, just as the body, the blood, and the Eucharist are. The paschal lamb has been sacrificed, and so we keep the feast. As depicted at Ravenna, Abraham and Isaac are the prototype for God the Father and this beloved Son (*monogenos* and *agapetos* in LXX). Jesus submits with obedient and joyous *Islam* (submission) to death, "even death on a cross" (Phil 2:8). Sacrifice henceforth no longer entails the human cutting and burning of the corpse of the *mouton*, human or animal, but the presentation of our bodies as living sacrifice—holy and acceptable to God, which is our reasonable service. (Rom 12.1)

The Hebrews letter is one of serene and clean blood and guts. The author glimpses an eternal altar, high priest, and sacrifice—one fashioned on faithful righteousness, the end point of Torah. The *Akedah* has become a heavenly perpetuity, sealed by one who has perfectly fulfilled the paradigm of Abraham—because he was before Abraham, because as Lord of the dead and the living, he lives in the company of Abraham, Isaac, and Jacob, and because as the perfect human One, he now lies in the bosom of Abraham effecting that spiritual/ethical transaction that is the kingdom of God in Earth as in heaven. The scriptural chain has found nuance and depth in Christian exegesis conducted in the grace and insight of Scriptural Reasoning.

Islam

In Sura 37, Islam has added its link to the chain of *Akedic* Scriptural Reasoning. Islam's rendition of this salient biblical theme is much in the line of the spiritualization explored in Romans and Hebrews. Muslims do not believe in sacrifice in order to achieve atonement. They do not follow Judaic exile theology or Christian crucifixion theology. Rather they interpose a theology of resurrection, reconstitution of the tradition of the martyr and of paradise.

The *dhabih*—the long tradition of prophetic martyr, sacrifice, and achievement of paradise—runs from Noah to Abraham through Moses and Jesus and forward through the prophet Muhammad. What is sought today in the *Eid al-Kabir* and *Eid al-Adha* is to interpret the *Akedah* as a parable of faithful submission for us today in this world. The Feast of Sacrifice at the conclusion of Ramadan is celebrated by observant Muslims as it is celebrated in the family of my Muslim interlocutor: cut and prepare the lamb, carry the roasted meat to neighbors (especially the poor), and ask for their forgiveness of sins committed and omitted.

Other points that arise from the Muslim contingent in Scriptural Reasoning on the *Akedah* chain are as follows:

- *Aslama*: Surrender of the will, obedience, and faith is seen as the essence of the narrative. The command of God is meant to be followed, as opposed to one's own distortions, aberrations, emendations, or retributions. Scriptures in all traditions find a subtlety in meaning so that our own intentions are often turned upside down. Processes of scriptural cross-referencing, community corroboration, and broad intra-faith and interfaith interactions clarify aberrant readings that we all know from empirical observation are widespread.

- When dealing with these primary narratives of the faith (Abraham, Isaac, Ishmael, Hagar), we find basic construals of all dimensions of the faith embedded in the text as if it were omni-explicatory—revealing the nature and will of God, human responsibility, and the requirements of faithfulness. Hagar and Ishmael are exiled, sent out into the wilderness: they wander, they are scapegoats, yet the delivering and succoring hand of God and blessing of Abraham follow them. Throwing stones during the *hajj* symbolizes this plight as it marshals resistance to the "evil one."

- In Islam, the wounded son from Abraham's sacrifice (or "near-miss") is carried off to paradise. Given the obviously authentic Aramaic contours of the crucifixion—*"Eloi, Eloi, lema sabachthani"* ("My God, my God, why have you forsaken me?"), quoting the victory Psalm 22 and the quite amazing promise from the cross, "today you will be with me in Paradise" (Luke 23.43)—Islam has preserved crucial elements of Christ's passion, even though the faith rejects the suffering and dying aspects of Jesus' life and ministry.

- When Muhammad's grandfather was tempted to sacrifice a son, the story's teaching appears thoroughly Semitic: "Who will be left when all my sons are gone? This will be a bad example to the other fathers."

- In Islam, the text also adds the demonic/satanic dimension, as the devil becomes a spokesperson for humanitarian values: "surely God did not say . . ."

In other words, Islam rejects the literalism of the suicide bombers and of *al-Zarqawi*. The tradition abhors killing, as do Judaism and Christianity. Scriptural Reasoning then holds the promise of diverting public reasoning and policy away from the present distortions so replete in Israel, Anglo-America, and in militant Islam. It exposes present suicidal bombing and war-on-terrorism strategies and tactics as deficient and totally contradictory to the religious, ethical, and political traditions being falsely invoked by the belligerents.

CHAINS OF SCRIPTURAL REASONING AND INTERFAITH DIALOGUE

This hermeneutical foundation and rationale now enables us to sketch what I have called "chains" of Scriptural Reasoning. A theme of interconnection in each of the three Abrahamic faiths is "the golden cord" or "chain." This would seem to mean that a ladder or link-chain ties together Earth and heaven, humanity and divinity. The three faiths of Abraham are, to me, a triple link-chain or a triple cord braid. My experience of some 30 years leads me to believe that there are certain connecting links that are natural, perhaps necessary, in the sense that a braided rope or linked chain belongs together and cannot break. I now review scriptural chains that testify to unbroken and unbreakable interconnectivity among Abraham's family of faiths.

Scriptural Chains

The first set of chains arises from texts themselves that witness to interactional enrichment and reach the "binding" (*Akedic*) conclusion that they belong together. Although in common scriptural usage in particular faith communities, these texts can stand apart as self-sufficient, self-explanatory, and revelatory, together they produce synergy and explanatory power.

Torah, Law of Christ, Taurut: Scripture, the Way, and Will of God
Scripture in all monotheistic faith conveys duty to God, neighbor, and world mediated through the word of sacred text which is *vox Dei*. The

way and will of God is a template of duty to God (obey, love, submit) and to fellow humans (justice, love, peace).

‡ Hebrew Bible: Exodus 20.1–13 ‡

¹And God spoke all these words, saying: ²I am the LORD thy God, who brought thee out of the land of Egypt, out of the house of bondage. Thou shalt have no other gods before Me. ³Thou shalt not make unto thee a graven image, nor any manner of likeness, of any thing that is in heaven above, or that is in the Earth beneath, or that is in the water under the Earth; ⁴thou shalt not bow down unto them, nor serve them; for I the LORD thy God am a jealous God, visiting the iniquity of the fathers upon the children unto the third and fourth generation of them that hate Me; ⁵and showing mercy unto the thousandth generation of them that love Me and keep My commandments. ⁶Thou shalt not take the name of the LORD thy God in vain; for the LORD will not hold him guilt-less that taketh His name in vain. ⁷Remember the Sabbath day, to keep it holy. ⁸Six days shalt thou labour, and do all thy work; ⁹but the seventh day is a Sabbath unto the LORD thy God, in it thou shalt not do any manner of work, thou, nor thy son, nor thy daughter, nor thy man-servant, nor thy maid-servant, nor thy cattle, nor thy stranger that is within thy gates; ¹⁰for in six days the LORD made heaven and Earth, the sea, and all that in them is, and rested on the seventh day; wherefore the LORD blessed the Sabbath day, and hallowed it. ¹¹Honour thy father and thy mother, that thy days may be long upon the land which the LORD thy God giveth thee. ¹²Thou shalt not murder. Thou shalt not commit adultery. Thou shalt not steal. Thou shalt not bear false witness against thy neighbour. ¹³Thou shalt not covet thy neighbour's house; thou shalt not covet thy neighbour's wife, nor his man-servant, nor his maid-servant, nor his ox, nor his ass, nor any thing that is thy neighbour's.

‡ Christian Gospels: Romans 13.7–10 ‡

⁷Pay to all what is due to them—taxes to whom taxes are due, revenue to whom revenue is due, respect to whom respect is due, honour to whom honour is due. ⁸Owe no one anything, except to love one another; for the one who loves another has fulfilled the law. ⁹The commandments, 'You shall not commit adultery; You shall not murder; You shall not steal; You shall not covet'; and any other commandment, are summed up in this word, 'Love your neighbour as yourself.' ¹⁰Love does no wrong to a neighbour; therefore, love is the fulfilling of the law.

‡ Islamic Qur'an: Sura 17.22–39 ‡

22. Take not with Allah another object of worship; or thou (O man!) wilt sit in disgrace and destitution.

23. Thy Lord hath decreed that ye worship none but Him, and that ye be kind to parents. Whether one or both of them attain old age in thy life, say not to them a word of contempt, nor repel them, but address them in terms of honour.

24. And, out of kindness, lower to them the wing of humility, and say: "My Lord! bestow on them thy Mercy even as they cherished me in childhood."

25. Your Lord knoweth best what is in your hearts: If ye do deeds of righteousness, verily He is Most Forgiving to those who turn to Him again and again (in true penitence).

26. And render to the kindred their due rights, as (also) to those in want, and to the wayfarer: But squander not (your wealth) in the manner of a spendthrift.

27. Verily spendthrifts are brothers of the Evil Ones; and the Evil One is to his Lord (himself) ungrateful.

28. And even if thou hast to turn away from them in pursuit of the Mercy from thy Lord which thou dost expect, yet speak to them a word of easy kindness.

29. Make not thy hand tied (like a niggard's) to thy neck, nor stretch it forth to its utmost reach, so that thou become blameworthy and destitute.

30. Verily thy Lord doth provide sustenance in abundance for whom He pleaseth, and He provideth in a just measure. For He doth know and regard all His servants.

31. Kill not your children for fear of want: We shall provide sustenance for them as well as for you. Verily the killing of them is a great sin.

32. Nor come nigh to adultery: for it is a shameful (deed) and an evil, opening the road (to other evils).

33. Nor take life, which Allah has made sacred, except for just cause. And if anyone is slain wrongfully, we have given his heir authority (to demand *qisas* or to forgive): but let him nor exceed bounds in the matter of taking life; for he is helped (by the Law).

34. Come not nigh to the orphan's property except to improve it, until he attains the age of full strength; and fulfill (every) engage-

ment, for (every) engagement will be enquired into (on the Day of Reckoning).

35. Give full measure when ye measure, and weigh with a balance that is straight: that is the most fitting and the most advantageous in the final determination.

36. And pursue not that of which thou hast no knowledge; for every act of hearing, or of seeing or of (feeling in) the heart will be enquired into (on the Day of Reckoning).

37. Nor walk on the Earth with insolence: for thou canst not rend the Earth asunder, nor reach the mountains in height.

38. Of all such things the evil is hateful in the sight of thy Lord.

39. These are among the (precepts of) wisdom, which thy Lord has revealed to thee. Take not, with Allah, another object of worship, lest thou shouldst be thrown into Hell, blameworthy and rejected.

One God, No Gods But God: First Principle

To hear and see (divine speech, grace, and deliverance) is in order to obey, follow, and submit first to God ("no other gods," idols) then to fellow humans. We submit to God by shunning idolatry and injustice and serving other.

‡ Hebrew Bible: Deuteronomy 6.4–7 ‡

[4]Hear, O Israel: the LORD our God, the LORD is one. [5]And thou shalt love the LORD thy God with all thy heart, and with all thy soul, and with all thy might. [6]And these words, which I command thee this day, shall be upon thy heart; [7]and thou shalt teach them diligently unto thy children, and shalt talk of them when thou sittest in thy house, and when thou walkest by the way, and when thou liest down, and when thou risest up.

‡ Christian Gospels: Matthew 19.16–22 ‡

[16]Then someone came to him and said, 'Teacher, what good deed must I do to have eternal life?' [17]And he said to him, 'Why do you ask me about what is good? There is only one who is good. If you wish to enter into life, keep the commandments.' [18]He said to him, 'Which ones?' And Jesus said, 'You shall not murder; You shall not commit adultery; You shall not steal; You shall not bear false witness; [19]Honour your father and mother; also, You shall love your neighbour as yourself.' [20]The young man said to him, 'I have kept

all these; what do I still lack?' ²¹Jesus said to him, 'If you wish to be perfect, go, sell your possessions, and give the money to the poor, and you will have treasure in heaven; then come, follow me.' ²²When the young man heard this word, he went away grieving, for he had many possessions.

‡ Islamic Qur'an: Sura 6.74–89 ‡

74. Lo! Abraham said to his father Azar: "Takest thou idols for gods? For I see thee and thy people in manifest error."

75. So also did We show Abraham the power and the laws of the heavens and the Earth, that he might (with understanding) have certitude.

76. When the night covered him over, He saw a star: He said: "This is my Lord." But when it set, He said: "I love not those that set."

77. When he saw the moon rising in splendour, he said: "This is my Lord." But when the moon set, He said: "unless my Lord guide me, I shall surely be among those who go astray."

78. When he saw the sun rising in splendour, he said: "This is my Lord; this is the greatest (of all)." But when the sun set, he said: "O my people! I am indeed free from your (guilt) of giving partners to Allah.

79. "For me, I have set my face, firmly and truly, towards Him Who created the heavens and the Earth, and never shall I give partners to Allah."

80. His people disputed with him. He said: "(Come) ye to dispute with me, about Allah, when He (Himself) hath guided me? I fear not (the beings) ye associate with Allah. Unless my Lord willeth, (nothing can happen). My Lord comprehendeth in His knowledge all things. Will ye not (yourselves) be admonished?

81. "How should I fear (the beings) ye associate with Allah, when ye fear not to give partners to Allah without any warrant having been given to you? Which of (us) two parties hath more right to security? (tell me) if ye know.

82. "It is those who believe and confuse not their beliefs with wrong—that are (truly) in security, for they are on (right) guidance."

83. That was the reasoning about Us, which We gave to Abraham (to use) against his people: We raise whom We will, degree after degree: for thy Lord is full of wisdom and knowledge.

84. We gave him Isaac and Jacob: all (three) guided: and before him, We guided Noah, and among his progeny, David, Solomon, Job, Joseph, Moses, and Aaron: thus do We reward those who do good:

85. And Zakariya and John, and Jesus and Elias: all in the ranks of the righteous:

86. And Isma'il and Elisha, and Jonas, and Lot: and to all We gave favour above the nations:

87. (To them) and to their fathers, and progeny and brethren: We chose them, and we guided them to a straight way.

88. This is the guidance of Allah. He giveth that guidance to whom He pleaseth, of His worshippers. If they were to join other gods with Him, all that they did would be vain for them.

89. These were the men to whom We gave the Book, and authority, and prophethood: if these (their descendants) reject them, Behold! We shall entrust their charge to a new people who reject them not.

Adam, Eve: Original Sin, Fall, Human Condition

A glory and darkness dwells within humans, personally and corporately, in their being and activity. Realism about human waywardness is requisite to receive the process of redemption. The God of justice is the God of grace and renewal. The Semitic poles of Abraham's trifecta accent endeavor, the conjoining Christian node accents grace and forgiveness.

‡ Hebrew Bible: Genesis 1.26–28 ‡

[26]And God said: 'Let us make man in our image, after our likeness; and let them have dominion over the fish of the sea, and over the fowl of the air, and over the cattle, and over all the Earth, and over every creeping thing that creepeth upon the Earth.' [27]And God created man in His own image, in the image of God created He him; male and female created He them. [28]And God blessed them; and God said unto them: 'Be fruitful, and multiply, and replenish the Earth, and subdue it; and have dominion over the fish of the sea, and over the fowl of the air, and over every living thing that creepeth upon the Earth.'

‡ Hebrew Bible: Genesis 2.5–25 ‡

⁵No shrub of the field was yet in the Earth, and no herb of the field had yet sprung up; for the LORD God had not caused it to rain upon the Earth, and there was not a man to till the ground; ⁶but there went up a mist from the Earth, and watered the whole face of the ground. ⁷Then the LORD God formed man of the dust of the ground, and breathed into his nostrils the breath of life; and man became a living soul. ⁸And the LORD God planted a garden eastward, in Eden; and there He put the man whom He had formed. ⁹And out of the ground made the LORD God to grow every tree that is pleasant to the sight, and good for food; the tree of life also in the midst of the garden, and the tree of the knowledge of good and evil. ¹⁰And a river went out of Eden to water the garden; and from thence it was parted, and became four heads. ¹¹The name of the first is Pishon; that is it which compasseth the whole land of Havilah, where there is gold; ¹²and the gold of that land is good; there is bdellium and the onyx stone. ¹³And the name of the second river is Gihon; the same is it that compasseth the whole land of Cush. ¹⁴And the name of the third river is Tigris; that is it which goeth toward the east of Asshur. And the fourth river is the Euphrates. ¹⁵And the LORD God took the man, and put him into the garden of Eden to dress it and to keep it. ¹⁶And the LORD God commanded the man, saying: 'Of every tree of the garden thou mayest freely eat; ¹⁷but of the tree of the knowledge of good and evil, thou shalt not eat of it; for in the day that thou eatest thereof thou shalt surely die.' ¹⁸And the LORD God said: 'It is not good that the man should be alone; I will make him a help meet for him.' ¹⁹And out of the ground the LORD God formed every beast of the field, and every fowl of the air; and brought them unto the man to see what he would call them; and whatsoever the man would call every living creature, that was to be the name thereof. ²⁰And the man gave names to all cattle, and to the fowl of the air, and to every beast of the field; but for Adam there was not found a help meet for him. ²¹And the LORD God caused a deep sleep to fall upon the man, and he slept; and He took one of his ribs, and closed up the place with flesh instead thereof. ²²And the rib, which the LORD God had taken from the man, made He a woman, and brought her unto the man. ²³And the man said: 'This is now bone of my bones, and flesh of my flesh; she shall be called Woman, because she was taken out of Man.' ²⁴Therefore shall a man leave his father and his mother, and shall cleave unto his wife, and they

shall be one flesh. ²⁵And they were both naked, the man and his wife, and were not ashamed.

‡ Christian Gospels: 1 Corinthians 11.3–12 ‡

³But I want you to understand that Christ is the head of every man, and the husband is the head of his wife, and God is the head of Christ. ⁴Any man who prays or prophesies with something on his head disgraces his head, ⁵but any woman who prays or prophesies with her head unveiled disgraces her head—it is one and the same thing as having her head shaved. ⁶For if a woman will not veil herself, then she should cut off her hair; but if it is disgraceful for a woman to have her hair cut off or to be shaved, she should wear a veil. ⁷For a man ought not to have his head veiled, since he is the image and reflection of God; but woman is the reflection of man. ⁸Indeed, man was not made from woman, but woman from man. ⁹Neither was man created for the sake of woman, but woman for the sake of man. ¹⁰For this reason a woman ought to have a symbol of authority on her head, because of the angels. ¹¹Nevertheless, in the Lord woman is not independent of man or man independent of woman. ¹²For just as woman came from man, so man comes through woman; but all things come from God.

‡ Christian Gospels: Romans 5.12 ‡

¹²Therefore, just as sin came into the world through one man, and death came through sin, and so death spread to all because all have sinned.

‡ Islamic Qur'an: Sura 2.29–37 ‡

29. It is He Who hath created for you all things that are on Earth; Moreover His design comprehended the heavens, for He gave order and perfection to the seven firmaments; and of all things He hath perfect knowledge.

30. Behold, thy Lord said to the angels: "I will create a vicegerent on Earth." They said: "Wilt Thou place therein one who will make mischief therein and shed blood? whilst we do celebrate Thy praises and glorify Thy holy (name)?" He said: "I know what ye know not."

31. And He taught Adam the nature of all things; then He placed them before the angels, and said: "Tell me the nature of these if ye are right."

32. They said: "Glory to Thee, of knowledge We have none, save what Thou Hast taught us: In truth it is Thou Who art perfect in knowledge and wisdom."

33. He said: "O Adam! Tell them their natures." When he had told them, Allah said: "Did I not tell you that I know the secrets of heaven and Earth, and I know what ye reveal and what ye conceal?"

34. And behold, We said to the angels: "Bow down to Adam" and they bowed down. Not so Iblis: he refused and was haughty: He was of those who reject Faith.

35. We said: "O Adam! dwell thou and thy wife in the Garden; and eat of the bountiful things therein as (where and when) ye will; but approach not this tree, or ye run into harm and transgression."

36. Then did Satan make them slip from the (garden), and get them out of the state (of felicity) in which they had been. We said: "Get ye down, all (ye people), with enmity between yourselves. On Earth will be your dwelling-place and your means of livelihood, for a time."

37. Then learnt Adam from his Lord words of inspiration, and his Lord Turned towards him; for He is Oft-Returning, Most Merciful.

Noah: Creation's Grace Renewed

The crisis of idolatry, immorality, and injustice has become ubiquitous and cosmic. Only upheaval, destruction, and renewal of creation will work out justice, grace, and forgiveness, can cleanse the disgrace, and renew the face of the Earth. Never again will iniquity manage to despoil creation.

‡ Hebrew Bible: Genesis 9.1–11 ‡

[1]And God blessed Noah and his sons, and said unto them: 'Be fruitful and multiply, and replenish the Earth. [2]And the fear of you and the dread of you shall be upon every beast of the Earth, and upon every fowl of the air, and upon all wherewith the ground teemeth, and upon all the fishes of the sea: into your hand are they delivered. [3]Every moving thing that liveth shall be for food for you; as the green herb have I given you all. [4]Only flesh with the life thereof, which is the blood thereof, shall ye not eat. [5]And surely

your blood of your lives will I require; at the hand of every beast will I require it; and at the hand of man, even at the hand of every man's brother, will I require the life of man. [6]Whoso sheddeth man's blood, by man shall his blood be shed; for in the image of God made He man. [7]And you, be ye fruitful, and multiply; swarm in the Earth, and multiply therein.'

[8]And God spoke unto Noah, and to his sons with him, saying: [9]'As for Me, behold, I establish My covenant with you, and with your seed after you; [10]and with every living creature that is with you, the fowl, the cattle, and every beast of the Earth with you; of all that go out of the ark, even every beast of the Earth. [11]And I will establish My covenant with you; neither shall all flesh be cut off any more by the waters of the flood; neither shall there any more be a flood to destroy the Earth.'

‡ Christian Gospels: 2 Peter 2.1–5 ‡

[1]But false prophets also arose among the people, just as there will be false teachers among you, who will secretly bring in destructive opinions. They will even deny the Master who bought them—bringing swift destruction on themselves. [2]Even so, many will follow their licentious ways, and because of these teachers the way of truth will be maligned. [3]And in their greed they will exploit you with deceptive words. Their condemnation, pronounced against them long ago, has not been idle, and their destruction is not asleep. [4]For if God did not spare the angels when they sinned, but cast them into hell and committed them to chains of deepest darkness to be kept until the judgment; [5]and if he did not spare the ancient world, even though he saved Noah, a herald of righteousness, with seven others, when he brought a flood on a world of the ungodly . . .

‡ Islamic Qur'an: Sura 71.1–5 ‡

1. We sent Noah to his People (with the Command): "Do thou warn thy People before there comes to them a grievous Penalty."

2. He said: "O my People! I am to you a Warner, clear and open:

3. "That ye should worship Allah, fear Him and obey me:

4. "So He may forgive you your sins and give you respite for a stated Term: for when the Term given by Allah is accomplished, it cannot be put forward: if ye only knew."

5. He said: "O my Lord! I have called to my People night and day:

‡ Islamic Qur'an: Sura 7.59–64 ‡

59. We sent Noah to his people. He said: "O my people! worship Allah. ye have no other god but Him. I fear for you the punishment of a dreadful day!

60. The leaders of his people said: "Ah! we see thee evidently wandering (in mind)."

61. He said: "O my people! No wandering is there in my (mind): on the contrary I am an apostle from the Lord and Cherisher of the worlds!

62. "I but fulfil towards you the duties of my Lord's mission: Sincere is my advice to you, and I know from Allah something that ye know not.

63. "Do ye wonder that there hath come to you a message from your Lord, through a man of your own people, to warn you, so that ye may fear Allah and haply receive His Mercy?"

64. But they rejected him . . .

Abraham, Hagar, Sarah: History of Salvation Begins

Judgment and grace entail God reaching out in love, suffering, dying, and effecting redemption. The complex tale of Abraham's two wives and two sons shows the profundity and intricacy of this saving redemption.

‡ Hebrew Bible: Genesis 16 ‡

¹Now Sarai Abram's wife bore him no children; and she had a handmaid, an Egyptian, whose name was Hagar. ²And Sarai said unto Abram: 'Behold now, the LORD hath restrained me from bearing; go in, I pray thee, unto my handmaid; it may be that I shall be builded up through her.' And Abram hearkened to the voice of Sarai. ³And Sarai Abram's wife took Hagar the Egyptian, her handmaid, after Abram had dwelt ten years in the land of Canaan, and gave her to Abram her husband to be his wife. ⁴And he went in unto Hagar, and she conceived; and when she saw that she had conceived, her mistress was despised in her eyes. ⁵And Sarai said unto Abram: 'My wrong be upon thee: I gave my handmaid into thy bosom; and when she saw that she had conceived, I was despised in her eyes: the LORD judge between me and thee.' ⁶But Abram said unto Sarai: 'Behold, thy maid is in thy hand; do to her that which is good in thine eyes.' And Sarai dealt harshly with

her, and she fled from her face. ⁷And the angel of the LORD found her by a fountain of water in the wilderness, by the fountain in the way to Shur. ⁸And he said: 'Hagar, Sarai's handmaid, whence camest thou? and whither goest thou?' And she said: 'I flee from the face of my mistress Sarai.' ⁹And the angel of the LORD said unto her: 'Return to thy mistress, and submit thyself under her hands.' ¹⁰And the angel of the LORD said unto her: 'I will greatly multiply thy seed, that it shall not be numbered for multitude. ¹¹And the angel of the LORD said unto her: 'Behold, thou art with child, and shalt bear a son; and thou shalt call his name Ishmael, because the LORD hath heard thy affliction. ¹²And he shall be a wild ass of a man: his hand shall be against every man, and every man's hand against him; and he shall dwell in the face of all his brethren.' ¹³And she called the name of the LORD that spoke unto her, Thou art a God of seeing; for she said: 'Have I even here seen Him that seeth Me?' ¹⁴Wherefore the well was called 'Beer-lahai-roi; behold, it is between Kadesh and Bered. ¹⁵And Hagar bore Abram a son; and Abram called the name of his son, whom Hagar bore, Ishmael. ¹⁶And Abram was fourscore and six years old, when Hagar bore Ishmael to Abram.

‡ Hebrew Bible: Genesis 17 ‡

¹And when Abram was ninety years old and nine, the LORD appeared to Abram, and said unto him: 'I am God Almighty; walk before Me, and be thou wholehearted. ²And I will make My covenant between Me and thee, and will multiply thee exceedingly.' ³And Abram fell on his face; and God talked with him, saying: ⁴'As for Me, behold, My covenant is with thee, and thou shalt be the father of a multitude of nations. ⁵Neither shall thy name any more be called Abram, but thy name shall be Abraham; for the father of a multitude of nations have I made thee. ⁶And I will make thee exceeding fruitful, and I will make nations of thee, and kings shall come out of thee. ⁷And I will establish My covenant between Me and thee and thy seed after thee throughout their generations for an everlasting covenant, to be a God unto thee and to thy seed after thee. ⁸And I will give unto thee, and to thy seed after thee, the land of thy sojournings, all the land of Canaan, for an everlasting possession; and I will be their God.' ⁹And God said unto Abraham: 'And as for thee, thou shalt keep My covenant, thou, and thy seed after thee throughout their generations. ¹⁰This is My covenant, which ye shall keep, between Me and you and thy seed after thee: every male among you shall be circumcised. ¹¹And ye shall be cir-

cumcised in the flesh of your foreskin; and it shall be a token of a covenant betwixt Me and you. [12]And he that is eight days old shall be circumcised among you, every male throughout your generations, he that is born in the house, or bought with money of any foreigner, that is not of thy seed. [13]He that is born in thy house, and he that is bought with thy money, must needs be circumcised; and My covenant shall be in your flesh for an everlasting covenant. [14]And the uncircumcised male who is not circumcised in the flesh of his foreskin, that soul shall be cut off from his people; he hath broken My covenant.' [15]And God said unto Abraham: 'As for Sarai thy wife, thou shalt not call her name Sarai, but Sarah shall her name be. [16]And I will bless her, and moreover I will give thee a son of her; yea, I will bless her, and she shall be a mother of nations; kings of peoples shall be of her.' [17]Then Abraham fell upon his face, and laughed, and said in his heart: 'Shall a child be born unto him that is a hundred years old? and shall Sarah, that is ninety years old, bear?' [18]And Abraham said unto God: 'Oh that Ishmael might live before Thee!' [19]And God said: 'Nay, but Sarah thy wife shall bear thee a son; and thou shalt call his name Isaac; and I will establish My covenant with him for an everlasting covenant for his seed after him. [20]And as for Ishmael, I have heard thee; behold, I have blessed him, and will make him fruitful, and will multiply him exceedingly; twelve princes shall he beget, and I will make him a great nation. [21]But My covenant will I establish with Isaac, whom Sarah shall bear unto thee at this set time in the next year.' [22]And He left off talking with him, and God went up from Abraham. [23]And Abraham took Ishmael his son, and all that were born in his house, and all that were bought with his money, every male among the men of Abraham's house, and circumcised the flesh of their foreskin in the selfsame day, as God had said unto him. [24]And Abraham was ninety years old and nine, when he was circumcised in the flesh of his foreskin. [25]And Ishmael his son was thirteen years old, when he was circumcised in the flesh of his foreskin. [26]In the selfsame day was Abraham circumcised, and Ishmael his son. [27]And all the men of his house, those born in the house, and those bought with money of a foreigner, were circumcised with him.

‡ Christian Gospels: Galatians 4.22–31 ‡

[22]For it is written that Abraham had two sons, one by a slave woman and the other by a free woman. [23]One, the child of the slave, was born according to the flesh; the other, the child of the free woman, was

born through the promise. ²⁴Now this is an allegory: these women are two covenants. One woman, in fact, is Hagar, from Mount Sinai, bearing children for slavery. ²⁵Now Hagar is Mount Sinai in Arabia and corresponds to the present Jerusalem, for she is in slavery with her children. ²⁶But the other woman corresponds to the Jerusalem above; she is free, and she is our mother. ²⁷For it is written, 'Rejoice, you childless one, you who bear no children, burst into song and shout, you who endure no birth pangs; for the children of the desolate woman are more numerous than the children of the one who is married.' ²⁸Now you, my friends, are children of the promise, like Isaac. ²⁹But just as at that time the child who was born according to the flesh persecuted the child who was born according to the Spirit, so it is now also. ³⁰But what does the scripture say? 'Drive out the slave and her child; for the child of the slave will not share the inheritance with the child of the free woman.' ³¹So then, friends, we are children, not of the slave but of the free woman.

‡ Islamic Qur'an: Sura 2.125–126 ‡

125. Remember We made the House a place of assembly for men and a place of safety; and take ye the station of Abraham as a place of prayer; and We covenanted with Abraham and Isma'il, that they should sanctify My House for those who compass it round, or use it as a retreat, or bow, or prostrate themselves (therein in prayer).

126. And remember Abraham said: "My Lord, make this a City of Peace, and feed its people with fruits, such of them as believe in Allah and the Last Day." He said: "(Yea), and such as reject Faith, for a while will I grant them their pleasure, but will soon drive them to the torment of Fire, an evil destination (indeed)!"

Jacob (Israel), Joseph, and His Brothers: Telescopic Redemption Begins

The Yussef story, like the story of Mary, Jesus' mother, is elaborately unfolded in the Qur'an, pointing to the particular/universal dialectic of scripture where these first historical persons of the patriarchal (matriarchal) epoch become the progenitors and promulgators of the universal scope of salvation and Earth redemption.

‡ Hebrew Bible: Genesis 41.38–42 ‡

[38]And Pharaoh said unto his servants: 'Can we find such a one as this, a man in whom the spirit of God is?' [39]And Pharaoh said unto Joseph: 'Forasmuch as God hath shown thee all this, there is none so discreet and wise as thou. [40]Thou shalt be over my house, and according unto thy word shall all my people be ruled; only in the throne will I be greater than thou.' [41]And Pharaoh said unto Joseph: 'See, I have set thee over all the land of Egypt.' [42]And Pharaoh took off his signet ring from his hand, and put it upon Joseph's hand, and arrayed him in vestures of fine linen, and put a gold chain about his neck.

‡ Christian Gospels: Matthew 1.1–17 ‡

[1]An account of the genealogy of Jesus the Messiah, the son of David, the son of Abraham. [2]Abraham was the father of Isaac, and Isaac the father of Jacob, and Jacob the father of Judah and his brothers, [3]and Judah the father of Perez and Zerah by Tamar, and Perez the father of Hezron, and Hezron the father of Aram, [4]and Aram the father of Aminadab, and Aminadab the father of Nahshon, and Nahshon the father of Salmon, [5]and Salmon the father of Boaz by Rahab, and Boaz the father of Obed by Ruth, and Obed the father of Jesse, [6]and Jesse the father of King David. And David was the father of Solomon by the wife of Uriah, [7]and Solomon the father of Rehoboam, and Rehoboam the father of Abijah, and Abijah the father of Asaph, [8]and Asaph the father of Jehoshaphat, and Jehoshaphat the father of Joram, and Joram the father of Uzziah, [9]and Uzziah the father of Jotham, and Jotham the father of Ahaz, and Ahaz the father of Hezekiah, [10]and Hezekiah the father of Manasseh, and Manasseh the father of Amos, and Amos the father of Josiah, [11]and Josiah the father of Jechoniah and his brothers, at the time of the deportation to Babylon. [12]And after the deportation to Babylon: Jechoniah was the father of Salathiel, and Salathiel the father of Zerubbabel, [13]and Zerubbabel the father of Abiud, and Abiud the father of Eliakim, and Eliakim the father of Azor, [14]and Azor the father of Zadok, and Zadok the father of Achim, and Achim the father of Eliud, [15]and Eliud the father of Eleazar, and Eleazar the father of Matthan, and Matthan the father of Jacob, [16]and Jacob the father of Joseph the husband of Mary, of whom Jesus was born, who is called the Messiah. [17]So all the generations from Abraham to David are fourteen generations; and from David to the deportation to Babylon, fourteen generations;

and from the deportation to Babylon to the Messiah, fourteen generations.

‡ Islamic Qur'an: Sura 12.1–60 ‡

1. A.L.R. These are the symbols (or Verses) of the perspicuous Book.

2. We have sent it down as an Arabic Qur'an, in order that ye may learn wisdom.

3. We do relate unto thee the most beautiful of stories, in that We reveal to thee this (portion of the) Qur'an: before this, thou too was among those who knew it not.

4. Behold! Joseph said to his father: "O my father! I did see eleven stars and the sun and the moon: I saw them prostrate themselves to me!"

5. Said (the father): "My (dear) little son! relate not thy vision to thy brothers, lest they concoct a plot against thee: for Satan is to man an avowed enemy!

6. "Thus will thy Lord choose thee and teach thee the interpretation of stories (and events) and perfect His favour to thee and to the posterity of Jacob, even as He perfected it to thy fathers Abraham and Isaac aforetime! for Allah is full of knowledge and wisdom."

7. Verily in Joseph and his brethren are signs (or symbols) for seekers (after Truth).

8. They said: "Truly Joseph and his brother are loved more by our father than we: But we are a goodly body! really our father is obviously wandering (in his mind)!

9. "Slay ye Joseph or cast him out to some (unknown) land, that so the favour of your father may be given to you alone: (there will be time enough) for you to be righteous after that!"

10. Said one of them: "Slay not Joseph, but if ye must do something, throw him down to the bottom of the well: he will be picked up by some caravan of travellers."

11. They said: "O our father! why dost thou not trust us with Joseph, seeing we are indeed his sincere well-wishers?

12. "Send him with us tomorrow to enjoy himself and play, and we shall take every care of him."

13. (Jacob) said: "Really it saddens me that ye should take him away: I fear lest the wolf should devour him while ye attend not to him."

14. They said: "If the wolf were to devour him while we are (so large) a party, then should we indeed (first) have perished ourselves!"

15. So they did take him away, and they all agreed to throw him down to the bottom of the well: and We put into his heart (this Message): 'Of a surety thou shalt (one day) tell them the truth of this their affair while they know (thee) not' . . .

16. Then they came to their father in the early part of the night, weeping.

17. They said: "O our father! We went racing with one another, and left Joseph with our things; and the wolf devoured him. . . . But thou wilt never believe us even though we tell the truth."

18. They stained his shirt with false blood. He said: "Nay, but your minds have made up a tale (that may pass) with you, (for me) patience is most fitting: Against that which ye assert, it is Allah (alone) Whose help can be sought".

19. Then there came a caravan of travellers: they sent their water-carrier (for water), and he let down his bucket (into the well). . . . He said: "Ah there! Good news! Here is a (fine) young man!" So they concealed him as a treasure! But Allah knoweth well all that they do!

20. The (Brethren) sold him for a miserable price, for a few *dirhams* counted out: in such low estimation did they hold him!

21. The man in Egypt who bought him, said to his wife: "Make his stay (among us) honourable: may be he will bring us much good, or we shall adopt him as a son." Thus did We establish Joseph in the land, that We might teach him the interpretation of stories (and events). And Allah hath full power and control over His affairs; but most among mankind know it not.

22. When Joseph attained His full manhood, We gave him power and knowledge: thus do We reward those who do right.

23. But she in whose house he was, sought to seduce him from his (true) self: she fastened the doors, and said: "Now come, thou (dear one)!" He said: "(Allah) forbid! truly (thy husband) is my lord! he made my sojourn agreeable! truly to no good come those who do wrong!"

24. And (with passion) did she desire him, and he would have desired her, but that he saw the evidence of his Lord: thus (did We order) that We might turn away from him (all) evil and shameful deeds: for he was one of Our servants, sincere and purified.

25. So they both raced each other to the door, and she tore his shirt from the back: they both found her lord near the door. She said: "What is the (fitting) punishment for one who formed an evil design against thy wife, but prison or a grievous chastisement?"

26. He said: "It was she that sought to seduce me from my (true) self." And one of her household saw (this) and bore witness, (thus): "If it be that his shirt is rent from the front, then is her tale true, and he is a liar!

27. "But if it be that his shirt is torn from the back, then is she the liar, and he is telling the truth!"

28. So when he saw his shirt, that it was torn at the back, (her husband) said: "Behold! It is a snare of you women! truly, mighty is your snare!

29. "O Joseph, pass this over! (O wife), ask forgiveness for thy sin, for truly thou hast been at fault!"

30. Ladies said in the City: "The wife of the (great) 'Aziz is seeking to seduce her slave from his (true) self: Truly hath he inspired her with violent love: we see she is evidently going astray."

31. When she heard of their malicious talk, she sent for them and prepared a banquet for them: she gave each of them a knife: and she said (to Joseph), "Come out before them." When they saw him, they did extol him, and (in their amazement) cut their hands: they said, "(Allah) preserve us! no mortal is this! this is none other than a noble angel!"

32. She said: "There before you is the man about whom ye did blame me! I did seek to seduce him from his (true) self but he did firmly save himself guiltless! . . . and now, if he doth not my bidding, he shall certainly be cast into prison, and (what is more) be of the company of the vilest!"

33. He said: "O my Lord! the prison is more to my liking than that to which they invite me: Unless Thou turn away their snare from me, I should (in my youthful folly) feel inclined towards them and join the ranks of the ignorant."

34. So his Lord hearkened to him (in his prayer), and turned away from him their snare: Verily He heareth and knoweth (all things).

35. Then it occurred to the men, after they had seen the signs, (that it was best) to imprison him for a time.

36. Now with him there came into the prison two young men. Said one of them: "I see myself (in a dream) pressing wine." said the other: "I see myself (in a dream) carrying bread on my head, and birds are eating, thereof." "Tell us" (they said) "The truth and meaning thereof: for we see thou art one that doth good (to all)."

37. He said: "Before any food comes (in due course) to feed either of you, I will surely reveal to you the truth and meaning of this ere it befall you: that is part of the (duty) which my Lord hath taught me. I have (I assure you) abandoned the ways of a people that believe not in Allah and that (even) deny the Hereafter.

38. "And I follow the ways of my fathers, Abraham, Isaac, and Jacob; and never could we attribute any partners whatever to Allah that (comes) of the grace of Allah to us and to mankind: yet most men are not grateful.

39. "O my two companions of the prison! (I ask you): are many lords differing among themselves better, or the One Allah, Supreme and Irresistible?

40. "If not Him, ye worship nothing but names which ye have named, ye and your fathers, for which Allah hath sent down no authority: the command is for none but Allah. He hath commanded that ye worship none but Him: that is the right religion, but most men understand not . . .

41. "O my two companions of the prison! As to one of you, he will pour out the wine for his lord to drink: as for the other, he will hang from the cross, and the birds will eat from off his head. (so) hath been decreed that matter whereof ye twain do enquire . . ."

42. And of the two, to that one whom he consider about to be saved, he said: "Mention me to thy lord." But Satan made him forget to mention him to his lord: and (Joseph) lingered in prison a few (more) years.

43. The king (of Egypt) said: "I do see (in a vision) seven fat kine, whom seven lean ones devour, and seven green ears of corn, and seven (others) withered. O ye chiefs! Expound to me my vision if it be that ye can interpret visions."

44. They said: "A confused medley of dreams: and we are not skilled in the interpretation of dreams."

45. But the man who had been released, one of the two (who had been in prison) and who now bethought him after (so long) a

space of time, said: "I will tell you the truth of its interpretation: send ye me (therefore)."

46. "O Joseph!" (he said) "O man of truth! Expound to us (the dream) of seven fat kine whom seven lean ones devour, and of seven green ears of corn and (seven) others withered: that I may return to the people, and that they may understand."

47. (Joseph) said: "For seven years shall ye diligently sow as is your wont: and the harvests that ye reap, ye shall leave them in the ear, except a little, of which ye shall eat.

48. "Then will come after that (period) seven dreadful (years), which will devour what ye shall have laid by in advance for them, (all) except a little which ye shall have (specially) guarded.

49. "Then will come after that (period) a year in which the people will have abundant water, and in which they will press (wine and oil)."

50. So the king said: "Bring ye him unto me." But when the messenger came to him, (Joseph) said: "Go thou back to thy lord, and ask him, 'What is the state of mind of the ladies who cut their hands'? For my Lord is certainly well aware of their snare."

51. (The king) said (to the ladies): "What was your affair when ye did seek to seduce Joseph from his (true) self?" The ladies said: "(Allah) preserve us! no evil know we against him!" Said the 'Aziz's wife: "Now is the truth manifest (to all): it was I who sought to seduce him from his (true) self: He is indeed of those who are (ever) true (and virtuous).

52. "This (say I), in order that He may know that I have never been false to him in his absence, and that Allah will never guide the snare of the false ones.

53. "Nor do I absolve my own self (of blame): the (human) soul is certainly prone to evil, unless my Lord do bestow His Mercy: but surely my Lord is Oft-forgiving, Most Merciful."

54. So the king said: "Bring him unto me; I will take him specially to serve about my own person." Therefore when he had spoken to him, he said: "Be assured this day, thou art, before our own presence, with rank firmly established, and fidelity fully proved!

55. (Joseph) said: "Set me over the store-houses of the land: I will indeed guard them, as one that knows (their importance)."

56. Thus did We give established power to Joseph in the land, to take possession therein as, when, or where he pleased. We bestow

of our Mercy on whom We please, and We suffer not, to be lost, the reward of those who do good.

57. But verily the reward of the Hereafter is the best, for those who believe, and are constant in righteousness.

58. Then came Joseph's brethren: they entered his presence, and he knew them, but they knew him not.

59. And when he had furnished them forth with provisions (suitable) for them, he said: "Bring unto me a brother ye have, of the same father as yourselves, (but a different mother): see ye not that I pay out full measure, and that I do provide the best hospitality?

60. "Now if ye bring him not to me, ye shall have no measure (of corn) from me, nor shall ye (even) come near me."

Prophets: Word to World

The Divine Word that has been Torah now amplifies into prophesy, which is Word spoken to World. Judgment against Israel becomes hope to all peoples; world calamity portends particular hope. *Akedic* theme and structure radiates from Torah into prophets, wisdom, and apocalyptic phases of sacred literature.

‡ HEBREW BIBLE: NUMBERS 6.4–7 ‡

⁴All the days of his Naziriteship shall he eat nothing that is made of the grape-vine, from the pressed grapes even to the grapestone. ⁵All the days of his vow of Naziriteship there shall no razor come upon his head; until the days be fulfilled, in which he consecrateth himself unto the LORD, he shall be holy, he shall let the locks of the hair of his head grow long. ⁶All the days that he consecrateth himself unto the LORD he shall not come near to a dead body. ⁷He shall not make himself unclean for his father, or for his mother, for his brother, or for his sister, when they die; because his consecration unto God is upon his head.

‡ CHRISTIAN GOSPELS: LUKE 1.76–77 ‡

⁷⁶And you, child, will be called the prophet of the Most High; for you will go before the Lord to prepare his ways, ⁷⁷to give knowledge of salvation to his people by the forgiveness of their sins.

‡ Islamic Qur'an: Sura 5.44–48 ‡

44. It was We who revealed the law (to Moses): therein was guidance and light. By its standard have been judged the Jews, by the prophets who bowed (as in Islam) to Allah's will, by the rabbis and the doctors of law: for to them was entrusted the protection of Allah's book, and they were witnesses thereto: therefore fear not men, but fear me, and sell not my signs for a miserable price. If any do fail to judge by (the light of) what Allah hath revealed, they are (no better than) Unbelievers.

45. We ordained therein for them: "Life for life, eye for eye, nose or nose, ear for ear, tooth for tooth, and wounds equal for equal." But if any one remits the retaliation by way of charity, it is an act of atonement for himself. And if any fail to judge by (the light of) what Allah hath revealed, they are (No better than) wrong-doers.

46. And in their footsteps We sent Jesus the son of Mary, confirming the Law that had come before him: We sent him the Gospel: therein was guidance and light, and confirmation of the Law that had come before him: a guidance and an admonition to those who fear Allah.

47. Let the people of the Gospel judge by what Allah hath revealed therein. If any do fail to judge by (the light of) what Allah hath revealed, they are (no better than) those who rebel.

48. To thee We sent the Scripture in truth, confirming the scripture that came before it, and guarding it in safety: so judge between them by what Allah hath revealed, and follow not their vain desires, diverging from the Truth that hath come to thee. To each among you have we prescribed a law and an open way. If Allah had so willed, He would have made you a single people, but (His plan is) to test you in what He hath given you: so strive as in a race in all virtues. The goal of you all is to Allah. it is He that will show you the truth of the matters in which ye dispute.

Wisdom and Logos

Wisdom also exhibits and elucidates the divine *Akedah*. Temptation marks life. Good and evil confront loyalties and decisions. Prophesy warms and recalls the Way of God. Persecution ensues. Suffering, death, and resurrection usher in redemption and new life.

‡ Hebrew Bible: Proverbs 10.1–29 ‡

¹The proverbs of Solomon. A wise son maketh a glad father; but a foolish son is the grief of his mother. ²Treasures of wickedness profit nothing; but righteousness delivereth from death. ³The LORD will not suffer the soul of the righteous to famish; but He thrusteth away the desire of the wicked. ⁴He becometh poor that dealeth with a slack hand; but the hand of the diligent maketh rich. ⁵A wise son gathereth in summer; but a son that doeth shamefully sleepeth in harvest. ⁶Blessings are upon the head of the righteous; but the mouth of the wicked concealeth violence. ⁷The memory of the righteous shall be for a blessing; but the name of the wicked shall rot. ⁸The wise in heart will receive commandments; but a prating fool shall fall. ⁹He that walketh uprightly walketh securely; but he that perverteth his ways shall be found out. ¹⁰He that winketh with the eye causeth sorrow; and a prating fool shall fall. ¹¹The mouth of the righteous is a fountain of life; but the mouth of the wicked concealeth violence. ¹²Hatred stirreth up strifes; but love covereth all transgressions. ¹³In the lips of him that hath discernment wisdom is found; but a rod is for the back of him that is void of understanding. ¹⁴Wise men lay up knowledge; but the mouth of the foolish is an imminent ruin. ¹⁵The rich man's wealth is his strong city; the ruin of the poor is their poverty. ¹⁶The wages of the righteous is life; the increase of the wicked is sin. ¹⁷He is in the way of life that heedeth instruction; but he that forsaketh reproof erreth. ¹⁸He that hideth hatred is of lying lips; and he that uttereth a slander is a fool. ¹⁹In the multitude of words there wanteth not transgression; but he that refraineth his lips is wise. ²⁰The tongue of the righteous is as choice silver; the heart of the wicked is little worth. ²¹The lips of the righteous feed many; but the foolish die for want of understanding. ²²The blessing of the LORD, it maketh rich, and toil addeth nothing thereto. ²³It is as sport to a fool to do wickedness, and so is wisdom to a man of discernment. ²⁴The fear of the wicked, it shall come upon him; and the desire of the righteous shall be granted. ²⁵When the whirlwind passeth, the wicked is no more; but the righteous is an everlasting foundation. ²⁶As vinegar to the teeth, and as smoke to the eyes, so is the sluggard to them that send him. ²⁷The fear of the LORD prolongeth days; but the years of the wicked shall be shortened. ²⁸The hope of the righteous is gladness; but the expectation of the wicked shall perish. ²⁹The way of the LORD is a stronghold to the upright, but ruin to the workers of iniquity.

‡ Christian Gospels: 1 Corinthians 1.17–29 ‡

[17]For Christ did not send me to baptize but to proclaim the gospel, and not with eloquent wisdom, so that the cross of Christ might not be emptied of its power. [18]For the message about the cross is foolishness to those who are perishing, but to us who are being saved it is the power of God. [19]For it is written, 'I will destroy the wisdom of the wise, and the discernment of the discerning I will thwart.' [20]Where is the one who is wise? Where is the scribe? Where is the debater of this age? Has not God made foolish the wisdom of the world? [21]For since, in the wisdom of God, the world did not know God through wisdom, God decided, through the foolishness of our proclamation, to save those who believe. [22]For Jews demand signs and Greeks desire wisdom, [23]but we proclaim Christ crucified, a stumbling-block to Jews and foolishness to Gentiles, [24]but to those who are the called, both Jews and Greeks, Christ the power of God and the wisdom of God. [25]For God's foolishness is wiser than human wisdom, and God's weakness is stronger than human strength. [26]Consider your own call, brothers and sisters: not many of you were wise by human standards, not many were powerful, not many were of noble birth. [27]But God chose what is foolish in the world to shame the wise; God chose what is weak in the world to shame the strong; [28]God chose what is low and despised in the world, things that are not, to reduce to nothing things that are, [29]so that no one might boast in the presence of God.

‡ Islamic Qur'an: Sura 2.1–21 ‡

1. A.L.M.

2. This is the Book; in it is guidance sure, without doubt, to those who fear Allah.

3. Who believe in the Unseen, are steadfast in prayer, and spend out of what We have provided for them;

4. And who believe in the Revelation sent to thee, and sent before thy time, and (in their hearts) have the assurance of the Hereafter.

5. They are on (true) guidance, from their Lord, and it is these who will prosper.

6. As to those who reject Faith, it is the same to them whether thou warn them or do not warn them; they will not believe.

7. Allah hath set a seal on their hearts and on their hearing, and on their eyes is a veil; great is the penalty they (incur).

8. Of the people there are some who say: "We believe in Allah and the Last Day;" but they do not (really) believe.

9. Fain would they deceive Allah and those who believe, but they only deceive themselves, and realise (it) not!

10. In their hearts is a disease; and Allah has increased their disease: And grievous is the penalty they (incur), because they are false (to themselves).

11. When it is said to them: "Make not mischief on the Earth," they say: "Why, we only Want to make peace!"

12. Of a surety, they are the ones who make mischief, but they realise (it) not.

13. When it is said to them: "Believe as the others believe:" They say: "Shall we believe as the fools believe?" Nay, of a surety they are the fools, but they do not know.

14. When they meet those who believe, they say: "We believe;" but when they are alone with their evil ones, they say: "We are really with you: We (were) only jesting."

15. Allah will throw back their mockery on them, and give them rope in their trespasses; so they will wander like blind ones (To and fro).

16. These are they who have bartered Guidance for error: But their traffic is profitless, and they have lost true direction,

17. Their similitude is that of a man who kindled a fire; when it lighted all around him, Allah took away their light and left them in utter darkness. So they could not see.

18. Deaf, dumb, and blind, they will not return (to the path).

19. Or (another similitude) is that of a rain-laden cloud from the sky: In it are zones of darkness, and thunder and lightning: They press their fingers in their ears to keep out the stunning thunderclap, the while they are in terror of death. But Allah is ever round the rejecters of Faith!

20. The lightning all but snatches away their sight; every time the light (Helps) them, they walk therein, and when the darkness grows on them, they stand still. And if Allah willed, He could take away their faculty of hearing and seeing; for Allah hath power over all things.

21. O ye people! Adore your Guardian-Lord, who created you and those who came before you, that ye may have the chance to learn righteousness.

Akedah: The All-Telling Parable

Eid al-Adha celebrates Abraham's sacrifice of his beloved child. As in the Hebrew text of Genesis 22, it is the paradigmatic proclamation of God's love for the world and responsive human trust.

‡ Hebrew Bible: Genesis 22.1–18 ‡

¹And it came to pass after these things, that God did prove Abraham, and said unto him: 'Abraham'; and he said: 'Here am I.' ²And He said: 'Take now thy son, thine only son, whom thou lovest, even Isaac, and get thee into the land of Moriah; and offer him there for a burnt-offering upon one of the mountains which I will tell thee of.' ³And Abraham rose early in the morning, and saddled his ass, and took two of his young men with him, and Isaac his son; and he cleaved the wood for the burnt-offering, and rose up, and went unto the place of which God had told him. ⁴On the third day Abraham lifted up his eyes, and saw the place afar off. ⁵And Abraham said unto his young men: 'Abide ye here with the ass, and I and the lad will go yonder; and we will worship, and come back to you.' ⁶And Abraham took the wood of the burnt-offering, and laid it upon Isaac his son; and he took in his hand the fire and the knife; and they went both of them together. ⁷And Isaac spoke unto Abraham his father, and said: 'My father.' And he said: 'Here am I, my son.' And he said: 'Behold the fire and the wood; but where is the lamb for a burnt-offering?' ⁸And Abraham said: 'God will provide Himself the lamb for a burnt-offering, my son.' So they went both of them together. ⁹And they came to the place which God had told him of; and Abraham built the altar there, and laid the wood in order, and bound Isaac his son, and laid him on the altar, upon the wood. ¹⁰And Abraham stretched forth his hand, and took the knife to slay his son. ¹¹And the angel of the LORD called unto him out of heaven, and said: 'Abraham, Abraham.' And he said: 'Here am I.' ¹²And he said: 'Lay not thy hand upon the lad, neither do thou any thing unto him; for now I know that thou art a God-fearing man, seeing thou hast not withheld thy son, thine only son, from Me.' ¹³And Abraham lifted up his eyes, and looked, and behold behind him a ram caught in the thicket by his horns. And Abraham went and took the ram, and offered him up for a burnt-offering in the stead of his son. ¹⁴And Abraham called the name of that place Adonai-jireh; as it is said to this day: 'In the mount where the LORD is seen.' ¹⁵And the angel of the LORD called unto Abraham a second time out of heaven, ¹⁶and said: 'By Myself have I sworn, saith the LORD, because thou hast done

this thing, and hast not withheld thy son, thine only son, ⁱ⁷that in blessing I will bless thee, and in multiplying I will multiply thy seed as the stars of the heaven, and as the sand which is upon the seashore; and thy seed shall possess the gate of his enemies; ¹⁸and in thy seed shall all the nations of the Earth be blessed; because thou hast hearkened to My voice.'

‡ Christian Gospels: Hebrews 11.17–20 ‡

¹⁷ By faith Abraham, when put to the test, offered up Isaac. He who had received the promises was ready to offer up his only son, ¹⁸of whom he had been told, 'It is through Isaac that descendants shall be named after you.' ¹⁹He considered the fact that God is able even to raise someone from the dead—and figuratively speaking, he did receive him back. ²⁰By faith Isaac invoked blessings for the future on Jacob and Esau.

‡ Christian Gospels: Romans 4 ‡

¹What then are we to say was gained by Abraham, our ancestor according to the flesh? ²For if Abraham was justified by works, he has something to boast about, but not before God. ³For what does the scripture say? 'Abraham believed God, and it was reckoned to him as righteousness.' ⁴Now to one who works, wages are not reckoned as a gift but as something due. ⁵But to one who without works trusts him who justifies the ungodly, such faith is reckoned as righteousness. ⁶So also David speaks of the blessedness of those to whom God reckons righteousness irrespective of works: ⁷'Blessed are those whose iniquities are forgiven, and whose sins are covered; ⁸blessed is the one against whom the Lord will not reckon sin.' ⁹Is this blessedness, then, pronounced only on the circumcised, or also on the uncircumcised? We say, 'Faith was reckoned to Abraham as righteousness.' ¹⁰How then was it reckoned to him? Was it before or after he had been circumcised? It was not after, but before he was circumcised. ¹¹He received the sign of circumcision as a seal of the righteousness that he had by faith while he was still uncircumcised. The purpose was to make him the ancestor of all who believe without being circumcised and who thus have righteousness reckoned to them, ¹²and likewise the ancestor of the circumcised who are not only circumcised but who also follow the example of the faith that our ancestor Abraham had before he was circumcised. ¹³For the promise that he would inherit the world did not come to Abraham or to his descendants

through the law but through the righteousness of faith. ¹⁴If it is the adherents of the law who are to be the heirs, faith is null and the promise is void. ¹⁵For the law brings wrath; but where there is no law, neither is there violation. ¹⁶For this reason it depends on faith, in order that the promise may rest on grace and be guaranteed to all his descendants, not only to the adherents of the law but also to those who share the faith of Abraham (for he is the father of all of us, ¹⁷as it is written, 'I have made you the father of many nations')—in the presence of the God in whom he believed, who gives life to the dead and calls into existence the things that do not exist. ¹⁸Hoping against hope, he believed that he would become 'the father of many nations', according to what was said, 'So numerous shall your descendants be.' ¹⁹He did not weaken in faith when he considered his own body, which was already as good as dead (for he was about a hundred years old), or when he considered the barrenness of Sarah's womb. ²⁰No distrust made him waver concerning the promise of God, but he grew strong in his faith as he gave glory to God, ²¹being fully convinced that God was able to do what he had promised. ²²Therefore his faith 'was reckoned to him as righteousness.' ²³Now the words, 'it was reckoned to him', were written not for his sake alone, ²⁴but for ours also. It will be reckoned to us who believe in him who raised Jesus our Lord from the dead, ²⁵who was handed over to death for our trespasses and was raised for our justification.

‡ Islamic Qur'an: Sura 37.99–113 ‡

99. He said: "I will go to my Lord! He will surely guide me!

100. "O my Lord! Grant me a righteous (son)!"

101. So We gave him the good news of a boy ready to suffer and forbear.

102. Then, when (the son) reached (the age of) (serious) work with him, he said: "O my son! I see in vision that I offer thee in sacrifice: Now see what is thy view!" (The son) said: "O my father! Do as thou art commanded: thou will find me, if Allah so wills one practising Patience and Constancy!"

103. So when they had both submitted their wills (to Allah., and he had laid him prostrate on his forehead (for sacrifice),

104. We called out to him "O Abraham!

105. "Thou hast already fulfilled the vision!" thus indeed do We reward those who do right.

106. For this was obviously a trial.

107. And We ransomed him with a momentous sacrifice:

108. And We left (this blessing) for him among generations (to come) in later times:

109. "Peace and salutation to Abraham!"

110. Thus indeed do We reward those who do right.

111. For he was one of our believing Servants.

112. And We gave him the good news of Isaac, a prophet, one of the Righteous.

113. We blessed him and Isaac: but of their progeny are (some) that do right, and (some) that obviously do wrong, to their own souls.

Magnificat

While Christian Mariology often visits havoc on Jews, Islam extends its great honor.

‡ Hebrew Bible: 1 Samuel 2.1–20 ‡

[1]And Hannah prayed, and said: my heart exulteth in the LORD, my horn is exalted in the LORD; my mouth is enlarged over mine enemies; because I rejoice in Thy salvation. [2]There is none holy as the LORD, for there is none beside Thee; neither is there any rock like our God. [3]Multiply not exceeding proud talk; let not arrogancy come out of your mouth; for the LORD is a God of knowledge, and by Him actions are weighed. [4]The bows of the mighty men are broken, and they that stumbled are girded with strength. [5]They that were full have hired out themselves for bread; and they that were hungry have ceased; while the barren hath borne seven, she that had many children hath languished. [6]The LORD killeth, and maketh alive; He bringeth down to the grave, and bringeth up. [7]The LORD maketh poor, and maketh rich; He bringeth low, He also lifteth up. [8]He raiseth up the poor out of the dust, He lifteth up the needy from the dung-hill, to make them sit with princes, and inherit the throne of glory; for the pillars of the Earth are the LORD'S, and He hath set the world upon them. [9]He will keep the feet of His holy ones, but the wicked shall be put to silence in darkness; for not by strength shall man prevail. [10]They that strive with the LORD shall be broken to pieces; against them will He thunder in heaven; the LORD will judge the ends of the Earth; and He will give strength unto His king, and exalt the horn of His anointed.

[11]And Elkanah went to Ramah to his house. And the child did minister unto the LORD before Eli the priest. [12]Now the sons of Eli were base men; they knew not the LORD. [13]And the custom of the priests with the people was, that, when any man offered sacrifice, the priest's servant came, while the flesh was in seething, with a flesh-hook of three teeth in his hand; [14]and he struck it into the pan, or kettle, or caldron, or pot; all that the flesh-hook brought up the priest took therewith. So they did unto all the Israelites that came thither in Shiloh. [15]Yea, before the fat was made to smoke, the priest's servant came, and said to the man that sacrificed: 'Give flesh to roast for the priest; for he will not have sodden flesh of thee, but raw.' [16]And if the man said unto him: 'Let the fat be made to smoke first of all, and then take as much as thy soul desireth'; then he would say: 'Nay, but thou shalt give it me now; and if not, I will take it by force.' [17]And the sin of the young men was very great before the LORD; for the men dealt contemptuously with the offering of the LORD. [18]But Samuel ministered before the LORD, being a child, girded with a linen ephod. [19]Moreover his mother made him a little robe, and brought it to him from year to year, when she came up with her husband to offer the yearly sacrifice. [20]And Eli would bless Elkanah and his wife, and say: 'The LORD give thee seed of this woman for the loan which was lent to the LORD.' And they would go unto their own home.

‡ Christian Gospels: Luke 1.46–56 ‡

[46] And Mary said,
'My soul magnifies the Lord,
[47]and my spirit rejoices in God my Saviour,
[48]for he has looked with favour on the lowliness of his servant.
Surely, from now on all generations will call me blessed;
[49]for the Mighty One has done great things for me,
and holy is his name.
[50]His mercy is for those who fear him
from generation to generation.
[51]He has shown strength with his arm;
he has scattered the proud in the thoughts of their hearts.
[52]He has brought down the powerful from their thrones,
and lifted up the lowly;
[53]he has filled the hungry with good things,
and sent the rich away empty.
[54]He has helped his servant Israel,
in remembrance of his mercy,

⁵⁵according to the promise he made to our ancestors,
to Abraham and to his descendants for ever.'
⁵⁶And Mary remained with her for about three months and then returned to her home.

‡ Islamic Qur'an: Sura 3.35–51 ‡

35. Behold! a woman of 'Imran said: "O my Lord! I do dedicate unto Thee what is in my womb for Thy special service: So accept this of me: For Thou hearest and knowest all things."

36. When she was delivered, she said: "O my Lord! Behold! I am delivered of a female child!" and Allah knew best what she brought forth. "And no wise is the male Like the female. I have named her Mary, and I commend her and her offspring to Thy protection from the Evil One, the Rejected."

37. Right graciously did her Lord accept her: He made her grow in purity and beauty: To the care of Zakariya was she assigned. Every time that he entered (Her) chamber to see her, He found her supplied with sustenance. He said: "O Mary! Whence (comes) this to you?" She said: "From Allah. for Allah Provides sustenance to whom He pleases without measure."

38. There did Zakariya pray to his Lord, saying: "O my Lord! Grant unto me from Thee a progeny that is pure: for Thou art He that heareth prayer!

39. While he was standing in prayer in the chamber, the angels called unto him: "(Allah) doth give thee glad tidings of Yahya, witnessing the truth of a Word from Allah, and (be besides) noble, chaste, and a prophet, of the (goodly) company of the righteous."

40. He said: "O my lord! How shall I have a son seeing I am very old and my wife is barren?" "Thus" was the answer "doth Allah accomplish what He willeth."

41. He said: "O my Lord! Give me a Sign!" "Thy Sign," was the answer, "Shall be that thou shalt speak to no man for three days but with signals. Then celebrate the praises of thy Lord again and again, and glorify Him in the evening and in the morning."

42. Behold! the angels said: "O Mary! Allah hath chosen thee and purified thee, chosen thee above the women of all nations.

43. "O Mary! worship Thy Lord devoutly: Prostrate thyself, and bow down (in prayer) with those who bow down."

44. This is part of the tidings of the things unseen, which We reveal unto thee (O Messenger.) by inspiration: Thou wast not with them when they cast lots with arrows, as to which of them should be charged with the care of Mary: Nor wast thou with them when they disputed (the point).

45. Behold! the angels said: "O Mary! Allah giveth thee glad tidings of a Word from Him: his name will be Christ Jesus, the son of Mary, held in honour in this world and the Hereafter and of (the company of) those nearest to Allah.

46. "He shall speak to the people in childhood and in maturity. And he shall be (of the company) of the righteous."

47. She said: "O my Lord! How shall I have a son when no man hath touched me?" He said: "Even so: Allah createth what He willeth: When He hath decreed a plan, He but saith to it, 'Be,' and it is!

48. "And Allah will teach him the Book and Wisdom, the Law and the Gospel,

49. "And (appoint him) an apostle to the Children of Israel, (with this message): "'I have come to you, with a Sign from your Lord, in that I make for you out of clay, as it were, the figure of a bird, and breathe into it, and it becomes a bird by Allah's leave: And I heal those born blind, and the lepers, and I quicken the dead, by Allah's leave; and I declare to you what ye eat, and what ye store in your houses. Surely therein is a Sign for you if ye did believe;

50. "'(I have come to you), to attest the Law which was before me. And to make lawful to you part of what was (Before) forbidden to you; I have come to you with a Sign from your Lord. So fear Allah, and obey me.

51. "'It is Allah Who is my Lord and your Lord; then worship Him. This is a Way that is straight.'"

Jesus

The earthly and eternal personage of Jesus is a deep tradition in Judaism and Islam and the central theme of Christianity. Themes such as "second God in heaven," *Logos*, Sophia (*hikmah*), Messiah (*Mahdi*), and others are found in the bookend Semitic traditions. For Christians, Jesus is "Son of Man," "Son of God," Savior, and Lord.

‡ Hebrew Bible: Isaiah 53 ‡

¹'Who would have believed our report? And to whom hath the arm of the LORD been revealed? ²For he shot up right forth as a sapling, and as a root out of a dry ground; he had no form nor comeliness, that we should look upon him, nor beauty that we should delight in him. ³He was despised, and forsaken of men, a man of pains, and acquainted with disease, and as one from whom men hide their face: he was despised, and we esteemed him not. ⁴Surely our diseases he did bear, and our pains he carried; whereas we did esteem him stricken, smitten of God, and afflicted. ⁵But he was wounded because of our transgressions, he was crushed because of our iniquities: the chastisement of our welfare was upon him, and with his stripes we were healed. ⁶All we like sheep did go astray, we turned every one to his own way; and the LORD hath made to light on him the iniquity of us all. ⁷He was oppressed, though he humbled himself and opened not his mouth; as a lamb that is led to the slaughter, and as a sheep that before her shearers is dumb; yea, he opened not his mouth. ⁸By oppression and judgment he was taken away, and with his generation who did reason? for he was cut off out of the land of the living, for the transgression of my people to whom the stroke was due. ⁹And they made his grave with the wicked, and with the rich his tomb; although he had done no violence, neither was any deceit in his mouth.' ¹⁰Yet it pleased the LORD to crush him by disease; to see if his soul would offer itself in restitution, that he might see his seed, prolong his days, and that the purpose of the LORD might prosper by his hand: ¹¹Of the travail of his soul he shall see to the full, even My servant, who by his knowledge did justify the Righteous One to the many, and their iniquities he did bear. ¹²Therefore will I divide him a portion among the great, and he shall divide the spoil with the mighty; because he bared his soul unto death, and was numbered with the transgressors; yet he bore the sin of many, and made intercession for the transgressors.

‡ Christian Gospels: Mark 8.27–31 ‡

²⁷Jesus went on with his disciples to the villages of Caesarea Philippi; and on the way he asked his disciples, 'Who do people say that I am?' ²⁸And they answered him, 'John the Baptist; and others, Elijah; and still others, one of the prophets.' ²⁹He asked them, 'But who do you say that I am?' Peter answered him, 'You are the Messiah.' ³⁰And he sternly ordered them not to tell anyone

about him. ³¹Then he began to teach them that the Son of Man must undergo great suffering, and be rejected by the elders, the chief priests, and the scribes, and be killed, and after three days rise again.

‡ Islamic Qur'an: Sura 4.155–165 ‡

155. (They have incurred divine displeasure): In that they broke their covenant; that they rejected the signs of Allah. that they slew the Messengers in defiance of right; that they said, "Our hearts are the wrappings (which preserve Allah's Word; We need no more)"; Nay, Allah hath set the seal on their hearts for their blasphemy, and little is it they believe;

156. That they rejected Faith; that they uttered against Mary a grave false charge;

157. That they said (in boast), "We killed Christ Jesus the son of Mary, the Messenger of Allah; but they killed him not, nor crucified him, but so it was made to appear to them, and those who differ therein are full of doubts, with no (certain) knowledge, but only conjecture to follow, for of a surety they killed him not:

158. Nay, Allah raised him up unto Himself; and Allah is Exalted in Power, Wise;

159. And there is none of the People of the Book but must believe in him before his death; and on the Day of Judgment he will be a witness against them;

160. For the iniquity of the Jews We made unlawful for them certain (foods) good and wholesome which had been lawful for them; in that they hindered many from Allah's Way;

161. That they took usury, though they were forbidden; and that they devoured men's substance wrongfully; we have prepared for those among them who reject faith a grievous punishment.

162. But those among them who are well-grounded in knowledge, and the believers, believe in what hath been revealed to thee and what was revealed before thee: And (especially) those who establish regular prayer and practise regular charity and believe in Allah and in the Last Day: To them shall We soon give a great reward.

163. We have sent thee inspiration, as We sent it to Noah and the Messengers after him: we sent inspiration to Abraham, Isma'il, Isaac, Jacob and the Tribes, to Jesus, Job, Jonah, Aaron, and Solomon, and to David We gave the Psalms.

164. Of some apostles We have already told thee the story; of others We have not; and to Moses Allah spoke direct;

165. Messenger. who gave good news as well as warning, that mankind, after (the coming) of the apostles, should have no plea against Allah. For Allah is Exalted in Power, Wise.

Baptism and Transfiguration

Noah and baptism, Isaac and crucifixion, suffering, death and resurrection are the interfaith substance.

‡ Hebrew Bible: Exodus 34.29 ‡

^{29}And it came to pass, when Moses came down from mount Sinai with the two tables of the testimony in Moses' hand, when he came down from the mount, that Moses knew not that the skin of his face sent forth beams while He talked with him.

‡ Christian Gospels: Matthew 17.1–8 ‡

^{1}Six days later, Jesus took with him Peter and James and his brother John and led them up a high mountain, by themselves. ^{2}And he was transfigured before them, and his face shone like the sun, and his clothes became dazzling white. ^{3}Suddenly there appeared to them Moses and Elijah, talking with him. ^{4}Then Peter said to Jesus, 'Lord, it is good for us to be here; if you wish, I will make three dwellings here, one for you, one for Moses, and one for Elijah.' ^{5}While he was still speaking, suddenly a bright cloud overshadowed them, and from the cloud a voice said, 'This is my Son, the Beloved; with him I am well pleased; listen to him!' ^{6}When the disciples heard this, they fell to the ground and were overcome by fear. ^{7}But Jesus came and touched them, saying, 'Get up and do not be afraid.' ^{8}And when they looked up, they saw no one except Jesus himself alone.

‡ Islamic Qur'an: Sura 17.1 ‡

1. Glory to (Allah) Who did take His servant for a Journey by night from the Sacred Mosque to the farthest Mosque, whose precincts We did bless, in order that We might show him some of Our Signs: for He is the One Who heareth and seeth (all things).

Spirit

Spirit is anchored in the Word and Way, the very active being of God. Pentecost is Shavuot and celebration of Taurut.

‡ Hebrew Bible: Numbers 11.21–25 ‡

[21]And Moses said: 'The people, among whom I am, are six hundred thousand men on foot; and yet Thou hast said: I will give them flesh, that they may eat a whole month! [22]If flocks and herds be slain for them, will they suffice them? or if all the fish of the sea be gathered together for them, will they suffice them?' [23]And the LORD said unto Moses: 'Is the LORD'S hand waxed short? now shalt thou see whether My word shall come to pass unto thee or not.' [24]And Moses went out, and told the people the words of the LORD; and he gathered seventy men of the elders of the people, and set them round about the Tent. [25]And the LORD came down in the cloud, and spoke unto him, and took of the spirit that was upon him, and put it upon the seventy elders; and it came to pass, that, when the spirit rested upon them, they prophesied, but they did so no more.

‡ Christian Gospels: Acts 2.1–21 ‡

[1]When the day of Pentecost had come, they were all together in one place. [2]And suddenly from heaven there came a sound like the rush of a violent wind, and it filled the entire house where they were sitting. [3]Divided tongues, as of fire, appeared among them, and a tongue rested on each of them. [4]All of them were filled with the Holy Spirit and began to speak in other languages, as the Spirit gave them ability. [5]Now there were devout Jews from every nation under heaven living in Jerusalem. [6]And at this sound the crowd gathered and was bewildered, because each one heard them speaking in the native language of each. [7]Amazed and astonished, they asked, 'Are not all these who are speaking Galileans? [8]And how is it that we hear, each of us, in our own native language? [9]Parthians, Medes, Elamites, and residents of Mesopotamia, Judea and Cappadocia, Pontus and Asia, [10]Phrygia and Pamphylia, Egypt and the parts of Libya belonging to Cyrene, and visitors from Rome, both Jews and proselytes, [11]Cretans and Arabs—in our own languages we hear them speaking about God's deeds of power.' [12]All were amazed and perplexed, saying to one another, 'What does this mean?' [13]But others sneered and said, 'They are filled with new wine.' [14]But Peter, standing with the eleven, raised

his voice and addressed them: 'Men of Judea and all who live in Jerusalem, let this be known to you, and listen to what I say. ¹⁵Indeed, these are not drunk, as you suppose, for it is only nine o'clock in the morning. ¹⁶No, this is what was spoken through the prophet Joel:

¹⁷"In the last days it will be, God declares,
that I will pour out my Spirit upon all flesh,
and your sons and your daughters shall prophesy,
and your young men shall see visions,
and your old men shall dream dreams.
¹⁸Even upon my slaves, both men and women,
in those days I will pour out my Spirit;
and they shall prophesy.
¹⁹And I will show portents in the heaven above
and signs on the Earth below,
blood, and fire, and smoky mist.
²⁰The sun shall be turned to darkness
and the moon to blood,
before the coming of the Lord's great and glorious day.
²¹Then everyone who calls on the name of the Lord shall be saved."

‡ Islamic Qur'an: Sura 5.32 ‡

32. On that account: We ordained for the Children of Israel that if any one slew a person, unless it be for murder or for spreading mischief in the land, it would be as if he slew the whole people: and if any one saved a life, it would be as if he saved the life of the whole people. Then although there came to them Our apostles with clear signs, yet, even after that, many of them continued to commit excesses in the land.

New World

Kingdom of God, eschatology, and paradise are common interfaith motifs representative of the world to come.

‡ Hebrew Bible: Isaiah 66.22–24 (see also verses 42, 53) ‡

²²For as the new heavens and the new Earth, which I will make, shall remain before Me, saith the LORD, so shall your seed and your name remain. ²³And it shall come to pass, that from one new moon to another, and from one Sabbath to another, shall all flesh

come to worship before Me, saith the LORD. ²⁴And they shall go forth, and look upon the carcasses of the men that have rebelled against Me; for their worm shall not die, neither shall their fire be quenched; and they shall be an abhorring unto all flesh.

‡ Christian Gospels: Revelation 21 ‡

²¹Then I saw a new heaven and a new Earth; for the first heaven and the first Earth had passed away, and the sea was no more. ²And I saw the holy city, the new Jerusalem, coming down out of heaven from God, prepared as a bride adorned for her husband. ³And I heard a loud voice from the throne saying,

'See, the home of God is among mortals.
He will dwell with them;
they will be his peoples,
and God himself will be with them;
⁴he will wipe every tear from their eyes.
Death will be no more;
mourning and crying and pain will be no more,
for the first things have passed away.'

⁵And the one who was seated on the throne said, 'See, I am making all things new.' Also he said, 'Write this, for these words are trustworthy and true.' ⁶Then he said to me, 'It is done! I am the Alpha and the Omega, the beginning and the end. To the thirsty I will give water as a gift from the spring of the water of life. ⁷Those who conquer will inherit these things, and I will be their God and they will be my children. ⁸But as for the cowardly, the faithless, the polluted, the murderers, the fornicators, the sorcerers, the idolaters, and all liars, their place will be in the lake that burns with fire and sulphur, which is the second death.' ⁹Then one of the seven angels who had the seven bowls full of the seven last plagues came and said to me, 'Come, I will show you the bride, the wife of the Lamb.' ¹⁰And in the spirit he carried me away to a great, high mountain and showed me the holy city Jerusalem coming down out of heaven from God. ¹¹It has the glory of God and a radiance like a very rare jewel, like jasper, clear as crystal. ¹²It has a great, high wall with twelve gates, and at the gates twelve angels, and on the gates are inscribed the names of the twelve tribes of the Israelites; ¹³on the east three gates, on the north three gates, on the south three gates, and on the west three gates. ¹⁴And the wall of the city has twelve foundations, and on them are the twelve names

of the twelve apostles of the Lamb. ¹⁵The angel who talked to me had a measuring rod of gold to measure the city and its gates and walls. ¹⁶The city lies foursquare, its length the same as its width; and he measured the city with his rod, fifteen hundred miles; its length and width and height are equal. ¹⁷He also measured its wall, one hundred and forty-four cubits⁻ by human measurement, which the angel was using. ¹⁸The wall is built of jasper, while the city is pure gold, clear as glass. ¹⁹The foundations of the wall of the city are adorned with every jewel; the first was jasper, the second sapphire, the third agate, the fourth emerald, ²⁰the fifth onyx, the sixth cornelian, the seventh chrysolite, the eighth beryl, the ninth topaz, the tenth chrysoprase, the eleventh jacinth, the twelfth amethyst. ²¹And the twelve gates are twelve pearls, each of the gates is a single pearl, and the street of the city is pure gold, transparent as glass. ²²I saw no temple in the city, for its temple is the Lord God the Almighty and the Lamb. ²³And the city has no need of sun or moon to shine on it, for the glory of God is its light, and its lamp is the Lamb. ²⁴The nations will walk by its light, and the kings of the Earth will bring their glory into it. ²⁵Its gates will never be shut by day—and there will be no night there. ²⁶People will bring into it the glory and the honour of the nations. ²⁷But nothing unclean will enter it, nor anyone who practices abomination or falsehood, but only those who are written in the Lamb's book of life.

‡ Christian Gospels: Revelation 22.14 ‡

¹⁴Blessed are those who wash their robes, so that they will have the right to the tree of life and may enter the city by the gates.

‡ Islamic Hadith: Sahil Collection of al-Bukhari, Chapter 2: The Book of Belief ‡

II. On matters concerning belief

And the words of Allah, "It is not devoutness to turn your faces to the East or to the West. , those with true devotion are those who believe in Allah and the Last Day, the Angels, the Book and the Prophets, and who, despite their love for it, give away their wealth to their relatives and to orphans and the very poor, and to travellers and beggars and to set slaves free, and who establish the prayer and pay zakat; those who honour their contracts when they make them, and are steadfast in poverty and in illness and in battle. Those are the people who are true. They are the godfearing . . ." (2:177) and the words of Allah, "The believers are successful . . ." (23:1)

XII: On part of belief being hating to revert to disbelief as much as being thrown into a fire.

21. It was related from Anas from the Prophet, may Allah bless him and grant him peace, "Whoever possesses three attributes will experience the sweetness of belief: whoever loves Allah and His Messenger more than anything else; whoever loves someone for the sake of Allah alone; and whoever hates reverting to disbelief as much as he would hate being thrown into a fire."

Exodus

Lessons of the Exodus event are infused in all three traditions—lessons about idolatry, right living, proper worship, and the power of God.

‡ Hebrew Bible: Exodus 18.13–22 ‡

[13] And it came to pass on the morrow, that Moses sat to judge the people; and the people stood about Moses from the morning unto the evening. [14] And when Moses' father-in-law saw all that he did to the people, he said: 'What is this thing that thou doest to the people? why sittest thou thyself alone, and all the people stand about thee from morning unto even?' [15] And Moses said unto his father-in-law: 'Because the people come unto me to inquire of God; [16] when they have a matter, it cometh unto me; and I judge between a man and his neighbour, and I make them know the statutes of God, and His laws.' [17] And Moses' father-in-law said unto him: 'The thing that thou doest is not good. [18] Thou wilt surely wear away, both thou, and this people that is with thee; for the thing is too heavy for thee; thou art not able to perform it thyself alone. [19] Hearken now unto my voice, I will give thee counsel, and God be with thee: be thou for the people before God, and bring thou the causes unto God. [20] And thou shalt teach them the statutes and the laws, and shalt show them the way wherein they must walk, and the work that they must do. [21] Moreover thou shalt provide out of all the people able men, such as fear God, men of truth, hating unjust gain; and place such over them, to be rulers of thousands, rulers of hundreds, rulers of fifties, and rulers of tens. [22] And let them judge the people at all seasons; and it shall be, that every great matter they shall bring unto thee, but every small matter they shall judge themselves; so shall they make it easier for thee and bear the burden with thee.

‡ Christian Gospels: Acts 4.23–31 ‡

[23] After they were released, they went to their friends and reported what the chief priests and the elders had said to them. [24] When they heard it, they raised their voices together to God and said, 'Sovereign Lord, who made the heaven and the Earth, the sea, and everything in them, [25] it is you who said by the Holy Spirit through our ancestor David, your servant: "Why did the Gentiles rage, and the peoples imagine vain things? [26] The kings of the Earth took their stand, and the rulers have gathered together against the Lord and against his Messiah." [27] For in this city, in fact, both Herod and Pontius Pilate, with the Gentiles and the peoples of Israel, gathered together against your holy servant Jesus, whom you anointed, [28] to do whatever your hand and your plan had predestined to take place. [29] And now, Lord, look at their threats, and grant to your servants to speak your word with all boldness, [30] while you stretch out your hand to heal, and signs and wonders are performed through the name of your holy servant Jesus.' [31] When they had prayed, the place in which they were gathered together was shaken; and they were all filled with the Holy Spirit and spoke the word of God with boldness.

‡ Islamic Qur'an: Sura 28.14–46 ‡

14. When he reached full age, and was firmly established (in life), We bestowed on him wisdom and knowledge: for thus do We reward those who do good.

15. And he entered the city at a time when its people were not watching: and he found there two men fighting, one of his own religion, and the other, of his foes. Now the man of his own religion appealed to him against his foe, and Moses struck him with his fist and made an end of him. He said: "This is a work of Evil (Satan): for he is an enemy that manifestly misleads!"

16. He prayed: "O my Lord! I have indeed wronged my soul! Do Thou then forgive me!" So ((Allah)) forgave him: for He is the Oft-Forgiving, Most Merciful.

17. He said: "O my Lord! For that Thou hast bestowed Thy Grace on me, never shall I be a help to those who sin!"

18. So he saw the morning in the city, looking about, in a state of fear, when behold, the man who had, the day before, sought his help called aloud for his help (again). Moses said to him: "Thou art truly, it is clear, a quarrelsome fellow!"

19. Then, when he decided to lay hold of the man who was an enemy to both of them, that man said: "O Moses! Is it thy intention to slay me as thou slewest a man yesterday? Thy intention is none other than to become a powerful violent man in the land, and not to be one who sets things right!"

20. And there came a man, running, from the furthest end of the City. He said: "O Moses! the Chiefs are taking counsel together about thee, to slay thee: so get thee away, for I do give thee sincere advice."

21. He therefore got away therefrom, looking about, in a state of fear. He prayed "O my Lord! save me from people given to wrong-doing."

22. Then, when he turned his face towards (the land of) Madyan, he said: "I do hope that my Lord will show me the smooth and straight Path."

23. And when he arrived at the watering (place) in Madyan, he found there a group of men watering (their flocks), and besides them he found two women who were keeping back (their flocks). He said: "What is the matter with you?" They said: "We cannot water (our flocks) until the shepherds take back (their flocks): And our father is a very old man."

24. So he watered (their flocks) for them; then he turned back to the shade, and said: "O my Lord! truly am I in (desperate) need of any good that Thou dost send me!"

25. Afterwards one of the (damsels) came (back) to him, walking bashfully. She said: "My father invites thee that he may reward thee for having watered (our flocks) for us." So when he came to him and narrated the story, he said: "Fear thou not: (well) hast thou escaped from unjust people."

26. Said one of the (damsels): "O my (dear) father! engage him on wages: truly the best of men for thee to employ is the (man) who is strong and trusty. . . ."

27. He said: "I intend to wed one of these my daughters to thee, on condition that thou serve me for eight years; but if thou complete ten years, it will be (grace) from thee. But I intend not to place thee under a difficulty: thou wilt find me, indeed, if Allah wills, one of the righteous."

28. He said: "Be that (the agreement) between me and thee: whichever of the two terms I fulfil, let there be no ill-will to me. Be Allah a witness to what we say."

29. Now when Moses had fulfilled the term, and was traveling with his family, he perceived a fire in the direction of Mount Tur. He said to his family: "Tarry ye; I perceive a fire; I hope to bring you from there some information, or a burning firebrand, that ye may warm yourselves."

30. But when he came to the (fire), a voice was heard from the right bank of the valley, from a tree in hallowed ground: "O Moses! Verily I am Allah, the Lord of the Worlds..."

31. "Now do thou throw thy rod!" but when he saw it moving (of its own accord) as if it had been a snake, he turned back in retreat, and retraced not his steps: O Moses!" (It was said), "Draw near, and fear not: for thou art of those who are secure.

32. "Move thy hand into thy bosom, and it will come forth white without stain (or harm), and draw thy hand close to thy side (to guard) against fear. Those are the two credentials from thy Lord to Pharaoh and his Chiefs: for truly they are a people rebellious and wicked."

33. He said: "O my Lord! I have slain a man among them, and I fear lest they slay me.

34. "And my brother Aaron, He is more eloquent in speech than I: so send him with me as a helper, to confirm (and strengthen) me: for I fear that they may accuse me of falsehood."

35. He said: "We will certainly strengthen thy arm through thy brother, and invest you both with authority, so they shall not be able to touch you: with Our Sign shall ye triumph, you two as well as those who follow you."

36. When Moses came to them with Our clear signs, they said: "This is nothing but sorcery faked up: never did we head the like among our fathers of old!"

37. Moses said: "My Lord knows best who it is that comes with guidance from Him and whose end will be best in the Hereafter: certain it is that the wrong-doers will not prosper."

38. Pharaoh said: "O Chiefs! no god do I know for you but myself: therefore, O Haman! light me a (kiln to bake bricks) out of clay, and build me a lofty palace, that I may mount up to the god of Moses: but as far as I am concerned, I think (Moses) is a liar!"

39. And he was arrogant and insolent in the land, beyond reason, He and his hosts: they thought that they would not have to return to Us!

40. So We seized him and his hosts, and We flung them into the sea: Now behold what was the end of those who did wrong!

41. And we made them (but) leaders inviting to the Fire; and on the Day of Judgment no help shall they find.

42. in this world We made a curse to follow them and on the Day of Judgment they will be among the loathed (and despised).

43. We did reveal to Moses the Book after We had destroyed the earlier generations, (to give) Insight to men, and guidance and Mercy, that they might receive admonition.

44. Thou wast not on the Western side when We decreed the Commission to Moses, nor wast thou a witness (of those events).

45. But We raised up (new) generations, and long were the ages that passed over them; but thou wast not a dweller among the people of Madyan, rehearsing Our Signs to them; but it is We Who send apostles (with inspiration).

46. Nor wast thou at the side of (the Mountain of) Tur when we called (to Moses). Yet (art thou sent) as Mercy from thy Lord, to give warning to a people to whom no warner had come before thee: in order that they may receive admonition.

Submission

The theme of submission—cornerstone of the Islamic tradition—appears prominently in Judaism and Christianity as well: submission to God in obedience, reverence, and love.

‡ Hebrew Bible: 2 Chronicles 30.7–9 ‡

[7]And be not ye like your fathers, and like your brethren, who acted treacherously against the LORD, the God of their fathers, so that He delivered them to be an astonishment, as ye see. [8]Now be ye not stiffnecked, as your fathers were; but yield yourselves unto the LORD, and enter into His sanctuary, which He hath sanctified for ever, and serve the LORD your God, that His fierce anger may turn away from you. [9]For if ye turn back unto the LORD, your brethren and your children shall find compassion before them that led them captive, and shall come back into this land; for the LORD your God is gracious and merciful, and will not turn away His face from you, if ye return unto Him.

‡ CHRISTIAN GOSPELS: HEBREWS 5.7 ‡

⁷In the days of his flesh, Jesus offered up prayers and supplications, with loud cries and tears, to the one who was able to save him from death, and he was heard because of his reverent submission.

‡ ISLAMIC QUR'AN: SURA 3.19 ‡

19. The Religion before Allah is Islam (submission to His Will): Nor did the People of the Book dissent therefrom except through envy of each other, after knowledge had come to them. But if any deny the Signs of Allah, Allah is swift in calling to account.

‡ ISLAMIC QUR'AN: SURA 3.85 ‡

85. If anyone desires a religion other than Islam (submission to Allah), never will it be accepted of him; and in the Hereafter He will be in the ranks of those who have lost (All spiritual good).

‡ ISLAMIC QUR'AN: SURA 2.133 ‡

133. Were ye witnesses when death appeared before Jacob? Behold, he said to his sons: "What will ye worship after me?" They said: "We shall worship Thy Allah and the Allah of thy fathers, of Abraham, Isma'il and Isaac, the one (True) Allah. To Him we bow (in Islam)."

Just War

Peoples of all three traditions are called to live in peace with other societies surrounding them, except when an attack against them makes it impossible to live peacefully.

‡ HEBREW BIBLE: 1 SAMUEL 15.13–26 ‡

¹³And Samuel came to Saul; and Saul said unto him: 'Blessed be thou of the LORD; I have performed the commandment of the LORD.' ¹⁴And Samuel said: 'What meaneth then this bleating of the sheep in mine ears, and the lowing of the oxen which I hear?' ¹⁵And Saul said: 'They have brought them from the Amalekites; for the people spared the best of the sheep and of the oxen, to sacrifice unto the LORD thy God; and the rest we have utterly destroyed.' ¹⁶Then Samuel said unto Saul: 'Stay, and I will tell thee what the LORD hath said to me this night.' And he said unto him: 'Say on.'

[17]And Samuel said: 'Though thou be little in thine own sight, art thou not head of the tribes of Israel? And the LORD anointed thee king over Israel; [18]and the LORD sent thee on a journey, and said: Go and utterly destroy the sinners the Amalekites, and fight against them until they be consumed. [19]Wherefore then didst thou not hearken to the voice of the LORD, but didst fly upon the spoil, and didst that which was evil in the sight of the LORD?' [20]And Saul said unto Samuel: 'Yea, I have hearkened to the voice of the LORD, and have gone the way which the LORD sent me, and have brought Agag the king of Amalek, and have utterly destroyed the Amalekites. [21]But the people took of the spoil, sheep and oxen, the chief of the devoted things, to sacrifice unto the LORD thy God in Gilgal.' [22]And Samuel said: 'Hath the LORD as great delight in burnt-offerings and sacrifices, as in hearkening to the voice of the LORD? Behold, to obey is better than sacrifice, and to hearken than the fat of rams. [23]For rebellion is as the sin of witchcraft, and stubbornness is as idolatry and teraphim. Because thou hast rejected the word of the LORD, He hath also rejected thee from being king.' [24]And Saul said unto Samuel: 'I have sinned; for I have transgressed the commandment of the LORD, and thy words; because I feared the people, and hearkened to their voice. [25]Now therefore, I pray thee, pardon my sin, and return with me, that I may worship the LORD.' [26]And Samuel said unto Saul: 'I will not return with thee; for thou hast rejected the word of the LORD, and the LORD hath rejected thee from being king over Israel.'

‡ Christian Gospels: Romans 12.12–21 ‡

[12]Rejoice in hope, be patient in suffering, persevere in prayer. [13]Contribute to the needs of the saints; extend hospitality to strangers. [14]Bless those who persecute you; bless and do not curse them. [15]Rejoice with those who rejoice, weep with those who weep. [16]Live in harmony with one another; do not be haughty, but associate with the lowly; do not claim to be wiser than you are. [17]Do not repay anyone evil for evil, but take thought for what is noble in the sight of all. [18]If it is possible, so far as it depends on you, live peaceably with all. [19]Beloved, never avenge yourselves, but leave room for the wrath of God; for it is written, 'Vengeance is mine, I will repay, says the Lord.' [20]No, 'if your enemies are hungry, feed them; if they are thirsty, give them something to drink; for by doing this you will heap burning coals on their heads.' [21]Do not be overcome by evil, but overcome evil with good.

‡ Islamic Qur'an: Sura 2.189–195 ‡

189. They ask thee concerning the New Moons. Say: They are but signs to mark fixed periods of time in (the affairs of) men, and for Pilgrimage. It is no virtue if ye enter your houses from the back: It is virtue if ye fear Allah. Enter houses through the proper doors: And fear Allah. That ye may prosper.

190. Fight in the cause of Allah those who fight you, but do not transgress limits; for Allah loveth not transgressors.

191. And slay them wherever ye catch them, and turn them out from where they have Turned you out; for tumult and oppression are worse than slaughter; but fight them not at the Sacred Mosque, unless they (first) fight you there; but if they fight you, slay them. Such is the reward of those who suppress faith.

192. But if they cease, Allah is Oft-forgiving, Most Merciful.

193. And fight them on until there is no more Tumult or oppression, and there prevail justice and faith in Allah. but if they cease, Let there be no hostility except to those who practise oppression.

194. The prohibited month for the prohibited month, and so for all things prohibited,- there is the law of equality. If then any one transgresses the prohibition against you, Transgress ye likewise against him. But fear Allah, and know that Allah is with those who restrain themselves.

195. And spend of your substance in the cause of Allah, and make not your own hands contribute to (your) destruction; but do good; for Allah loveth those who do good.

Veiling and Modesty

Head coverings and veils for women are common motifs in all three traditions—signifying modesty and protection and, in some cases, self-respect and social status.

‡ Hebrew Bible: Genesis 24.57–67 ‡

[57]And they said: 'We will call the damsel, and inquire at her mouth.' [58]And they called Rebekah, and said unto her: 'Wilt thou go with this man?' And she said: 'I will go.' [59]And they sent away Rebekah their sister, and her nurse, and Abraham's servant, and his men. [60]And they blessed Rebekah, and said unto her: 'Our sister, be thou the mother of thousands of ten thousands, and let thy seed possess the gate of those that hate them.' [61]And Rebekah arose,

and her damsels, and they rode upon the camels, and followed the man. And the servant took Rebekah, and went his way. ⁶²And Isaac came from the way of Beer-lahai-roi; for he dwelt in the land of the South. ⁶³And Isaac went out to meditate in the field at the eventide; and he lifted up his eyes, and saw, and, behold, there were camels coming. ⁶⁴And Rebekah lifted up her eyes, and when she saw Isaac, she alighted from the camel. ⁶⁵And she said unto the servant: 'What man is this that walketh in the field to meet us?' And the servant said: 'It is my master.' And she took her veil, and covered herself. ⁶⁶And the servant told Isaac all the things that he had done. ⁶⁷And Isaac brought her into his mother Sarah's tent, and took Rebekah, and she became his wife; and he loved her. And Isaac was comforted for his mother.

‡ Hebrew Bible: Genesis 38.13–19 ‡

¹³And it was told Tamar, saying: 'Behold, thy father-in-law goeth up to Timnah to shear his sheep.' ¹⁴And she put off from her the garments of her widowhood, and covered herself with her veil, and wrapped herself, and sat in the entrance of Enaim, which is by the way to Timnah; for she saw that Shelah was grown up, and she was not given unto him to wife. ¹⁵When Judah saw her, he thought her to be a harlot; for she had covered her face. ¹⁶And he turned unto her by the way, and said: 'Come, I pray thee, let me come in unto thee'; for he knew not that she was his daughter-in-law. And she said: 'What wilt thou give me, that thou mayest come in unto me?' ¹⁷And he said: 'I will send thee a kid of the goats from the flock.' And she said: 'Wilt thou give me a pledge, till thou send it?' ¹⁸And he said: 'What pledge shall I give thee?' And she said: 'Thy signet and thy cord, and thy staff that is in thy hand.' And he gave them to her, and came in unto her, and she conceived by him. ¹⁹And she arose, and went away, and put off her veil from her, and put on the garments of her widowhood.

‡ Hebrew Bible: Isaiah 47.1–3 ‡

¹Come down, and sit in the dust, O virgin daughter of Babylon, sit on the ground without a throne, O daughter of the Chaldeans; for thou shalt no more be called tender and delicate. ²Take the millstones, and grind meal; remove thy veil, strip off the train, uncover the leg, pass through the rivers. ³Thy nakedness shall be uncovered, yea, thy shame shall be seen; I will take vengeance, and will let no man intercede.

‡ Christian Gospels: 1 Corinthians 11.1–16 ‡

¹Be imitators of me, as I am of Christ. ²I commend you because you remember me in everything and maintain the traditions just as I handed them on to you. ³But I want you to understand that Christ is the head of every man, and the husband is the head of his wife, and God is the head of Christ. ⁴Any man who prays or prophesies with something on his head disgraces his head, ⁵but any woman who prays or prophesies with her head unveiled disgraces her head—it is one and the same thing as having her head shaved. ⁶For if a woman will not veil herself, then she should cut off her hair; but if it is disgraceful for a woman to have her hair cut off or to be shaved, she should wear a veil. ⁷For a man ought not to have his head veiled, since he is the image and reflection of God; but woman is the reflection of man. ⁸Indeed, man was not made from woman, but woman from man. ⁹Neither was man created for the sake of woman, but woman for the sake of man. ¹⁰For this reason a woman ought to have a symbol of authority on her head, because of the angels. ¹¹Nevertheless, in the Lord woman is not independent of man or man independent of woman. ¹²For just as woman came from man, so man comes through woman; but all things come from God. ¹³Judge for yourselves: is it proper for a woman to pray to God with her head unveiled? ¹⁴Does not nature itself teach you that if a man wears long hair, it is degrading to him, ¹⁵but if a woman has long hair, it is her glory? For her hair is given to her for a covering. ¹⁶But if anyone is disposed to be contentious—we have no such custom, nor do the churches of God.

‡ Islamic Qur'an: Sura 24.30–31 ‡

30. Say to the believing men that they should lower their gaze and guard their modesty: that will make for greater purity for them: And Allah is well acquainted with all they do.

31. And say to the believing women that they should lower their gaze and guard their modesty; that they should not display their beauty and ornaments except what (must ordinarily) appear thereof; that they should draw their veils over their bosoms and not display their beauty except to their husbands, their fathers, their husband's fathers, their sons, their husbands' sons, their brothers or their brothers' sons, or their sisters' sons, or their women, or the slaves whom their right hands possess, or male servants free of physical needs, or small children who have no sense of the shame of sex; and that they should not strike their feet in order to draw

attention to their hidden ornaments. And O ye Believers! turn ye all together towards Allah, that ye may attain Bliss.

‡ Islamic Qur'an: Sura 33.59 ‡

59. O Prophet! Tell thy wives and daughters, and the believing women, that they should cast their outer garments over their persons (when abroad): that is most convenient, that they should be known (as such) and not molested. And Allah is Oft-Forgiving, Most Merciful.

IV

Interfaith Action

The Common Work—Conflicts in a Global World

CITY AND COUNTRY: TWO CITIES[1]

IT IS INDEED A TALE OF TWO CITIES—full of damnation and redemption —fully Dickensian. A several-month sojourn in Europe recently had made me aware of a coalescence of global forces that portend such a double-edged sword during the fateful election year of 2008. An uncanny and most uncomfortable instinct told me that the world was gathering into two clashing communities—the U.S. and Israel on the one hand and Europe and Islam on the other (in what is now being called "Eurabia").[2]

A possible intermediacy third party—among Russia, India and Pakistan, China, Africa, and the Muslim world—is standing in the wings. As Iran tests her rocket delivery systems, Israel and the U.S. discuss preemptive strike, and Pakistan becomes a cauldron where the once munificent medieval *madrassas* (Islamic religious schools) now become smoking factories for insurgents and terrorists. Western "torture schools" (with their Catholic links) contort the bitter legacy of old Franco-Algerian colonial systems into something now commensurable with Islamic "suicide

---

1. This section is excerpted from Vaux, *America in God's World*, 105–118.
2. See Jenkins, *God's Continent*.

schools," as the noble Abrahamic residue of Avicenna, Maimonides, and Aquinas whirls into a Dante-like Inferno.

The gathering storm is far different from that envisioned by a "clash of civilizations" between the West and Islam or America and the Hispanic world in Huntington's last Manichean apocalypse. This crisis is focused in the very heartland of Euro-American culture. Let us glance into this crisis through the eyes of two important new studies in biblical theology—referring also to two religious developments that seek to engage dialogue on the Christian/Muslim issue. My purpose is to endorse the interfaith dialogue, all the while calling for a firmer commitment to begin trialogue with attention to biblical and historical Israel. Israel's absence from pan-Abrahamic sharing now takes the theological heart away from public discourse and threatens to render it vacuous and irrelevant.

I have become aware in these precarious years of something Israel has known for 4,000 years—how fragile its existence is in the world. One of every two Jews born since the earthly life of Jesus the Jew has been killed and not allowed to live out his or her God-given life. Today, the American misadventure in the invasion and occupation of Iraq and the further, equally misinformed venture contemplated in Iran, has accelerated again the centripetal cleansing and refugee process. To this is added the Israeli attack, occupation, and dismemberment of Palestine and the furtive and futile attack on Lebanon (2006) and Gaza (2008–2009) that makes it feel that America is the only friend Israel has left in the world. Ninety percent of all Jews left in the world are now in America and Israel. This is something like the concentration of global Jewry exiled in Eastern Europe 150 years ago. I am told that there are only some 30 Jews left in Cairo, a once-thriving synagogue city, and that pattern holds throughout the Islamic world.

Equally disturbing to the *Shoah* and the de-Judification of *Dar al-Islam* is the de-Christianization of Israel and Palestine. A once-20-percent population is now less than 1 percent. Long gone is the pattern of centuries past when the "Peoples of the Book" harbored each other in freedom and safety as in medieval *Al-Andalus*. Though the Jewish community is impressive in France, England, and Holland (4,000, 2,000, and 100,000, respectively), these communities are feeling increasingly embattled and uncomfortable, especially as Islam surges into the spiritual vacuum that is modern secularized and materialistic Europe.

The immediate background to this crisis is obviously the tripartite, fratricidal intra-Abrahamic conflict caused by the mania in Israel for a security state, tenored by a terrible Holocaust revenge. This is seconded by the same craving for an idolatrous security state in the U.S., tinged by an insufferable and ill-targeted revenge and belligerence animated by the events of September 11th. This theo-global mania, we must remember, is fueled as much by dispensational Christian theology and militant Islam as by the "Israel lobby."

And finally, swept into the cauldron are the blasphemous, yet *Mullah*-unchallenged and unhindered suicide bombings of innocent civilians by militant Muslims in every corner of the world. What is anathema and unethical along all of the lineaments of Abrahamic faith and ethics has been glorified as heroic martyrdom.

So where can we look for hope, justice, peace, and salvation? My thesis throughout this writing is that the confession of the Jewish people and the name of the God of Israel must endure in the world for the world itself, so that the soul of humanity can continue and fulfill its redemptive destiny. Judaism conveys into history the theological and ethical substance of both Christianity and Islam. A bilateral Christian-Muslim dialogue is not only insufficient—it sends an ominous signal to the world. To insure a broader triune context, the Abrahamic family of faiths must reverse its recent historical course of enmity as we now offer amity and go to the wall for Israel, opposing the wall, as Dietrich Bonhoeffer did in that "greater love . . . for his friends." (John 15.13). Conceptually and ethically, we must reanchor our convictions, not in hatred and supercessionism, but in the truth of God and in the derivative humanistic ethical substance.

The Common Biblical Matrix

The resolution of this conflict can only come by the combined power of revelatory and rational ethics. We must take the deep pacific meanings of biblical apocalyptic (*e.g.*, Mark 13, Daniel, and Revelation), and join them to the canons of just-war theory to find this synergy. I derive this synthesis from two of the salient biblical and historical works now circulating: Robert Jewett's *Hermeneia* Commentary on Romans and Martin Goodman's landmark *Rome and Jerusalem*.[3] Each, in his own way, is dealing with a contemporary interpretation of what Goodman presciently calls

---

3. See Jewett, et al., *Romans*; Goodman, *Rome and Jerusalem*.

"an ancient clash of civilizations." Along with Rodney Stark's *Cities of God*,[4] these works encourage the search for a modern relevance of their work.

Robert Jewett: The Synergistic Destiny of Judaism and Christianity

Robert Jewett had to be barred by his colleagues from taking another five years to add an Italian bibliography to a work that was already 25 years in the making and bring his "Romans" to a close. The conclave was in our living room in Evanston. At the end of that night, we acknowledged that the quarter century was well spent, as the book could now join the historically crucial commentaries of the same epistle by Luther and Barth—to say nothing of Augustine and Wesley—all of which helped guide the world through ominous times.

Acutely aware of Greco-Roman rhetorical theory and finding evidence of a modern sociological template of honor and shame, Jewett has cleared up long-standing biases by those who appropriated the passages from the Greek Septuagint and deliberately changed the meanings of the Hebrew text. With his protégée James Dunn, he also has forged a fully affirmative treatment of the people Israel in the world, free from the now-embarrassing anti-Judaic tone of previous German scholarship.

Two features of his study bear on my thesis. He first takes a view toward religious zeal expressed in terms of violence and then offers a positive perspective of Israel's political destiny in world history and the country's enduring provenance in the care and purposes of God. He also addresses America's pretensions to power in the world.

Knowing this good colleague for many years has convinced me of the theology about violence that undergirds all of his work. He is a disciple of the peaceful Christ. Convicted by the non-retaliative forgiveness of *Ecce Homo*, the cross of Christ in its Pauline construal becomes the *sine qua non* of all Jewett's exegesis. I often have heard him reflect on Judas and the zealots and how they wrongly and abruptly sought to rupture the kingdom into premature being. In his many studies preliminary to *Captain America and the Crusade Against Evil* (with John Lawrence),[5] he has forwarded a position of Pauline conciliation with the powers of Rome—resistance to Rome's blasphemy and Judacide, yes, but otherwise living in equanimity with the powers that be as the Jewish people did under Babylon and Persia where the great *Talmudic* period would flourish.

---

4. See Stark, *Cities of God*.
5. See Jewett and Lawrence, *Captain America and the Crusade Against Evil*.

It is true that Jesus seemed to believe that state violence was inevitable in the concourse of the Gospel, and that he and his disciples would be killed no matter how pacifist their response to Rome. This was part of the larger concession to divine plan wherein with Peter's confession he turns his face "steadfastly toward Jerusalem" (Mark 10.33). But Jewett takes numerous passages: "put up your sword" (Matt 26), the prediction of the fall of the walls of Jerusalem (Mark 13), and the cleansing of the temple (Luke 19.45) to indicate that Jesus sought to avert the calamity Goodman depicts in his lachrymose history where Jewish (and Christian) blood flowed like rivers down from Mount Zion (Josephus).[6]

Beyond the first level of argument that is pacifist and consequentionalist, Jewett moves to a deeper theological argument that embraces the ethical. Rejecting the radical apocalyptical line of Pauline/Augustinian clash of two cities for a more irenic cohabitation, Jewett develops his argument in two further steps to show that Israel and the church have a synergistic destiny to complement each others' unique place in the plan of God.

He first shows that the offering for the poor of Judea (Rom 15.25–26) reveals the inextricable reciprocity of thanksgiving toward one's ancestral people and the further success of the Gospel. If the mission to Spain is to go forward, if one day those gladiatorial lands are to know of the righteousness of God, the mission of help to the poor of Jerusalem—a Gentile offering—must go back to Judea and Paul will deliver it in person. The Jerusalem community, we can believe, included James, Jesus' brother, with whom Paul had undergone such strife (Acts 15), the Jewish Christians (if such a designation is possible), Jesus' extended family, and the associated Jewish community with whom archeology shows Christians may have shared a common *mikvah*/baptismal bath and perhaps even worship quarters at the Western gate of the city. Jewett finds Paul's explication of a divine theology of Jerusalem and Rome one of reciprocity rather than mutual recrimination. The apostle develops this theology in Romans (ch. 10–11).[7]

Building on the foundational argument of Jesus Messiah as the purveyor of righteousness and peace and the pastoral/ethical imperative of mutual, physical aid, within and beyond the particular faith community,

---

6. Goodman, *Rome and Jerusalem*.
7. See Facultés jésuites de Paris, *L'exégèse patristique de Romains 9–11*.

Jewett next traces Paul's contentions about Judeans (Jews) and Romans (Gentiles) to a subtle camaraderie they share in the sacrifice offering of Messiah and the radical brotherhood this engenders in the *hikmah* (wisdom) of God. The position unfolds in three parts: 1) the equality of Jew and Gentile under divine justice and grace; 2) the "call" therefore to Jew and Greek to present worship as "bodies as a living sacrifice" (Rom 12.1); since 3) this "political formation" is the pattern of divine life for this world.

Equality of Jews and Gentiles

The stated purpose of Paul's Letter to the Romans, writes Jewett, is to set forth "the equality of Jew and Gentile under sin and grace and stress the inclusive rule of faith." While this may sound like all the other "Lutheran" works on Romans, it marks a radical departure. Jewett is arguing for a radical parity among the offspring of Abraham in the absolute fairness, equity, and desire of God for the righteousness and salvation of His Jewish and Gentile children. This radical equity and parity is all the more remarkable given Paul's experience of being:

- attacked in Galatia by "the Judaizers";
- confronted by sharp exchange with Peter at Antioch (Gal 2.14);
- attacked by Jewish/Christian missionaries at Corinth (2 Cor 10–13); and
- physically tortured by fellow Jews (2 Cor 11.24).

Like Jesus, Paul was considered a criminal. The 39 lashes—administered five times—left gashes (*stigmata tou Jesou*) on his body (*cf.* Isa 53). He was accused of breaking synagogue custom, claiming Torah was no longer effectual. In Goodman's view, Jesus was accused of repudiating and invalidating Jewish religion, *per se*, which was precisely what the Roman Empire attempted when they desecrated and destroyed Jerusalem and did not rebuild it—as had been their custom in other conquests.[8]

Rome's pogrom sought to eradicate Judaism itself, not just the Jewish people. But Paul forcefully objects: "far be it," "God forbid," "No way!" and "this is not what I'm about." His conviction and commission was the exact opposite. Throughout his correspondence, he seeks to "uphold the law."

---

8. Goodman, *Rome and Jerusalem*.

His ministry as such seeks to fulfill the Abrahamic vision of Israel (Torah, Moses, the Prophets, and Psalms). His proclamation is the "Gospel of God" (Rom 1.1)—the charter of righteousness and salvation, forgiveness of sin, and the renewal and rectification of life.[9]

Not only in apocalyptic writings but in legal and ethical literature, Judaism searches out the connection between righteousness, duty, death, resurrection, and the historical-worldly context of redemption—this world and the world to come. Rome's genocide of Jews, like that of 20th-century Christendom in Europe, is a blasphemous assault on the "God of Israel"—on God's self.

In this light, both Jewett and Goodman are correct. The accusation against Paul was unjust. The Roman judgment was wrong—a "tragic accident."[10] The "parting of the ways" was an historical calamity, and the Jew and Gentile covenants of life under the God of Israel and in Jesus Messiah remain intact. Indeed, the wider family of Jew and Gentile that arose from the rift—Sarah and Hagar, Isaac and Ishmael—remains a synergistic work of Torah and task, grace and Gospel, *Taurut* and *Injil*. In the enigmatic words of Dietrich Bonhoeffer, written days before his execution, fundamentally rejecting "the final solution," he wrote, "Israel is delivered out of Egypt so that it may live before God as God's people on Earth."[11] Israel is woven into the very fabric of Christ's messianic redemption of the world.

Living Sacrifice

This persuasion leads to Paul's theology of body-sociologic, ecclesiologic, and politic. Jewett proceeds to explore the cosmic divine rationale behind this sublime concord, now so obfuscated by historical inter-religious strife so profound that it mimics the divine entry into time and space in creation and incarnation. The proper offering (*logikon*) of Israel and extended Israel in this messianic age is an atmosphere of justice and rapport where our "bodies" are presented unto God as a "living sacrifice" (Rom 12.1).

Martin Buber affirmed in his study, *On Zion*, that the singular purpose of Israel in history is to witness to the light of justice and "love of the

---

9. See Levenson, *The Death and Resurrection*; *Sinai and Zion*; *Resurrection and the Restoration of Israel*.

10. Goodman, *Rome and Jerusalem*.

11. Bonhoeffer, *Letters and Papers from Prison*, 336.

other."[12] Christians share that eternal bond with Jews—a marturial (living sacrifice) witness against the genocidal and Judacidal pretensions, idolatries, and violence of Rome and all her imperial successors. The bodily offering of Jewish and Christian resistance in the three-century span—Maccabees–*Bar Kokhba* (150 b.c.e. to 150 c.e.)—now is transfigured into a spiritual worship, a theocentric way of life. Sacrifice has been made ethical as the parochial cult realizes its universal destiny and opportunity. Christian Rome is built within the bosom of Diaspora Judaism. Rome is God's judgment and forgiveness on paganism, within which a Godless world is restored to the "Bosom of Abraham." Now—as in the story of Dives and Lazarus—righteousness and the "world beyond" is restored to the continuum of "here-and-now" sufferings and pains of this world.

Legacy of Abrahamic Theology
Today, if we indulge in a bit of conjecture, we find three imperial or quasi-imperial entities contending for political and economic preeminence and influence in the world. There is the Americo-Israeli world—very tenaciously holding its sway in the Middle East and in the global economy. Europe or Eurabia is emerging as a strong, but still precarious entity, given the enormous diversity of nations being swept formatively together out of an agonizing Eurasian history—including the ethically and theologically signature event of the Jewish *Shoah*. Then there are the rapidly developing and formidable neutral nations of Russia, China, India (scene of the most acute spiritual/cultural exacerbation), and the poorest of the poor and sickest of the sick—Africa.

I believe that monotheistic or Abrahamic faith holds the sway of the future. Of course Hinduism, Buddhism, and secularism, as well as the Chinese ways of life—all exert enormous global influence along with their precursors and successors. I see these as great universal, humanistic philosophies or ethics of life rather than theologies in the strict sense or monotheisms.

In one way or another, the seed or offspring of Israel will determine the shape of world history given the enormous energy of evangelical and Pentecostal Christianity and of global Islam—especially in the epicenters of Indonesia and Asia, the Middle East, Africa, India/Pakistan, and Europe. I believe that the legacy of Abrahamic theology and justice is now becoming a singular phenomenon and has a chance to renew this inhab-

12. Buber, *On Zion*.

ited and technologically unified world by muting violence, materialism, and exploitation and extending stewardship, justice, care, and hope—the phenomenon of redemption. Will we turn from enmity to amity—before it is too late? That is the question.

From the foundation of the Earth—in the universal annunciation of the destiny of Abraham, in the selection and formation of the people of Israel by her God in Moses and the prophets, in the opportunity of the Greco-Roman *oikumene* and the broad universal cosmos it has formed and is yet forming in world history—the One God is seeking. Through the Hebrew, then universal messianic Being (*kaine ktisis* or new creation) of humanity, God seeks to craft *tikkun olam*, the kingdom of God, the way the world was meant to be and will in the certainty of redemption surely be. In this offering, the self-giving God and responsive humanity find "satisfaction of the soul" (Isa 53) as in the gift of *agapetos*—"He who did not spare his only beloved Son but freely gave him up, now in him freely gives the world all things" (Rom 8.23).

Martin Goodman: A Jewish Perspective

In his two cities, Martin Goodman explores the same theology of history from a Jewish perspective.[13] Following his work for many years as the professor of Jewish history in the train of his mentor Géza Vermès at Oxford, I have had the privilege of watching his perspective unfold as he oversaw the Cambridge History of Judaism, taught the Jewish Diaspora, and incorporated those dimensions into the new phenomenon of the State of Israel and the new Americo-European Jewish reality. Consider Goodman's reading of the ancient "clash of civilizations" exemplified in biblical Jerusalem and imperial Rome—and the legacies of empires and the perennial plight of the Abrahamic families of faith.

Clash of Civilizations

Goodman reflects on the history of Emperor (to be) Vespasian sending his son Titus to end the uprising in Judea and Palestine, with supposedly no intent to destroy the temple, only to have the attack end with its total destruction. A bloodbath of unprecedented fury by marauding soldiers ended with a declaration of the defeat of the Jewish religion, the taking of the paraphernalia of the temple (including the great Menorah candelabra and the Holy scrolls), parading them through the streets of Rome and

---

13. Goodman, *Rome and Jerusalem*.

displaying them on *l'Arc de Triomphe*. The *herem* (accursed) signaled that the Jews and their faith were totally reviled. Genocide had accomplished Deicide—or had it?

Rather than rebuilding the temple as was customary, the Emperor Hadrian built a pagan city, *Aelia Capitolina* in 132 c.e., from which all Jews were banned. This total ostracizing of Jews, Goodman reasons, caused Christians to distance themselves from what was left of the Jewish community. Despite this point, it must be acknowledged that the New Testament never saw the destruction of the temple as a sign of God's judgment on Israel. At the same time, though, the Jewish Diaspora in Syria, Egypt, Asia Minor, and Rome did not join the zealot uprising. Perhaps Appian's record of 240,000 Jews being massacred in Cyprus would explain this reluctance. Before long, Jews and Christians would anathematize and excommunicate each other and the modern travail—crusade and ghetto, reformation and reviling, trifurcation and Holocaust—would be underway.

Perennial Plight of Abrahamic Faiths
It may be the case then, if this argument is valid, that a pagan empire projected its blasphemy, idolatry, and immorality—its composite violence toward God and humanity—toward the destruction of faith and the obliteration of the Divine Name from Israel. Here we see the importance of our marturial witness (*martys* in Greek or martyr), as each Abrahamic faith lays down its life for the validity and perpetuity of the Name of the One God of Israel, Jesus as Messiah, and Allah. Against this deicidal propensity and holocaust of empire, Synagogue, Church, and Mosque must cry "never, never again!" Late Judaism and early Christianity are born in apocalyptic literature Richard Horsley sees as theological response to imperial oppression.

Note must be made here of very recent efforts at *rapprochement* among the three sibling faiths. In the contemporary language of war crimes against God and humanity—in truth commissions, repentance, reparations, and forgiveness—the churches have acknowledged sins and crimes against the Jews. Reconciliation documents have come from the Catholics, Lutherans, and Presbyterians, among others. Response documents including Vatican II (1960s), "*Dabru Emet*" (2000), and "A Common Word" (2006) from Jewish and Muslim leaders have furthered the reconciliation process.

One is forced to wonder, in light of my analysis of the very recent literature represented by Jewett and Goodman, whether this ecclesiastical remonstrance really carries much weight. Has anti-Semitism, anti-Islamism and anti-Christianity seeped into the secular waters of empire where they now pollute all culture despite the lachrymose confessions and pleadings of religious bodies and well-intentioned scholars? Has society had enough—30 years, 100 years—of wars of religion?

Two camps, two cities—where do they leave us? Two scenarios it would seem lie before us. Scenarios are dreams, constructions, imaginations, films. They are confabulations or construals within the human mind—personal and collective. The mind is always the receptor, interceptor, and conceptor of wide ranging impressions, ideas, divinities, and interpretations. Various subconscious or subliminal patterns and processes intercede and involve—depending on how one assesses psychological process, (*e.g.*, Freud)—with this array of impulses. My pre-dawn dreams are the most vibrant, creative and regrettably, also most distorted versions of reality within my imagination. Dawn brings depression, but also graceful release.

Most human thoughts, theories, literatures, songs, ideas, and other expressions flow from this wellspring. The Book of Revelation is a film—a running stream of consciousness and conscientiousness. The Book of Daniel, Mark 13, and all pieces of apocalyptic literature are dramas. Hearing Scottish actor Alan McCown recite Mark's Gospel in a West End theatre makes this clear. Apocalypses—apparently bad dreams—capture very sensible ethical wisdom such as that embodied in the Decalogue.[14] Utopias, dystopias, and plans are more comprehensive attractions or aversions. Scenarios are replays or foreplays of such irrepressibly human impulses. As persons and communities, we live in faith and hope that become the modalities by which we challenge the unknowns of daily reality. We also confront omnipresent temptations that activate the vector of goodness or justice that is love.

We are also idealists as well as naturalists—Platonists and Aristotelians. Like Augustine, we know that the city of Earth drops down from heaven as the city of heaven arises from the Earth. We transfigure immanence by transcendence as well as transcendence by immanence.

---

14. See *Die Dekalogische Struktur der Apokalypse* to explore how Bible passages reflect the Ten Commandments.

The scenarios that follow from the reflections on Jerusalem and Rome—the two paradigmatic urban utopia/dystopias, of earthly or heavenly good or bad place—therefore follow Augustine's rather than Tertullian's more severe interpretation. Here, Jerusalem is the symbol of the city of peace, the city of God, and Rome symbolizes the earthly city, the city of conflict.

City of Peace

The city of peace is the place where justice grounds concord because trust prevails over fear. For sixty years now, an interfaith reconciliation has been sought in the state of Israel, with Palestinian and Arab/ Muslim neighbors—guaranteed by the world community of nations. The present discord of faiths and peoples reflects a millennial/ perennial crisis and yearning. *Civitas Dei*—being about Church in the world—is an old woman who is becoming a young bride. It is the field of wheat and tares, sorting of sheep and goats, the old becoming new, the possible, actual—the proleptic, ontic—as Being itself transfigures being and "the kingdoms of this world become the kingdom of our God and of His messiah and He shall reign forever" (Rev 11).

In penultimate terms, which is the grammar of the Letter to the Romans, a justification and righteousness is being fashioned here and now upon the Earth as people become just and righteous in the new being known as *Logos*, *hikmah*, Sophia, Messiah. New being in God enables persons and peoples to live in care, respect, forgiveness, and forbearance rather than the much easier and more pleasurable (Augustine) rage, revenge, power, and violence—what Jewett characterizes as "shame" culture. The two-way process (Deut 8, Prov 14, Matt 5–7) is that described in Torah and Prophets, in Gospel—in *Taurut* and *Injil*—of annunciated goodness, of temptation, of grace-borne awareness of injustice and sin, of forgiveness, death and resurrection, of new being and new life—the completion of creation and kingdom. "New Earth" is realization of what the world was meant to be. Now the Earth brings forth its fruit, and justice and peace flourish.

The Worldly City

The worldly city—as Reinhold Niebuhr and the political realists rightly point out—is a place of treachery, deceit, and exploitation. Scriptural Reasoning among faith adherents has a better chance of tipping the scales toward heavenly Jerusalem than do Versailles, Yalta, The Hague, and Annapolis. Yet try we must. American apocalyptic must be corrected by European (*e.g.*, Kant-Habermas) logic.[15] There may be rhyme, reason, even revelation, in the polar antinomy with which I began this essay. Eurabia and Americo-Israel may be providential configurations in the One in whose hands are the times and places of persons and peoples (Matt 16.3). Better to venture peace than crave animosity, to love and lose, than to choose not to love at all.

Two Provisional Moments

To conclude, I touch on two efforts in our earthly city to effect part of the called-for "coming together" under one "Common Word." Don Wagner, former Director of the Center of Middle East Studies at North Park University, leads a group of "evangelical" Christian leaders in dialogue with Muslims through his partner—Mahmoud Ayoub, formerly of Temple University. A major conference in Libya brought together scholars from Britain and the U.S., as well as leaders from the Middle East. If this conference can help evangelicals sort out how its own belief structures and preaching are fueling inter-Abrahamic animosity and derivative discord in the world, the venture will have been well worth the effort. The belief that Messiah is resurrected and Logos reigns eternally may be fully orthodox, even to our Abrahamic sibling faiths. The elaborate Middle Eastern end-time eschatology is mischievous and theologically suspect. If evangelical faith can be cleansed of its nationalistic and cultural biases and find release in authentic biblical convictions, great strides toward world concord will have been made.

Our Scriptural Reasoning movement—radiating out of Cambridge, Virginia, and Princeton with cells and outposts around the world—has now assisted in the preparation of and presented responses to "A Common Word" from world Muslim leaders.[16] Thousands of official and informal house groups around the world now supply this endeavor. In my own experience, the simple sharing of viewpoints, both learned and "common sense" insights—which arise from a comparative read of cognate texts from Jews, Christians and Muslims—offers extraordinary enlightenment.

15. See Habermas, *The Divided West*.

16. See Ochs, "Speaking the Truth (*Dabru Emet*)" and Vaux, "Comment on the Document 'Common Word.'"

LIFE AND DEATH: AKEDAH AND BIOETHICS

Akedah as Symbol for Human Possibility

Abraham's offering of Isaac, and the broader literary and artistic motif identified by Jon Levenson as *The Death and Resurrection of the Beloved Son*, is the most powerful symbol common to Judaism, Christianity, and Islam. As such it offers a deep metaphor to illuminate the human and divine nature and action. It is therefore an imperative symbol for the human plight and possibility—suffering, sacrifice, and death, as well as the redemption and renewal of life. *Akedah* also speaks to the reality of God, especially in the theodicy function (rationalizing divine goodness in a world filled with evil). Because of this anthropomorphic and theologic currency, *Akedah* is a salient and deep metaphor for bioethics. As a meta-ethical symbol, it ponders "what is" in light of "what ought to be."

In this brief statement, offered to elicit debate on its theological merits and provoke discussion of its practical ramifications, I first delineate the *Akedah* symbol, show its theological and ethical significance, and finally suggest its bioethical applications.

First, a proviso. It has been argued by Stan Van Hooft that the Western enterprise of imbuing suffering with meaning has a tendency to trivialize and distort the profound reaches of that experience. ". . . Western thinkers have generally falsified our experience of suffering in trying to make sense of it. In a postmodern age, these accounts seem implausible."[17] It is my conviction that the search for redemptive meaning—principally fathoming meaning in human suffering and in satisfactorily construing the matter of theodicy (divine goodness in a world of suffering)—is the primary ethical activity of theology and the essence of religion's contribution to medicine. Indeed, as Van Hooft goes on to show ". . . Our bodies might suffer maladies, we suffer pain, our zest for life might be lost, our relationships shattered, our projects failures, our suffering real, and yet we can think of it as for the ultimate good."[18] *Akedah* is the most salient symbol of the Abrahamic faiths, those traditions now embracing three-quarters of the world's people.

---

17. Van Hooft, "The meaning of suffering," 13.
18. Ibid., 15.

Akedah in Popular Culture

Akedah is a picture that captures the composite divine actions and human reaction of love, command, giving over, suffering, resurrection, and joy. Some moving pictures of *Akedah* are:

- Schweitzer's image of the Nazarene on the wheel of the world;[19]
- Abraham's sacrifice of Isaac in Genesis 22;
- the seer John's vision in the Book of Revelation (ch. 5) of the enthroned immolated lamb holding the Torah (*Biblion*);
- the Islamic vision of the universal travail of Ishmael in the Qur'an (Sura 37);
- Elie Wiesel asking the haunting question in *Night*, "Where is God?," "He is there," pointing to the young man on the gallows at Auschwitz;
- John Gunther, in *Death Be Not Proud*, holding his son dying from brain cancer; and
- Oliver Stone's film, *Platoon*, or Terrence Malick's *The Thin Red Line*.

These pictures have in common the premise that goodness evokes violence in the world as redemption ensues. They assume a moral reality in the world—conceived either as deontological structure or natural law—a command or way of life incumbent on and implicit in our living and dying. The pictures assume reality beyond reality. They also assume that a deviation from that way—*peccata mundi* (sins of the world)—has been the consequence of two *sequellae* of love: freedom and fall. The command has been broken. Persons fall short of their full humanity: reason, justice, health, piety. The dynamic of sacrifice—God's gift and human offering—reconstitutes the way of life, truth, and good. This journey of the soul and cosmology of collective conscience is depicted by *Akedah*.

Love, command, and joy—this is the ligature of human yearning and divine coming that binds humanity back to its moral home. The two central metaphors of *Akedah* are *Akedah* as binding of ropes in freely willed servitude and as splitting deliverance through catastrophic seas of life. In Judaism, the symbol pertains to the Abraham saga, to the liberating

---

19. See Schweitzer, *The Quest for the Historical Jesus*.

splitting of the seas in oppression in Exodus, the agony of human aging, the vicissitudes of the human pilgrimage, and the resurrection blessing of progeny (Abraham's seed). In Christianity, it is the crucifixion, which the evangelist John saw as the *Logos*—the key to discerning the meaning of the cosmos. The visionary John, still a Jewish Christian, saw the *Akedah*-Torah complex as the world's ultimate narrative symbol (Rev 5). Teilhard de Chardin saw crucifixion/*Akedah* (one bound to the tree) as the clue to all natural process: "The world of nature resembles nothing so much as the way of the cross."[20] Islam, the newest of Abrahamic faiths, focuses on *Akedah*, the continuing travail of Ishmael that is not only the natural wisdom of the Qur'an (Sura 37) as it discerns the sacrament of life, the witness (*Jihad*) of sacrifice and death, but also the historical travail of crusade and revenge. This crusade still can be felt today in Serbian slaughters in Albanian Kosovo, American-induced infanticide (embargo of food and medicine) in Iraq, the bombing of Sudan's most important factory for medicaments, or the quest for justice and peace within the Christian-Muslim crisis in Sudan or Indonesia. *Akedah* is first of all a symbol of human travail against the fierce antagonistic powers of the world. War, persecution, oppression, and harsh violence toward women and children—all reflect the animosity that invokes the giving of the beloved son (John 3.16). *Akedah* also stands for suffering in the flesh, sickness in the body, refraction of reality in the brain and mind, lethal genetic flaws in the amnion (lamb), the sacrifice of life wrought by malignancy in the axis of life and delight—in sexuality and procreation in women and men, breast and cervix, prostate and testes. It anticipates Kurosawa's venture of the elders up the Mount Moriah of death. Life seems to extract a sacrifice. Human response to such insult is dread (angst). In Malick's film, *The Thin Red Line*, he offers numerous scenes of Japanese and American young men on Laguna Point and Cape Esperance on Guadalcanal trembling uncontrollably—bizarre laughter, shell-shock, shaking-sobs, shuddering pain, dying shiver.

One's mind goes to sources of inspiration for this philosopher-filmmaker:

- Kierkegaard's *Fear and Trembling* (and essay on *Akedah*);
- Buddhist *askesis* as serene suffering; and

---

20. Teilhard de Chardin, *Le Phenomena Humaine*, 73.

- the excruciating African-American spiritual "Were You There When They Crucified My Lord?" (that sometimes causes me to tremble).

The travail of the human condition and the trust in vindication and victory are the essence of the symbol of *Akedah*.

Medicine and Akedah

The enterprise of medicine, especially in the last four centuries, has been a grand act of sacrifice, appeasement of animosity from deity and world, all in an attempt to secure life against death. The saga of the biomedical epoch is, in Teilhard de Chardin's words, a "Mass Upon the Earth." Examples of this saga include quelling respiratory distress in the newborn, assuaging the quaking of depression with tricyclic anti-depressants, implanting fetal amygdal cells to still the tremors of Parkinson's, quieting seizures secondary to epilepsy or brain lesions, and injecting morphine to still the rattles and shudders of death-throws. I remember vividly in the 1960s, the days of Drs. Frei and Freireich, pioneer pediatric oncologists in Houston. Like ancient priests, they drew from the altar of animal and child research the life-blessing of the first multi-drug cures for leukemia. In the 60s, I debated Emil Freireich on a most current question—prophylactic mastectomy for the female-child or adult woman genetically vulnerable to cancer. From *Akedah*, this saga of sacrifice and salvation in medicine's sublime century has wrought resurrection in its bodily dimension (progeny [*cf.* Abraham's offspring] and longevity). Kierkegaard and René Girard have rightly shown that all Abrahamic faiths have sealed the book and that the lamb—that divine provision of a substituting sacrifice of work (worship)—forever ends the need for, indeed forever forbids, human sacrifice. The human project of safeguarding and strengthening life in biomedicine and the broader cultural enterprise is not honorific living sacrifice. Does the blessing of gene therapy justify offering a human subject? How do we transact and transcend the *Akedic* agony of inequitable distribution of care?

Akedah and Ethics

How does *Akedah* become an instrument of ethical evaluation? I have noted how it deals with meta-ethical reality—matters we associate with human suffering, theodicy, righteousness (theoretically conceived), and ultimate judgment (blessing and curse, life and death). How does it take on practical currency? Here the connection of *Akedah* and Torah (way of life) in Abrahamic faiths needs to be ascertained. Let me make this connection with an insight from Alan F. Segal:

> The problem of martyrdom—the man who dies a painful death precisely because he stays true to the commands of God—is a Hebrew expression of a broad ethical and moral question which was being debated actively in the Hellenistic world.[21]

The martyr—Yitzak or Jeshua ben Joseph—dies for the Torah. They die by the force of *peccata mundi*, fulfilling the way or will of God the Father against a resistant world. Jewish, Christian, and Muslim martyrs die for *mitzvah*, especially for sanctifying the name, resisting idolatry, blasphemy and immorality, even at the cost of death. The powers of evil, what Paul calls principalities and powers, seeks to kill the good of God in the world. The virulence of the demonic is pronounced despite its ultimate proleptic defeat in the cross. Resurrection is the ultimate vindication of life against the force of evil. The agonizing question in the Hellenistic world—in the foundational philosophy of Platonic and Aristotelian schools and in Judaism and early Christianity—is the connection of judgment and mercy, obligation and salvation. In my view, Christianity inclines toward antinomianism and immorality in its rejection of Judaism. This becomes a demonic force in Constantine and crusading Christianity. In Serbia today, we see the demonic excesses of a crusader Christendom that must expel both Judaism and Islam. Judaism in turn forsakes its strong salvific piety and universality and settles for xenophobic parochialism in its excommunication of Christianity. Islam can become a hideous anomaly as it rejects its two parent faiths.

If the *Akedah*/Torah conjunction animates the faith/life vitalities of our human community, a moral structure like the Decalogue comes to inform personal, parish, and public life. I offer an example from my biomedical career.

I began my work in bioethics with a study of the Holocaust, the medical crimes of the Nazi physicians and the Nuremburg Code. I was intrigued that this proceeding searched for a "universal law," "a law of humanity," an ethical structure transcending national, political, and positive law, which was vacated by the Third Reich. It sought a normative structure that transcended Jews and Christians, one that held both communities

---

21. Segal, "He who did not spare his own son," 176.

to transcending responsibility. The Nazi physicians, indicted for medical crimes, claimed that they were only following the law (and orders) when they killed persons in the "execution" of sterilization, euthanasia, and human experimentation statutes. The Universal Code of Humanity today—in Nuremberg, Helsinki, and Hague pronouncements on human experimentation, war crimes, laws of the seas, etc.—are articulations of the Noachic universality code—the *Akedic* ethic of Abrahamic faith.

A universal ethical structure can therefore be formulated against the template of the Decalogue (the moral system, for example, of the *Akedic* text of the Book of Revelation).[22] A fitting responsibility today, what the apostle Paul calls "a living sacrifice" (Rom 12), is righteous living.

A Practical Akedic Bioethic

The foregoing theoretical analysis makes possible a bioethic suggested in the following application tables. I list the ten commandments in positive mode synoptically developed from the many scriptural versions (*e.g.*, Exod 20, Deut 5, Ezek 18).

Principle	Specific Imperatives in Health Care
I. Loyalty to God alone	• Respecting the faith and values of patients • Acceding to the ultimate wisdom of God beyond health and life, suffering and death
II. Iconoclasm	• Money, prestige, hierarchy—even health and life—are not ultimate values
III. Sanctify the Name	• Subscribing only to the ultimate and to nothing penultimate
IV. Honor parents and children	• Affirming and honor the parental bond • Strengthening respect of children • Condemning child and elder abuse

---

22. See Kerner, *Die Ethik der Johannes*.

Principle	Specific Imperatives in Health Care
V. Work and rest	• Imperatives from leisure to ultimate Sabbath—rest, death, serene acceptance • Work as the affirmation of an ameliorative, not a renovative, biomedical project • No superman
VI. Choose life	• Right to life at inception and conclusion
VII. Be faithful	• No harassment of colleagues or sexual exploitation of patients • Honoring marriage and family in sexual and reproductive therapies
VIII. Respect property	• Integrity of body
IX. Veracity	• Informed consent
X. Care for needs of others	• Access to care regardless of wealth

To conclude, *Akedah* joined to Torah, embedded in Abrahamic faith, provides a symbol linking the salvific with the axiomatic in human experience. The two qualities illuminate biomedical decision-making because the confrontation with phenomena of life and death requires attention to both relationship and rule as normative and interpretative instruments. Simply put, dealing with matters of birth, health, life, pain, suffering, and death as parents, families, professionals or publics, encourages belief and ethics—the yield in experience of *Akedah*/Torah. This writing has sought to be suggestive and provocative of critique or corroboration, impressionistic rather than analytic, tentative and probing rather than finished. Your response is invited.

WAR AND PEACE: RUMOR AND RULES OF WAR

Just-war teaching has always addressed the crucial aspect of bringing an end to war with truth and justice, as much as this is humanly possible. The facts of guilt and hope, punishment and forgiveness, widows, orphans and prisoners, and death and life render *jus post bellum* (concerning the justice of peace agreements in the termination of war) issues irresistibly theological and ethical. That we face matters such as war crimes, apologies, reparations, reconciliations, and rebuilding evidences the inevitable political dimensions of *jus post bellum* (JPB).

Wars have always shuddered to some end, perhaps glorious, more likely ambiguous, even this one which, as we have seen, is spoken of as permanent and unending. A scholar of the Germanic invasions in antiquity rehearses the solemn aftermaths and mourning of the *Aeneid, Iliad,* and *Odyssey* when he speaks of those so-human ones we call "barbarians" who sat down and wept at what they had done after the killing, raping, and pillage of their conquests. Fascinating reflections accompany the conclusion of wars (from ancient times until the present day) involving Jews, Christians, and Muslims dispelling the old saw that it is the gods who crave and command war. God, it becomes clear from brute human experience, abhors war and requires justice and peace: "he breaks the bow, and shatters the spear." (Ps 46.9)

Jus post bellum arises in our consciousness and discourse through many experiences:

- In 2006, George McGovern writes his book *Out of Iraq* using the tools of both philosophical and theological pacifism and just-war theory.

- In various speeches, former Secretary of State Colin Powell invokes the old ethic: "you break it, you own it."

- Historical precedents are called to mind: Bonhoeffer's implied call for confession and repentance for the German "Final Solution" in *Ethics*; Willy Brandt and President von Weizsäcker's confession of the "Nazi sins" of the Third Reich; Japanese Premier's apologizes after World War II; Guatemala; African Truth and Reconciliation Commissions; War Crimes proceedings in the World Court (Bosnia, Serbia, Rwanda, etc.); President Bush Sr.'s apologies and proposal for reparations for Japanese-American internments; President Pinochet (praised by Prime Minister Thatcher) being condemned by his own government for war crimes and other "crimes against humanity" against his own people.

What are the meanings of these actions and how do they relate to the history of this doctrine?

In *The City of God*, Augustine lays the foundation of *jus post bellum* when he says that the only worthy purpose of war is to "make peace." If that is not the purpose, war should not be engaged. "It is an established fact that peace is the desired end of war. For every man is in quest of peace, even in waging war, whereas no one is in quest of war when making peace."[23] Kant extends this tradition and becomes the most important modern proponent of *jus post bellum*:

> International right (or justice) is thus concerned partly with the right to make war, partly with the right of war itself and partly with the questions of right after the war, i.e. with the right of states to compel each other o abandon their war-like condition and to create a constitution which will establish an enduring peace.[24]

These anthropological assertions provide the groundwork of a doctrine of *jus post bellum* from the twin pillars of human ethics: theology and philosophy. It must be noted that these underlying premises are posited on the nobility of man and other approaches; *e.g.*, Hobbes or Clausewitz would start with the contrary premise of inherent human malice.

The Stanford Encyclopedia of Philosophy defines the endeavor of *jus post bellum* as the justice sought "during the third and final stage of war: that of war termination." While there is little law extant (except occupation law and human rights treaties) on the matter of *jus post bellum*, there is much moral tradition on several themes:

- *Proportionality and publicity.* The settlement should be reasonable, not vengeful, unconditional, and should be publicly presented.

- *Rights vindication.* Abrogated rights that made the war justifiable should be restored: human rights to life and liberty, territory and sovereignty.

- *Discrimination.* If punishments are to be meted out, a distinction should be made between leaders (politicians and military/strategists, not those under command) and innocent civilians. No sweeping sanctions should be made

---

23. Augustine, *The City of God*, 866.
24. Kant, *The Metaphysics of Morals*, 167.

that affect the poor and weak rather than those responsible: "to beggar thy neighbor is to insure future fights." Reform, disarmament, structural and infrastructural transformation becomes possible.

An orderly exit strategy that suggests long-range care for what happens to the people is essential. Hasty departure (as when the state of Israel was created)—either because the departing party fears ensuing chaos or because there is something wrong about the preceding invasion or conquest—becomes self-fulfilling prophesy that things will go wrong. The Marshall Plan to rehabilitate Europe, particularly Germany, after World War II, is exemplary in this regard. The *jus post bellum* foreseen in Iraq is accompanied by impulses of guilt, wrong-doing, the "hell-with-them, let-them-kill-each-other" rage that portends ensuing calamity.

A more noble and effective *jus post bellum* is found in the Catholic approaches to Hispanic colonialism where there was acknowledgement of wrong, apology and confession in the deep theological sense (*i.e.*, the presumption of grace, mercy and forgiveness), and the succeeding intent to make things right in the aftermath, rather than attempting to get out fast and hope that no post-mortem is conducted.

Asking for international cooperation in the *jus post bellum* is crucial in order to ensure an honest assessment of fault, a just settlement, and a workable restoration and renewal plan. In Iraq, for example, we should shoulder our own Anglo-American responsibility, invite the full participation of the neighboring Arab and Middle East neighbors—even Christian Lebanon and Armenia and ("God-forbid") Israel. We then can solicit the full cooperation and subsidy of the world community. A destabilized Iraq will endanger everyone else, and enlightened self-interest should prompt everyone to help. As part of this hoped-for stability, wealth should be ensured for the emerging government and people so that they, in turn, can return to the dignity of being able to help others (an old Calvinist principle used with welfare for Protestant refugees). Oil revenues and restoration of what we have stolen from Iraq may provide a portion of the needed largesse. Along with this, treaties for non-aggression, non-proliferation, and mutual protection should be provided.

In South America, the Spanish could identify certain goods—acts of justice and love—that were embedded within the more general act of exploitation and violation. The saving Gospel had been preached—noncoercively, we hope. Idolatry, immorality (including native violence) had been challenged; elevation of dignity had been achieved. These salutary benefits of missionary work are obvious and evident, even though they are sadly discolored by the pervading context of colonial exploitation, degradation, and brutality. As in all human interaction after the fall, the brilliance and beauty of goodness and righteousness are always sullied and discolored by our overdoing and misdeeds in thought, will, and act.

THREE INTERFAITH VOICES

This philosophical and political heritage is amplified by the theological dimension. I have chosen three individuals who have each thought and felt deeply about the tragedy of Iraq (and on this subject, they agree with me). The three have vaguely and indirectly reflected a faith tradition in their convictions and proposals and they each now pray, plan, and work for *jus post bellum* in this world so sadly contorted toward evil by history.

Leslie H. Gelb

I know nothing of Gelb's theological background—if he is Jewish or how good a Jew he may be. I only know this: as writer and commentator on the subject matter in the *New York Times*, he was unexcelled, and as president emeritus of the Council on Foreign Relations, he exemplifies a philosophical and theological ecumenism. His review of one of the very few honest and provocative books about these matters—*The Israel Lobby and U.S. Foreign Policy*—reflects the passion of Judaism for truth, freedom, and justice as well as anything I've read on the subject.[25]

In a feisty argument, John Mearsheimer and Stephen Walt, professors of political science at Chicago and Harvard respectively, tackle an unspoken subject of how Jewish (and Zionist/Dispensationalist Christian) ideologues have perversely shaped American foreign policy—especially in Iraq. In my view, it is the transformation of attitudes among proponents of this theo-political world view—in the U.S., Israel, and to a lesser extent Great Britain—that is our best hope for an exit strategy, a hope for a humane future under renewed theological vision, a genuine *jus post bellum*.

Gelb cites the indictment of Mearsheimer and Walt of "the Conference of Presidents of Major American Jewish Organizations, the

---

25. See Gelb, "Dual Loyalties."

Anti-Defamation League" (whose major strategy I interpret as "defamation" of proponents of the "just rights" of Palestinians and Muslims in the world) "and the neoconservatives." With a blind eye to what his fellow political scientists from George Kennan to Rashid Khalidi exposed courageously—Mearsheimer and Walt let the "Christian Right" off the hook.

Agreeing with the authors and politico-theologians like George McGovern and Jimmy Carter, Gelb sees the fanatically one-sided support of Israel in American policy and the failure to name and condemn the violence that verges toward Amalekite-type genocidal cleansing (I Samuel 15) of the Muslim and even Christian presence in Palestine as a principal cause of Muslim terrorism against the United States. I have argued this etiology of terrorism and the war on terrorism, going to theology as the core phenomenon, ever since the events of September 11th.[26]

Gelb endorses Mearsheimer and Walt's position, but finds the issue going deeper:

> Of course, America's close ties with Israel compound its problems with Arabs and Muslims. But at a deeper level, one ignored by Mearsheimer and Walt, these problems would not disappear or seriously lessen if Washington abandoned Israel. The main source of anti-Americanism and anti-American terrorism is America's deep ties with highly unpopular regimes in countries like Saudi Arabia and Egypt, not to mention the war in Iraq.[27]

Rather than hurling the epithet "anti-Semite" at scholars, Gelb believes—like my son and I, who genuinely support the people of Israel in the world and believe that the Holocaust and its precursor genocide of the Armenian peoples at the beginning of the century is the signature evil of the modern world—that the affinities of Jews and Muslims and the wisdom that these peoples share with Christians is a solid hope for a way out of the morass and for constructing a better world—*jus post bellum*.

So what do Mearsheimer and Walt say that we should do to wind down Iraq in light of the broader context in the Middle East? My view, which I hope is concordant with the long-range political interests of the State of Israel and of the crucial and indispensable endurance of the voice of Hebrew Scripture and tradition to theology and ethics in the world, is that this nation's future be secured alongside that of its neighbor, Palestine.

---

26. See Vaux, *Ethics and the War on Terrorism*.
27. Gelb, "Dual Loyalties."

Jus post bellum in Iraq must now be pursued in tandem with the U.S. secretary of State's agenda for dialogue between Israel and Palestine—with security assurance for both peoples given by the U.S. and the great powers, as well as the Middle East and global communities of nations. The sometimes rapport of the three faiths in *Terra Sancta* must be restored, if at all possible, so that reciprocal flourishing might resume. I believe, and my experience confirms, that the vitality and integrity of the faith of Jews worldwide and of the people of *Ha'retz Israel* is crucial to the identity and development of Christianity and Islam, and these faiths vitally contribute to Judaism and to each other.

Jewish conviction, pertinent to *jus post bellum*, would include Torah adherence that would advocate values like truth-telling (commandments 1 and 7), restraint from killing (commandment 6), and robbery and land-grabbing (commandments 8, 9, and 10). It would recognize our subservience to the sovereign Lord of history, to whom we are responsible in judgment and mercy. The Jewish tradition, unlike Christianity, does not have a strong pacifist strand. God fights for the people's survival, for the viability of the Divine Name, and for the diminution of idolatry and apostasy. In sum, however, Hebrew ethics contends that God is One, holy, zealous, just, good, merciful and compassionate, caring for the poor and needy. Human behavioural ethics must imitate this divine character as humans enact divine image in being holy, doing justice, and loving mercy, loving neighbors, and caring for the poor, widows, orphans and strangers (Deut 10.17–20, 14.28–29, and 15.7–11). These core values, discolored by a cultural Islamophobia today, can take ominous direction in time of war, forgetting that Israel's God "breaks the bow, and shatters the spear." (Ps 46.9)

A footnote to these reflections on *jus post bellum* is found in an important thinker: Noah Feldman in his book, *What We Owe Iraq*.[28] The diplomat and constitutional adviser to the formative government and constitution in Iraq is a sophisticated philosophical and theological thinker. He argues that, for our own protection, we need to undertake nation-building in what will be this post-invading, post-occupying period in Iraq with a new, humbler approach. The author of *After Jihad: America and the Struggle for Islamic Democracy*,[29] he draws lessons on

---

28. See Feldman, *What We Owe Iraq*.
29. See Feldman, *After Jihad*.

jus post bellum from Haiti, Somalia, Kosovo, and Afghanistan. Central to the book is a thought experiment that Feldman draws from the libertarian philosopher Robert Nozick, in which he asks what we will do when confronted with anarchy. We will help create a protective association, a neighborhood, he concludes. A decimated and demoralized people must not be left to suffer in isolation—the world must not leave Iraq alone. I agree with Feldman here, especially for his caring justice for this great people who gave the world, in ancient Babylonia and Persia, figures like Abraham, Hammurabi, and Avicenna. I offer several critiques to his approach, however. Nation-building, especially in the neoconservative concept of the "new American agenda," is highly questionable. Allowing the Iraqi people to reconstruct their noble ancient civilization with help and resources as well as genuine good will is a life-giving understanding of justice. As far as anarchy is concerned, we have contributed greatly to that present disarray as did, of course, the Saddam Hussein regime. *Jus post bellum* will acknowledge our culpability along with our resolve to now stand alongside the Iraqi people as they fashion their new existence in the community of nations. I will stand, and we must stand, unequivocally with Israel. We also stand with Palestine and Iraq. If we don't stand together, we surely will "hang" separately.

The foundation we seek to lay down in this groundwork discussion of *jus post bellum* is offered by the "hands-down" authority on just-war in our time, Michael Walzer of Princeton's Institute for Advanced Study, whose present intellectual work is on Jewish political philosophy. (I have stood in awe of the Advanced Institute since I was just down the road at the seminary and was asked by a scholar there to present my college oration that won a collegiate competition. My talk was something of an *hors d'oeuvre* before the main course, which was a lecture by Fellow Robert Oppenheimer of Manhattan Project fame. He spoke on—of all subjects—Sanskrit poetry.) Walzer has distinguished himself with salient books such as *Just and Unjust Wars, Spheres of Justice*, and *Arguing About War*.[30] A rare scholar who combines expertise on the Puritan revolution, prophetic theology, Thomistic philosophy, and political science, he has addressed nuanced public philosophy with fine-grained analysis of the detailed casuistry of war. Stressing themes such as "self-determination, popular legitimacy, civil rights, the idea of common good, and distribu-

---

30. See Walzer, *Just and Unjust Wars*; *Spheres of Justice*; *Arguing About War*.

tion of benefits" in his *jus post bellum*, he feels that peace at the end (not just stalemate or restoration of the status quo) is the purpose of just-war processes. The meting out party and the recipient party of such justice each have rights grounded in such principles, and they must be honored in the *jus post bellum* activities. The victor (if such polar terms still have any meaning), for example, might expect that another attack by the unjust assailant will not occur. Assurance of such might be guaranteed by imposed demilitarization, limitation on the size of army, limitation of rearmament, etc. Walzer is profoundly committed to the cache of values and concrete principles that arise from Hebraic and biblical faith and democratic, human rights-oriented political order—truth, justice, freedom, self-determination, fair process, the rights of victims, etc. His now evolving convictions about Iraq are central in our formulated position.

George McGovern

A graduate of our seminary, Garrett-Evangelical, and our sister university Northwestern, in Evanston, Illinois, Senator McGovern has formulated his concrete proposal for *jus post bellum*—*Out of Iraq*. Though not couched in theological language, *per se*, implicit and often explicit reference to his Christian world-view is made by the one-time presidential candidate, history teacher, combat pilot, and minister-in-training. Here are his points:

- Why we must leave: injury and death to thousands of American youth and hundreds of thousands of Iraqis; costs that will ultimately reach $2 trillion, a faulty *jus ad bellum* policy (*e.g.*, the charge of weapons of mass destruction); and *jus in bello*—*Abu Ghraib*; apocalyptic rather than reasonable rhetoric such as "axis of evil," and "not for but against us."

- Values ought to now determine our course of action.

Although a big-time loser in his presidential run (he won only in Mitt Romney's home state), McGovern, along with Jimmy Carter, are my greatest heroes in American politics—right there with James Madison, Abraham Lincoln, and Woodrow Wilson—all exhibiting qualities I hold dear. I flag McGovern as an exemplar of the cardinal values I listed at the outset of this piece regarding war and peace, theology and ethics—an inveterate peacemaker with strenuous realism. His essay *Out of Iraq* is ignored by all the pundits and professors writing about concluding this war, which may be some evidence for the veracity of his position. I distill his central points with comments on the implicit, though non-stated, theological presuppositions.

"The Kingdom of God is Among You" or peace with justice as *status quo ante*
The historian and student of history's most important foundational text, Augustine's *The City of God*, begins with the human yearning for and divine requirement of peace on Earth, good will among men. McGovern's starting point is *Civitas Dei* approximated in the midst of *Civitas Terrena*. The pastor-politician seeks to reconcile warring parties, demanding truth in place of propaganda, justice, and mutual respect in the place of hegemony and exploitation, "getting on" rather than giving ultimata, working together rather than pursuing self-interest independently. He counters all of the operative rules of politics, yielding to the politics of God and the good—the realm of God. His political theology is not highly conceptual Schlesingerian Niebuhrianism or Hobbesian Tertullianism; instead it is simple "love your neighbor as yourself," "do justice, love mercy, and walk humbly with your God" (Mic 6.8)—straightforward Dakota ethics, before the present generation of unsavory characters would come out of those black hills.

"The truth shall make you free" or "Why did Al Jazeera so infuriate the American command?
Northwestern, in McGovern's day, was the home of truthful and thoughtful, free-press journalism. We struggle to make it so again in this age of corporate sponsorship/censorship of the media. There is something of the Quaker in McGovern—demanding truth in order to achieve strenuous social action. Most studies show that, after the events of September 11th, the American press and media was in the firm ideological hand of the White House and the war-justifying and war-prosecuting agenda. While that has liberalized slightly after the democratic election victories of 2006, it remains the case, as I see clearly when living abroad as I am now on sabbatical in England. America's large, recent-immigrant community and (increasingly marginalized) intellectual elite had access to the international media, thanks to the liberty blessing of global electronic access, but the folks in the American heartland were left at the mercy of Fox news and the networks where, it is said, media moguls with their Wall Street proclivities kept in place the "party-line" agenda. Truth, truth commis-

sions, and getting the story straight will be central to reconstructed *jus ad bellum* and *jus in bello* in the coming *jus post bellum* period. It may not happen at home, but will be accomplished somewhere, and we will know about it.

"Let all the World in Every Corner Sing/ My God and King" or Who are the Iraqis?

Of the myriad array of excellences in McGovern's approach to *jus post bellum* in Iraq, which hint of theological influence, I point to the esteem and respect he pays to the ancient and honorable people of Iraq. Here in the ancient world are Mesopotamia and the Babylonian Empire of Hammurabi, where some of the world's first justice codes were struck. Here, in the eighth century, in concert with Syriac Christians, a philosophical, medical, and theological heritage sprung from the bosom of Muslim culture, one that would transform the still barbarian West and make the Renaissance, modern science, and religious learning possible. Not protecting the Baghdad antiquities will be one of the grievances our side must face in the *jus post bellum* proceedings.

The larger conviction McGovern is commending to the world in these pending proceedings is the integrity and dignity of all peoples and nations of the world and the correlate notion of involving the largest possible international authority in settling disputes among peoples of the world. In the Acts of the Apostles, Luke the physician tells the world about a new post-ethnic, post-parochial *oikumene* (world house) that is appearing in the world through Jesus—dead and now risen—conceived as *Christos* (anointed Messiah), *Logos* (eternal Word and Wisdom) and *Kurios* (sovereign Lord of the world and its history). This new (yet old) and past (yet future) arbiter within the world's domains describes a theology of history and lands where God has fashioned:

> From one ancestor he made all nations to inhabit the whole Earth, and he allotted the times of their existence and the boundaries of the places where they would live, so that they would search for God and perhaps grope for him and find him—though indeed he is not far from each one of us. For "In him we live and move and have our being." (Acts 17.26–28)

In this theology of nations (to which I believe, but have no evidence, that McGovern subscribes, except that he is a graduate of one of the better "global-mission" seminaries in the world), countries are bound together in one human blood-bond and under one sovereign God of history. From this premise flows the requirement of mutual understanding and respect between nations. In this case, it means simply that we need to get to know them—their language, culture, faith, and feelings—and they us. In terms of the *jus post bellum* issue, this means in the very least that we seek cosmopolitan analyses and answers to the issues. In terms of just-war in particular, it means that we seek the widest, most global authority possible for resolution of the conflict. Though there is much to be said for national sovereignty and the necessity of individual nations tackling the issues squarely and decisively, we also need to enlist the United Nations, regional associations of nations, and proximate neighbors to help and be willing to accept the authority of these cosmopolitan entities.

In conclusion, McGovern's proposal rings with Christian theology and resonates with the themes of Christian global ethics. If Christ is the *way*, the *truth*, and the *life*, these three dimensions of his proposed policy deserve the support of those who bear this Name in their own personal, ecclesial, and national worlds. One who wrote more lucidly than any other of this new global understanding put it this way:

> Finally, beloved, whatever is true, whatever is honourable, whatever is just, whatever is pure, whatever is pleasing, whatever is commendable ... Keep on doing the things that you have learned and received and heard and seen in me, and the God of peace will be with you. (Phil 4.8–9)

Good *jus post bellum* counsel!

Timothy Winter (Abdal Hakim Murad)

We might wonder why one would draw thoughts of *jus post bellum* from an essay on suicide bombing. The bitter truth is that America, I believe, has been forced to the disengagement table by this frightful, though quite common case phenomenon in just-war history. In the same way, Israel has been encouraged to the negotiating table on a Palestinian state by the same phenomenon. Winter, as one of two professors of Islamic studies on the Cambridge divinity faculty, decries terrorism and suicide bombings, but acknowledges that it is the only defensive recourse left in David-and-Goliath-like occupations. Though suicide, like murder, is anathema to each of the Abrahamic faiths—in contrast to Vietnamese Buddhism or Kashmir Hinduism and Japanese Shintoism—it has become the weapon of choice in the Palestinian *intifada* and the Iraqi insurgency. To "die for God" in the three monotheisms is, however, an act of martyrdom, as evidenced with the Jews at Masada, in executions of Christians in the Coliseum, and in the martyring of Muslims at Hebron.

Extrapolating Winter's argument on *jus post bellum*, *Bombing Without Moonlight: The Origins of Suicidal Terrorism*,[31] provides a glimpse at the rationale as the Muslim tradition ponders just war. At one level, just-war theory in Islam is taken over from Augustine and Aquinas, as well as from modern philosophical understandings. At another level, Islamic *jus post bellum* is drawn from particular Qur'anic and *hadith* materials that bear some resemblance to Hebrew Holy War and *herem* (extinguishing the enemy), but that also possess striking irenic accent in drawing on traditions such as Muhammad's disarmed final journey from Medina to Mecca.

For Muslims, ending war is a matter of restoring peace. As Henry Kissinger, a cold-warrior if there ever was one, said in his ruminations on ending the Cold War, that which is sought in *jus post bellum* is peace and the absence of war, not military victory. Kissinger might have added that, since ending World War II with treaties of surrender and Marshall Plans for reconstitution of the vanquished, there has never been what could be called a victory in war. Muslims recognize that there always remains the realm of war *(dar al-Harb)* and the realm of peace *(dar al-Islam)*, or in the words of Koholeth (the Preacher), "a time for war, and a time for peace" (Eccl 3.8). The greater *jihad* (strenuous mental and cultural striving) endures long after the lesser *jihad* of war has ceased. What Kissinger called restoring equilibrium and stability was actually the moral meaning of war in just-war tradition from its beginning.

In a troubling final paragraph, after rehearsing the sad history of the suicide bombers along with the candor of tragic reality that all other options for resistance against invasion and occupation had been exhausted and then removed by Israeli and American control, Winter writes, ". . . Liberalism will prove too weak to prevent one form of Enlightenment Chauvinism—carceral Islamism (autonomic lashing out)—from triggering a sudden revival of another form—Hitlerian essentialism (American/Israeli policies of repression). The prosperity of the far-right across the liberal west shows how far this march has already come. Postmodernity is methodically incapable of resisting this, and monotheism must step

---

31. See Murad, *Bombing Without Moonlight*.

into the breach."³² *Jus post bellum*, claims one of our best contemporary Islamic scholars, must rest on the sure foundation of Abrahamic monotheism, the very crucible from which the fanaticism and derived violence on all three sides has arisen. Winter is correct. Only the cause can effect the cure. Fraternity can only quell the fratricide as younger and elder brothers learn to feast together and as Daniel Barenboim and Edward Saïd discover and show the world that they are brothers in one God.³³

Conclusion

We have reviewed three case studies of interfaith work that illustrate the creative and fruitful yield of common theological, ethical, and scriptural explorations. We looked at the general conditions of strife and concord in society at large, of health and medicine, and, in conclusion, of war and peace. Many other areas, including economics and business and marriage and family, will be explored in a set of practical workshops within a major interfaith project beginning in 2010.

---

32. Ibid., 113.

33. Daniel Barenboim is an Argentine pianist and conductor. The grandson of Russian Jews, he has been a supporter of Palestinian rights and outspoken in his criticism of the Israeli settlements. Barenboim became close friends with Edward Saïd, a Palestinian American political activist and, although the two men might have been enemies, they formed a friendship and collaboration based on a shared vision of peace in Israel.

V

Corroborations

Explorations of Related Topics

THE PRESIDENT AND KING: INTERFAITH CONCILIATION

THE FOLLOWING IS THE TEXT OF A KEYNOTE SPEECH *delivered at the Fourth Annual Interfaith Dinner, sponsored jointly by the Northern Illinois Conference of the United Methodist Church and the Council of Islamic Organizations of Greater Chicago (March 31, 2009 at North Central College in Naperville, Illinois).*

As we meet tonight, the world is divided in darkness. Half the world agrees with President Obama—now at the G20 London Summit—that the greatest danger to the U.S. and the world lies in Muslim AfPak (Afghanistan and Pakistan). Much of the rest of the world finds great danger in the U.S. and Israel. We tonight stand against that darkness illumined by the light of Abraham's myriad stars of heaven. In this age of increasing darkness, we search for some glimmer of light.

Dateline Peshawar, Pakistan: at least 50 of our own family and neighbors are killed at the holiest Muslim place, Rahman Baba shrine. The *masjid* was packed with worshippers. In clear stigmata of holocaust, sandals lay scattered on the ground. The great *masjid* lay near the Khyber

Pass on the road to Afghanistan, a clear signal to America now poised to enlarge efforts in AfPak.

Dateline ancient biblical Gaza in a brutal war: only one adversary has armies, battleships, an air force, tanks, and bulldozers (a war in which Israeli soldiers now confess atrocities), and the world asks Arno Mayers' old question of Auschwitz, "Why did the heavens not darken?"[1]

It is an age of Iraqi rehabilitation, Afghani insurgence, and Pakistani complicity, an age of Iranian insolence and American political and global reconstitution—all gravely complicated by a global economic calamity—we take heart from an event like this dinner tonight and from a similar little-known event in New York City, convened by Secretary-General Ban Ki-moon at the United Nations this past winter.

Like our evening, it was an event of interfaith dialogue, a Muslim and a Jew brought together by a Buddhist. It was a haunting reminiscence of the holy moment in 1978 at Camp David, when Muslim Egyptian President Anwar Sadat and Jewish Israeli Prime Minister Menachem Begin unclenched fists and joined clasped hands outstretched by U.S. President Jimmy Carter, a Christian.

Ha'retz made the report on November 17, 2008. The backdrop setting was the great scriptural tableau we all know. It is from the prophet we share, Isaiah: ". . . and they shall beat their swords into plowshares, and their spears into pruning hooks . . ." (Isa 2.4)

Israeli President Shimon Peres spoke first: "This initiative for peace from King Abdullah is a serious opening for real progress." He spoke of the proposal for peace coming from several years' work of Arab leaders. Being offered in the context of a Scriptural Reasoning ritual, the proposal bears a special solemnity and recognition that in this world of great political powers, we all stand responsible before God—accountable for our deeds and misdeeds, our justice and injustice. It also recognizes that true justice, reconciliation, and peace belonged alone to the One God—the One over and within us all.

The proposal promises peace and security to Israel in return for their promise of non-invasion and occupation and their reversion to the pre-1967 war boundaries. It parallels a document we all know, which was brokered by the Cambridge Inter-faith Programme where I am a fellow. Called "A Common Word," this plea for peace with justice—love of God

---

1. See Mayer, *Why Did the Heavens Not Darken?*

and our neighbors—seeks to end the prevalent animosity in order to "give peace a chance." The Web site for A Common Word offers a powerful backdrop for our own interfaith work and for the unfolding political drama now happening in God's world.

President Peres continued by saying—in clearly scriptural speech—that this interfaith encounter might help to "Stop the further shedding of blood, enabling the Arab countries and Israel to live in peace and good neighborliness, and provide future generations with security, stability, and prosperity."[2]

These words are encouraging, given the fact (as I have developed in *Ethics and the War on Terrorism*) that Israel/Palestine is the epicenter of the Earth-shaking quake we call the war on terror, and given that the fault running from Sinai through Jerusalem to Damascus has the power to tear the world asunder or bind up its wounds in Abrahamic/*Akedic* healing.

The Scriptural Reasoning chains we call on in these circumstances are those about blessing and curse, revenge and forgiveness, which convey "'... I will repay,' says the Lord," (Rom 12.19) clearly the divine prerogative on retribution and caution against our following the impulses of political and economic expediency. Most Abrahamic scripture is about social ethics. The bilateral peace conference convened as interfaith dialogue at the United Nations tells me that we are becoming aware that only God can temper our warring madness and transfigure that *elan* into forgiveness, love, and mutual upbuilding. Grace, justice, and peace are spiritual impulses, anchored in the reality of God, which are given for and mediated into the public spheres of economic, political, and military action. Secular spheres cannot make it happen on their own, and religious spheres cannot implement those values in God's world without the secular orders.

Now I'm aware of the provocation and danger of this activity. The devil roams around quoting scripture, and bizarre scriptural inference flows from the snarled lips and twisted hearts of the likes of Baruch Goldstein at Hebron, Pastor Hagee in Dallas, and Osama bin Laden in his cave in Pakistan. This is why we must insist on reading scripture in community with interfaith, cross-referential, and corroborative search. All this must be undertaken with clean hands and pure hearts, humble and responsive to our One God and Lord.

---

2. For the full text, see http://www.haaretz.com.

This fourth interfaith banquet of Northern Illinois Methodists and Muslims stirs warm inspiration in our hearts. It challenges our complacency and alienation. It gives us an agenda for the common work so urgently needed in the world around us. Before we turn to our table dialogues, let us explore three areas of critical importance for this activity:

- the *political* meaning—the King Abdullah/President Peres interfaith dialogue points to the global impact of this local act in which we engage tonight;
- the *parochial* meaning of interfaith dialogue in this holiday season; and
- the *personal* gift that such activity holds for each one of us here tonight.

Political Meaning

This faith-sponsored encounter between king and president is striking, in the same way as that of Tony Blair as he becomes mediator of the Middle East Quartet (the United Nations, Europe, Russia, and the U.S.) with a side portfolio of his interfaith agenda. We seem to be learning that politics without faith, justice, and hope is manipulation, just as faith without public policy is only pious subjectivity. The Earth-shaking realization behind Scriptural Reasoning and interfaith contemplation and action at all levels of our public life—high schools, colleges, neighborhood groups and the like—is that here is the sphere in which the secular and sacred are inextricably intertwined.

King Abdullah put the imperative this way, "It is high time that the world has learned the harsh lesson of history that differences between followers of different religions and cultures have engendered intolerance, causing devastating wars and considerable bloodshed without any sound logical or ideological justification." Honest feedback into our faith traditions will be crucial. We cannot abide without protesting the bad preaching, incitement of violence, and sectarianism that goes along with religion claiming their way the only way to God and proposing we live in fear of and antagonism toward any other view. In my new book, *America in God's World*, I have addressed this lethal demonization of the "other," as well as the ideas of exceptionalism, materialism, and chosenness. Let me be very clear. We will not stop border wars—as we now witness as the border of the U.S. and Mexico—while we are sending the guns and craving the drugs. Street preachers and politicians cause wars. So do our passions and animosities. If we have ears, let us hear.

Here is the way President Peres addressed the issue at the United Nations, "In order to stand up against those who instigate discord and violence, we must bear the flags of brotherhood and peace." By this, he meant the flags of nations and factions, as well as the flags of faith.

King Abdullah also captured the issue precisely, "Terrorism is the enemy of religion." Despite the fact that the 16 bombers responsible for the events of September 11th came from Saudi Arabia, along with the six masterminds from Egypt, the king called for "a united front to combat terrorism and promote tolerance." In this statement, he seems to be calling for a *jihad* of mind and spirit.

He continued, "We state with a unified voice (of scripture) that almighty God sought to bring happiness to mankind (and those gifts) should not be turned into instruments of misery." This scriptural reference should prompt us to ask why the poor suffer so in the affluent Muslim Middle East. For that matter, wealthy Jews also make their home in the Middle East, as do affluent Christians in Hispanic America. Scriptural study is a call to economic duty.

President Peres took with him to the Scriptural Reasoning a rabbi, a mullah, and a Christian priest. Israel hopes to restore an interfaith population, although the Christian population has nearly disappeared there. Islam and Judaism have some heavy lifting ahead. But there is a bright ray of hope. I've been amazed how often in interfaith study, these two Semitic communities seem to understand each other, while both of them find Christians baffling and exasperating. The Christian/Muslim activity is also encouraging, given the mutual fear and demonization between these two bodies.

To my mind and experience with the Cambridge Inter-faith Center, activities of a Common Word, and high-level political/faith dialogue, Ambassadors Blair, Carter—the king and president—are reasons for hope. I regret that our own country in the past has been so non-religious in geopolitics, even though the dispensationalist "Christian right" has major impact on Israeli policy, on an anti-Islamic slant in international life, and on the apocalyptic belligerence toward Palestine, Iran, Darfur, and other nations. We must deconstruct these causal impulses toward Armageddon craving and apocalyptic yearning that are embedded in

American religiosity. I explore this Manichean mania of American policy in *America in God's World*.

Parochial Meaning

Scriptural Reasoning and interfaith dialogue not only offer public goods and global impacts by holding our world leaders and decision-makers to their transcending vocations, they indeed demand that we transform our particular faith traditions. In the 25 years I've been involved in these activities, starting groups around the world and sustaining others, the first result I've seen everywhere is that we are sent back to the drawing board of our own particular parish faith. We do not settle on some new syncretistic, least-common-denominator religion, but we are driven to study our own traditions, perhaps for the first time, seeking to mine each particular genius in order to share that with the wider world.

While some would lament such resorting to provincial faiths, wishing rather for a Comtean shedding of all religious consciousness from the human soul and from public affairs, I, for one, celebrate this revival of real, personal faith. I do agree with post-religious thinkers that religion has wrought havoc in the long history of human affairs. I also celebrate the presence of secularists and humanists at the table of sharing bread, word, and steering of the world because I recognize that holy agnosticism and passionate iconoclasm—"you shall have no other gods before me"—is the first article of true faith. I also know that secular humanists bring great wisdom to the world. If we have learned anything throughout these recent years of global crisis, it is surely that Anglo-American militarism, capitalism, and environmentalism—or, for that matter, Chinese or Russian or pan-Islamic domination—is not good for God's world; what is called for is a new universal justice and peace under the will of the one God of creation and redemption.

We Christians are especially challenged as we learn this new craft by the disciplined scripture study known in the *yeshiva* and *madrassas* and at home and hearth in daily litany (the five pillars) by our fellow Jews and Muslims. Christians also hope that the world will one day again recognize us, as was true with the primitive church, by our love: "See how they love one another."[3]

---

3. Tertullian's words, written in the third century (*Apology* 39.6), were quoted by people of the time about Christian communities.

Our own scriptural acquaintance is quite shallow. All too common is the student who, when asked to identify Moses, answered that he played for the 76ers and when asked if he had read the Bible, responded "no," but that he had seen the movie. Nominal, occasional, "little-dab'll-do-ya" faith is too small for times such as these.

As interfaith groups form, I've often heard the testimony that after the pain and initial confrontation, after the confessions and *mea culpas*, and after the forgiveness, a challenge is felt to go back and recover our own faith roots. Sometimes the interfaith groups adjourn to work unilaterally back home—then to come back together. Often I've heard the testimony, "I finally discovered what it is to be truly a Christian, a Jew, a Muslim."

In my major study, *Jew, Christian, Muslim*, I offer an even stronger thesis. I argue that something is amiss in each tradition, that each faith remains imperfect and incomplete. I ask, in particular, whether cutting ourselves off from each other—what scholars call a parting of the ways— has distorted the pristine power of our original faiths and pushed us to suspicion, anger, and ultimately a death-wish toward those we consider other. Since we are siblings of the One God, this estrangement can only be blasphemy. I've argued that God has deliberately fashioned the three children of Abraham in *Heilsgeschichte*, the holy history of the human race. I believe God also has blessed each faith tradition with a passion for universality and a global mission. We each believe that God has made us stewards of truth about God and good, and we are right in that stewardship. In talks like this, I often quote my good friend and brother, Tariq Ramadan, now professor at Oxford, who says, "listen to my story of faith, and I will ask you to tell me of Jesus." Such reciprocity is no longer a luxury—it is a life-and-death necessity.

Fundamental theological issues abound and remain unanswered. I urge this company tonight—a high-powered, insightful, faithful, college- and community-based fellowship—to take up some of these issues. In *Jew, Christian, Muslim*, I've argued that we will either find a way to hang together in faithful unification or hang separately in fateful trifurcation.

We may find in this endeavor that, at the deepest levels, we are one, as God is One. *Yitzhak* (Isaac), Jesus, and Ishmael enhance, complement, correct, and enrich each other. *Christos*, Messiah, Wisdom is the second God in heaven—*Emmanuel*—God with us.

Personal Meaning

I finally refer to the liberation and transformation afforded each of us personally by the interfaith dialogue. What we practice here tonight—and ideally carry with us to our churches, synagogues, *masjids*, colleges, dormitories, homes, and neighborhoods—is nothing short of a new vocation for persons of faith in this new millennium of salvation history we are called to, nothing less than to fashion under One God one world of justice, love, and new life for all. Faith alive is scriptural; it is the gift to humanity from the One God in order to bring about human unity; it is highly ethical and world transformative. Interfaith activity meets these tests. Other faith expressions today leave the personal soul empty and disappointed. Piety that is self-serving will not work at this moment in God's world. Faiths that are xenophobic, which nurture triumphalism and disdain for strangers, set back the kingdom of God. Mega-church prosperity gospel destroys the poor and disturbs the equilibrium of the Earth and cosmos. We must learn the tropism toward the poor of global Islam and the Wesleyan Holiness movement in Africa, for example. The zone of Christian political expansion is also the zone of the world's most concentrated populations and the zone of world Islam. This geological and historical enigma should give us pause.

Together, we must relearn the wisdom of the rabbi of *midrash* who, when he found Elijah standing at the entrance to a cave, asked "When will the Messiah come?" Elijah's response was that the Messiah, the *Mahdi*, "sits among the diseased poor, at the gate of the city disguised as our neighbor among the poor and sick, a destitute leper." In today's idiom, he is with the starving poor and those with HIV.

Here, at the membrane of time and eternity, are Lazarus and Dives and Abraham:

> The sun is low, the hour is late; let us enter the gates at last.
>
> When a man begins life, countless gates stand waiting to be opened. But as he walks through the years, gates close behind him, one by one.
>
> Remember the unopened gates. Open them before they are locked.
>
> The gates do not stay open forever. We walk through the years and they shut behind us. And, at the end, they are all closed, except the final one gate which we must enter.

Today, I shall come, says Messiah, if only all of you would listen to my voice. Before it is too late, let us open the gates that lead to blessing and beauty, enter the gates of Torah and tranquility, of grace and peace, of *Taurut* and *Injil*, of the stars of Abraham's skies and the sands of his seashores, go through the gates of kindness and compassion—these are the gates to the eternal in this life.

My friends, my prayer for your inspiring mission this night is that we enter these gates.

LUTHER AND INTERFAITH DIMENSIONS: GIFT OF THE BELOVED SON

The following remarks are in response to an address presented by Bishop Munib Younan of Israel/Palestine: "Reforming Luther: Toward Prophetic Interfaith Dialogue for Life"—as part of "The Global Luther" international conference on February 21-23, 2008 at Northwestern University in Evanston, Illinois.

The global Luther construes and constitutes God as the One God, the beloved God, whose judgment is love and whose love is judgment. This God manifests being as the beloved Son, for a beloved world, and in beloved community. These three themes—and the divine *ego eimi*—(I am that I am or I will be who I will be) are respectively developed in Judaism, Christianity, and Islam, which constitute nearly three-quarters of the world's population. My comment on this interfaith panel argues that the provocative assertions of the historical Luther on Jews and Muslims need now to be transfigured, in the global Luther, to a reciprocity and synergy, where each faith of Abraham makes an indispensable gift to the others.

As the one God of the *Shema* of *Adonai* binds the covenant people of Israel, and as the high priestly prayer of Jesus in John 17 ("so that they may be one, as we are one") forms the church, and as the *Shahada* of Allah is the gateway for the Holy *Ummah*, God's own redeemed world (or concurrent worlds, as the case may be) is being fashioned within world history. This divine gift to the world condemns and confounds our propensity to anathematize each other and even eliminate the other—especially the faith other. In the one God, our Babel and our dissociation from the other are muted and transmuted into the one reality, which is the divine will for this free and rebellious world. In this light, to my poor presbyopic eyes, only two futures are possible—either fateful trifurcation (which will eventually destroy the world) or a faithful unification of Abraham's family.

So tonight, as we take our leave of one another, as our friends return to Africa, to Europe, and to the Middle East, what is transpiring before us in Darfur, in the new Kosovo, in Palestine and Israel bears out this impending decision that we must make—to come together or to witness the disintegration of God's world.

I offer reflection with a brief *midrashic* comment on Psalm 122, a favorite of Luther. Jesus was the church for him; for post-*Shoah* and post-Crusade faith, we can say Zion is the church only if we are prepared to say the church is Zion. You remember the words:

> I was glad when they said to me . . . "Let us go to the house of the Lord . . . To the tribes go up, the tribes of the Lord, as was decreed for Israel, to give thanks to the name of the Lord. For there, the thrones of judgment were set up, the thrones of the house of David. Pray for the peace of Jerusalem: May they prosper who love you." (Ps 122.1–6)

The two walls of Bethlehem and the Gaza are an offense to the One God. I believe that Jerusalem symbolizes the connection of heaven and Earth—of eternity and time. I've learned this from Martin Buber, for whom Zion can only be Zion and in contact with the thou of the other and the eternal Thou if it is tri-faith. If I forget you, O Zion, if I forget you, O Golgotha, If I forget you, O *Akedic Ka'bah*, let my right hand that has failed to be extended in justice and in peace wither away.

Zion attaches here to there, we to thou and to eternal Thou. Zion is, insisted Buber, the home of Jews, Christians, and Muslims. In prophetic speech that bridges these spheres, Jerusalem, the city of fire and earthquake, is the residence of the "still, small voice," the city of walls and tears, the residence of hope and peace.

In the agonal cross of Luther, time and modernity, of Crusades along the Rhine and expulsions from Spain where Jews and Muslims are slain together, to the *Schwert* (sword) of Christendom, to Armenia and Auschwitz, to Algeria and *Abu Ghraib*, we slash with the sword of hate in the face of the beloved God. We even have the audacity to politicize John the Seer's terrible, pacifying sword of the Spirit in the Book of Revelation to a white horse mowing down heathens, idolaters, and apostates, a slashing sword from the messianic throat. The *Akedic* peace of the beloved God is symbolized in the Judaic gift of the beloved Son. This I take from Jon Levenson, who wrote his wonderful book here in our Garrett-Evangelical Theological Seminary Library, *The Death and Resurrection of the Beloved Son*. I commend to you also his book on resurrection in Judaism.[4]

The beloved Son and the beloved world are in the text of John 3.16, well-known to all of us, but most of us do not understand its links to Genesis 22. Every time you see the words *agapetos monogenos* (beloved child or only-begotten child), know that they come from the Abraham story. In this high holy season, we Christians again mark John 3.16: God so loved this beloved world that he gave his *monogenos agapetos*.

And the Holy *Ummah* is one of the most powerful divine pictures of the one World that the *Shema* and the high priestly prayer of Jesus are about.

Today, Muslims are the despised and rejected in that fallen world, a world so loved—now they are the demonized and anathematized of this world. Now these least of these become the *Akedic* lamb of God—to the grief of Yahweh, God, and Messiah Christ. Palestinians, as Bishop rightly cries out, shout this cry from Mitri Raheb in Christmas Lutheran Church in Bethlehem and his other remaining congregations in the disappearing Christian people in Palestine and Israel. Remember Osterlamm in *Christ lag in Todesbanden* (Christ lay in death's bonds).

So, my friends, let us march in justice with peace, to the victory of the slain lamb, singing the songs of Zion, where nations are healed as they stream up together to Jerusalem, breaking sword into plowshare. And let us remember with the passion of the speaker the message of the Psalms:

> I will not forget the law . . .
> I will not forget thy Word . . .
> I will not forget thy commandment . . .
> . . . If I forget thee . . . O Jerusalem
> If I fail to extend my hand in justice and peace,
> Let that hand wither away, it has become useless. (Pss 119, 137)

---

4. See Levenson, *Resurrection and the Restoration of Israel*.

LUTHER, JEWS, AND MUSLIMS: THE PRE-EMINENT COMMANDMENTS

The following is the text of a sermon delivered at Garrett-Evangelical Theological Seminary in Spring, 2007.

If you're a street person like me and hang out downtown, you're always ready for a surprise. And there it was last week, a die-hard Cubs fan wearing his blue cap in mid-October. He eyeballed my Bears hat with some snide remark: "Dusty Baker's 'cool' didn't work," he sneered. "Now we've got Lou Piniella's 'heat'—it's the Cubs in '07." I agreed! Perhaps the most ejected manager in baseball history really could light a fire under the Cubs. Going into Barnes & Noble, I found an even greater surprise as I entered the warming center with the other homeless, when I picked up the news journal, *The American Interest*, and saw that the lead article was by our old friend, Peter Berger. "Neither relativism or fundamentalism can ground moral and theological reason," the old Lutheran sociologist wrote.[5] We need a revitalized "Protestant" middle way. "Yes!" I shouted to shushing all around: No more Pat Robertson—let's get Martin Luther in the White House!

I began writing this Reformation message last summer in the great Pompidou Library in Paris; I had just begun my research on inter-Abrahamic Scriptural Reasoning as a fellow at Cambridge's Centre for Advanced Religious and Theological Studies (CARTS). The library was filled with émigrés from all over the world—especially the Middle East and Africa—and we watched nervously as CNN covered the outbreak of war in Lebanon. It tore at my heart as I saw cluster bombs made in America rip that nation to shreds. Where on Earth could justice and peace be found? Could this Moabite Ruth have a bomb strapped under her *burqa*? Were we catering to an unending permanent religious war—the clash of civilizations Huntington forecast? Tonight our "War and Peace" class will consider such dialogue on war scriptures with Jewish and Muslim colleagues from Northwestern University. You are welcome to join us.

But today, we still see the *shalom* that ever eludes Jerusalem. That "could-be" brought tears to the rabbi who secreted that elusive peace in his heart and purpose as he looked over the city of Jerusalem the other day. In this homily, I feel the press of his Passover soliloquy in John 17 where he prayed "that they may be one, as we are one"—an obvious re-

---

5. See Berger, "Between Relativism and Fundamentalism."

prise of *Shema*: "Hear, Israel, the Lord is our God, the Lord is One . . . and you shall love the Lord your God with all your heart and with all your soul and with all your might." (Deut 6.4–9)

Which brings us to the Reformation. Though instrumental in the great unification of humanity born in the Renaissance, the Protestant Reformation has played no small part in the seemingly endless schism and balkanization both of the human family and Abraham's faith heritage.

Martin Luther epitomized the blessing and curse of that profound historical revolution that spawned the 400 years from Wycliffe to Wesley. The benefits have transfigured society and revitalized faith, allowing for:

- reading scripture in the vernacular;
- comprehending faith as personal and vital, not just cultural and nominal;
- the renewal of the Gospel of God: *sola gratia, sola scriptura, sola fide*;
- the rise of democracy;
- the Protestant ethic and Weber's mediation of the sacred and secular; and
- blessing the world with theistic and humanistic impulse.

But the dark side is also there, resulting in:

- subjective individualism that negates community and eventually becomes our virtual age;
- *Kapitalismus savage* (savage capitalism), which brings an unspeakable chasm and violence between rich and poor and in which greed, exploitation, and mendacity have flourished;
- the tortuous history of colonialism based on Manifest Destiny and disdain of the other as infidel.

Luther was blamed for Hitler and the Holocaust, for the Danish cartoons, Bergman's cinematic atheism, and skinhead terror throughout the Nordic world. Luther would last about five minutes today before being arrested for ethnic slurs and crudity. Luther believed fervently that Jews and Muslims would convert to Christ as the evangelical Reformation gained strength. When that didn't happen, he got mad as hell!

Luther personified this fratricidal rage. A Jew-hater and Turk-hater, for him, Jews and Muslims were despicable heretics, Unitarians, secular humanists, anti-Christ. The only good thing he could say was that they were not as bad as Catholics. Like today's dispensationalists, his gospel fervor turned to vitriolic hatred of infidels as anti-Christ. Like so many in America today—from televangelists to politicians—for Darby's followers, there must be an enemy of God. In the past, it's been Amerindians, Nazis, and communists, Catholics, Africans, or Hispanics—now it's Muslims. The world of God of Revelation 19 gallops across history on a white horse, and from his larynx protrudes a sword mowing down the evil empire.

To avoid such treacherous human remonstrance, recover the authentic evangelical awakening, and rescue Jesus as messiah of the whole world, consider three pictures—Martin Luther, Tariq Ramadan (who has been called the Muslim Martin Luther), and one lesser light (resembling only in baldness and belly), yours truly—Ken Vaux.

On closer look, Luther was not a bad guy. In fact, he was a real *mensch*, and worthy of being the most biographed human since that first Christian. Luther's greatest treasure, he often said, was the human Jesus. He was an anti-Manichean, par excellence. The Hebrew Bible was not an Old Testament—a secularly Anglican idea—it was *Heilige schrift*—holy writings of Earth-shattering news. The God of Israel was God; the psalms were his *jihad*, and Jesus' incarnation assured creation and the victory of the triune God. For Martin, the Christian faith was holistic, no severable body and soul, no disdain for flesh and family, no split between God and nature. When *Decolam padius* confronted him with this humanism, he shouted, "I know no God except the one who became man and I want none other." Pointing to the intense prayer of persecuted Jews, Luther said, "I'd give goblets worth 200 guilder to pray as they do," and the Muslims drew praise for their love and care of children. When he prefaced the Bibliander's 1543 Edition of the Qur'an in Latin, he encouraged Christians to study the book to sharpen their interactions—both condemnatory and conciliatory—with that community.

Thoroughly orthodox, Luther saw Jews and Muslims as sustaining the Unitarian heresy of preaching the unity of the One God rather than the triune God and emphasizing the humanity of Christ or the divinity of man. Yet Luther himself persisted, as Barth would emphasize in his later work, with the humanity of God. Johann von Staupitz, the greatest of pastoral counselors, advised his protégé on the Lord's Supper—"the Father is too sublime" (Martin). So God the Father said, "I'll give you a new way to come to me, namely Christ—believe in him, hang upon Christ, then you will find out who I am, in good time."

Luther concurred, "wherever you put God, you must also place humankind. They can't be put apart. Jesus came as one being. You can't peel humanity off and throw it down like your jacket at bedtime. You can't peel divinity of humanity and put it out there somewhere in the closet where there are no humans."

Again, Luther says, "if Christ was able to suffer and die on Earth while he was part of the Godhead, why can't he suffer with us here today even though he's in heaven? No, Christ was in heaven while he walked on Earth—so were the apostles and we ourselves. We are now in heaven just as long as we have faith in Christ. Wouldn't that stir up a tempest in Zwingli's bag of tricks?"[6]

Jesus was a real, down-to-earth person—Hebrew's High Priest—so like us, sublime grace in so human investiture. Such formulation, a kenotic God, saves the biblical God and Christ—the God of Abraham, Isaac, and Jacob—from the labyrinth of Greek philosophy.

The second portrait in the triptych is Tariq Ramadan. *Time* magazine named him one of the 100 most important intellectuals of the 21st century, right up there with our Professor Steve Long. Some of you remember his stirring message to the Council for a Parliament of the World's Religions, from which he was banned in Barcelona. Last year, he was denied a visa by U.S. Homeland Security to receive a professorship at Notre Dame. His grandfather, whose thought he disavows, founded the Egyptian brotherhood. He also advocated *Hamas*, no sweet gang to be sure, but surely better than the demonization of the CIA and IDF, the only social-service arm of the beleaguered Palestinian people and their elected government. He now teaches at Oxford—a new seed bed for radicals since Brent and Oliver O'Donovan left—and some of our Northwestern students there work with him. Ramadan is a European Muslim, an Enlightenment Muslim. Probing his connection with Martin Luther, John Carroll asked for the 95 theses he would tack on the Great Christ church doors. He had only three:

- *Understand what a text is that comes from God*. What are the universal meanings and truths of our sacred texts? Scriptures are the seed bed, the seminary of "the kingdom of God."

---

6. See Luther, *D. Martin Luther's Werke*, 26:345.

- *Understand how these texts express universal values.* Let's abandon, he says, *dar al- Islam, dar al-Harb,* the realms of Muslims and war. Let's tear down the barricades between Israel and Islam, between *corpus Christianum* Constantinian and Islam. Let's recover our sacred brotherhood and sisterhood as in 13th-century Cordova, the birthplace of Seneca, Averroës, Maimonides. Here, Muslims and Christians both worship to this day in the Great Cathedral and Mosque at Mesquite, and Maimonides' study is just down the street. Let's find, he continues, one house of testimony, as he told me at AAR some years ago, "listen to my story of faith, and I will ask you to tell me of Jesus." Each time he concludes an e-mail, he writes, in Andalusian wisdom, "May the light protect you and go with you and all the people you love."
- *Do Abraham's jihad.* In teaching, preaching, evangelizing, and praying, we remember Ruth Duck's good words, that we cherish our own traditions and find ourselves in each other. Only on the path of understanding will our common search find blessing.

The last door on the triptych is a mirror. Meet Ken Vaux. As I view myself in the glass of Scriptural Reasoning, I am aware of the precariousness of my own location and the fragility and holy agony of my witness. Sufi wisdom is terrifying, it's only when you are old and broken, only then can you be teacher and mentor (sans teeth, sans hair, sans everything) and bring together Jews, Christians, and Muslims arm-in-arm against godlessness and unrighteousness.

I have come to realize that I live in a world where nearly two-thirds of the population is comprised of the children of Abraham:

- 1 billion Protestant and Orthodox Christians;
- 1 billion Roman Catholics;
- nearly 1 billion Pentecostals in the West, Africa, South America, and Asia; and
- more than 1 billion Muslims on that belt of poverty that stretches across "the middle of the world," the 10–40 parallel.

I have come to know and believe that Christian faith derives from the faith of Israel. This fact, let's be honest, has not been recognized until after the signature Christian violence in human history, the Holocaust. I therefore now believe that we must prevent the annihilation of our parental people Israel from the face of the Earth and, for me, this has scary and uncomfortable meanings for events like Palestine, Iraq, and Lebanon.

I believe that our scriptures are embedded in the *Tanakh* and are incomprehensible without that seminary, the seed bed of the Torah; without the law, prophets, and writings, there is no gospel. We now know that most Christian scriptures stand as links on a chain between Hebrew texts and Islamic *midrash*. Take any text: creation, fall, *Akedah*, the Joseph or Jacob narrative, Job, the Sermon on the Mount, the woman taken in adultery, Mary, Jesus—really, any New Testament text. We are chained together in vexing scriptural links to our sister Abrahamic faiths. These monkey-ropes will either unite the world in justice and peace, or precipitate some final apocalyptic blistering or blizzarding holocaust on Earth. Therefore, we must call the Earth from near-calamity to *shalom*—to feed, clothe, heal, and teach the world.

As we celebrate this week the Renaissance Reformation of Luther, let us reflect on the tremendous and terrible energy released into world history by the faith he pioneered. And let us vow to be "Jesus people," listening to the corroboration and criticism from our sister Abraham faiths. Let us ponder anew what it is to be "evangelicals," evangelical people of the Reformation in this dynamic world. Peter Berger is right: *Sola fide*, Luther's *Evangelische Ethos*, or Tillich's "Protestant Principle" can serve our radicalized world well.

Let us resolve, in Pope Benedict's good words, that *Deus Caritas Est*, that the world needs a restful pause of peace, justice, and good will, that women and children, justice and life, must rise to the top of our agenda—above invasion, occupation, and violence, and that those who die young of hunger, AIDS, and preventable disease, poverty, and war are our trust. And let us now and for all our days live for Him who died and ever lives for us. Alleluia, Alleluia. In the name of the Father, the Son, and the Holy Spirit, One God—world without end. Amen.[7]

---

7. See Pope Benedict, *Paraphrase of Pope Benedict XVI's First Encyclical Letter*, December 25, 2005.

DO JEWS, CHRISTIANS, AND MUSLIMS WORSHIP THE SAME GOD?

This essay is part of the course reading for the "Doctrine of God" class at Garrett-Evangelical Theological Seminary, Spring 2009. The third section—addressing historical continuity in the three Abrahamic faith traditions—appears on pages 82–107.

It may take an historical calamity to ask an old question in a new way. Many around the world, because of religious undertones and overtones (particularly Jews, Christians, and Muslims) have been forced by the events of September 11th to examine the interstitial theologies and ethics between the faiths of Abraham. This introspection about whether we love, hate, or just respect and avoid each other is even more the case as a result of the profound concomitant tragedies of Iraq and Israel/Palestine that have come to define contemporary theological history. If Holocaust is an event of biblical moment for Jews, then what of the cleansing and genocide now proceeding in Iraq under the tutelage of Christian Anglo-America? And as military surge ensues in defiance of the American electorate, we ask if we are witnessing again events of religious significance, now with Muslims, Christians, and even Jews stirring the furies of Holy War.

The global religio-political crisis is further exacerbated as Pope Benedict lets slip in Regensburg, then Istanbul, a frightful Islamophobia and theological disdain for our sister Abrahamic faiths. Rather than shock the world, we shake off his gaffs to the resurgent orthodoxy and enmity found rising today in all three faith traditions. All this prompts me to ask again an ancient theological question: Do Jews, Christians and Muslims worship and serve the same God? If we do, is the present violence fratricidal, even blasphemous? In the *jus post bellum* we hope now draws near as the war on terrorism shudders from acute conflict into a chronic permanence, should there be charges of religious murder as well as war crimes? If we decide that we are not accountable to the same God, then what are the implications for religious and public policy, local and global?

These pragmatic issues hinge on the ultimate question: Is the God of Abraham and Israel, the God and Father of the Lord Jesus Christ, and Allah of Muhammad and Islam—one and the same? Though each faith asserts shared origins, historic continuities, and affinities, the strong aniconic (anti-idol)—even fratricidal—impulse within each becomes fervent, especially in such times of trouble as today.

Despite the current drift, I contend that one God is the focal power of the three faiths. Calling on motifs central to the logic and substance of these great faith tradition, I present four lines of evidence to establish the case:

- the Name of God;
- the singularity and unity of God;
- historical derivation and continuity; and
- the experience of interfaith dialogue.

The Name of God

As we have noted with our consideration of Pseudo-Dionysius and Soskice, the Name of God goes to the heart of the matter of the reality of God. "One God" is at the essence of the being, speaking, and hearing of the *Memra*, the Word, and Name in the faiths of Abraham. Starting with *Shema*—"Hear Israel, the Lord is our God, the Lord is One"—we are commanded to have no other gods. The *Hashem* reminds us that the Name is not to be taken lightly or manhandled. The third facet of the first Word of the three faiths is "You shall not take the name of the Lord your God in vain" (Exod 20.7) These are the true faith commandments.

Names are potent, especially the Name of God. To be given the Name, or to use the Name, is fraught with privilege and danger. A human name bestows meaning and possession. In ancient Rome, children were not named until they were claimed. To place a name on God is highly dangerous. It is to locate, define, and control. Jews will not utter or spell the Name—a refreshing silence in the blathering, babbling age of God-talk in which we live. Many religions believe that God, the ineffable, indefinable, and unnamable One, gives over his Name—as password—to his beloved, a holy and righteous people. God now presumably goes on call by that Name to that people. As Harold Bloom has shown in *Jesus and Yahweh: The Names Divine* that Yahweh, Jesus, and Allah are interweaving, inter-illuminating designations.[8] To belong to this Name is to belong to each other. An inveterate Shakespearean, Bloom cites the Anglo-literary epitome of this name-calling as William Tyndale's New Testament

---

8. See Bloom, *Jesus and Yahweh*.

of 1526, smuggled over from Antwerp to sustain his beloved, nascent English church with its epicenters in Cambridge and London.

To take a name or to become known by a name was something like the outgiving of God's self by which the creation came into being. As Ivan Illich has shown in his studies of Medieval friars munching on the Word,[9] naming imparts *exousia* or bread—the very substance and sustenance of the giver. *Kabbalah*, and its precursor archaic cosmogonies according to Mircea Eliade, affirms that a primal fullness (*pleroma*) is emptied in order to make room and give freedom for responsive creation and humanity.

In Christianity, Philippians 2 develops this *kenosis*, the voiding of namesake in the name of love: "... though he was in the form of God, did not regard equality with God ... but emptied himself ... therefore God also highly exalted him and gave him the name that is above every name ..." (Phil 2.5–9) You know the parallel texts in Judaism and Islam.

There is something glorious yet tragic in *kenosis*—in Name-giving. In Kitamori's language, it involves the theology of the pain of God. It is pain to God, that rather than being met by outflow and generosity to mimic the Divine self-giving, all human religions, including those of Abraham, tend to clam up, shut in, and exclude—the bright world goes dark. Separatism or supercessionism then leads one and all of our three faiths to part ways with the others by saying "we worship another God."

Here we must confront the human tragedy or the divine mystery of Judaism and Christianity excommunicating and un-naming each other from the first century until the final venom of the *Shoah*. We must also ponder the enigma of Islam rejecting and being rejected by its heritage in Crusade and Inquisition, ancient and modern. Our political and religious leaders today look as foolish as the administrators of Trinity College excoriating Jewish student Abrams in the film *Chariots of Fire*: "another mountain, another God," they snidely observe at his impieties. Much more commendable is Clint Eastwood's pair of films on *Iwo Jima*, in which inter-perspective empathy is sought.

Though affirming an affinity with Israel, evangelical Christians today have great difficulty acknowledging that Jews worship and serve the same God. And Muslims are not even on the radar. This, even though Jesus likely addressed God with the Aramaic *El Lah*—the name Muslims invoke today.

---

9. See Illich, *In the Vineyard of the Text*.

Though the Divine Name is always defamed by those called by that Name, the Name remains sovereign. In his metaphysical historical theology, Wolfhart Pannenberg argues that humans do not project soul, name, goodness, or justice onto transcendence as the Enlightenment, Feuerbach, Marx, and Freud held. Rather, the Divine Name creates soul and contains body and creation. In this holistic view, Spirit initiates and contains body. This more biblical view overturns the Greek ontology in which body contains and confines soul. An Abrahamic ontology—one in accord with Ibn Sina (Avicenna), Maimonides, and Aquinas, where the divine Name shines within world, body, and community—is the first evidence that we worship the same God.

I will go farther and offer an even more radical thesis for which I may be the only proponent even among the broad spectrum of theology found here at Cambridge. I believe that Christianity does and should resonate the inner meaning of Judaism and Islam. In the same way Judaism resonates the inner meaning of Christianity and Islam, and Islam bears out the inner meaning of Judaism and Christianity. The thesis of my book *Jew, Christian, Muslim* is that we will either rediscover or discover for the first time a vital and reciprocally illuminating tri-unity or we will perish in fateful trifurcation. More on this inter-religious eschatology in a moment.

For now, painfully, we live in a world crisis where anti-Semitism, anti-Christianism, and anti-Islamism abound. Holy Warrior Jews kill innocent Muslims in a housing block in Gaza or at prayer in a Hebron *masjid*. Christian crusaders kill Jews in skinhead attacks in Europe or Muslims in Afghanistan, Iraq, or Somalia; Muslim suicide-bombers kill themselves and innocent Jews and Christians at a Tel Aviv bus station and London or Christian children at a Beslan school in Russia. In Iraq now, we witness the final apocalyptic violence as Muslims devour their own children and betray and kill their own.

Against this fratricidal impulse, the Name of the One God insists that God visits and is adored and served by all of his flocks. The Name of God signals proleptically, if not actually, the inner coherence and unity of those bound in faith and service.

The Singularity and Unity of God

The second argument for the same-God thesis is the singularity and unity of God. Beyond the obvious insight that we live in a manifest *universe* not *pluri-verse*—where we all see, hear, and comprehend the same objects and phenomenon and that these sensations are commonly knowable and explicable by reason, mathematics, causality and science—we also live in a religious salience that allows us to apprehend, as Whitehead has shown, that unified realm of space and time, eternity and infinity. Voting for Polkinghorne instead of Dawkins, I contend that God is One and is behind all knowledge and faith, all science and theology.

Hebrew Faith Constructed on Shema
"Sh'ma Yis'ra'eil Adonai Eloheinu Adonai echad"—"Hear, Israel, the Lord is our God, the Lord is One ..." (Deut 6.4–9)

Like Name, this is the most disturbing and transforming Word ever sent out to this world and its people. It writes the world's history. It sets off tumult in space and time. It creates the history of Israel, the rise of Christianity, the emergence of Islam and recently the rise of a planetary, cosmopolitan, scientific, and economic world and a universal history. The One God of all life signals the Apostle Paul in Romans 8, sets off a redemptive labor in the cosmos whose birth pangs and delivery, though yet to be received, are inevitably coming into being.

Even though this new world arises from polytheism and pluralism, in God-induced- apperception, Abraham senses a singular and ethical God. *Gott* (God) and *gut* (good), in etymology, are interchangeable words—a unified neuro-linguistic heritage.

How do singularity and unity arise? The influences of Egypt, Sumeria, Persia, and India, Julius Lipner would show us, are unmistakable. The idea of the high and Holy, mighty and good One—out there and in here, One who is Lord of all, One who demands awe, association and allegiance—is manifestly evident. And, as Brahms meditated on the North Sea rocks one day in his *Schicksaalied*, the human heart perennially longs for such singular strength and purpose, despite the crashing waves of seemingly blind destiny all around.

Like the *kenotic* element found in the phenomenon of Name, the God who finally acts on Abraham in Genesis 12–25 condescends into history and nature. Abraham's father Terah had felt some beckoning and moved from Chaldea to Haran. His sons were now poised toward Canaan. High God is becoming Earth-God with the purification of each pagan preparation. This new God not only succors and provokes obeisance, He companions and guides. He befriends and chides. He is *Akbar* and full of *Hesed*. He is *Ramah*, great and good in demand, love, and mercy.

Tikkun olam has begun—mending the unraveling state of affairs. Recreation is undertaken to restore the disturbed creation. Some primal remembrance as echoed in Gilgamesh or Hammurabi, memory that will be recollected in the exile, is at work: creation/fall, Adam/Eve, Cain/Abel, Noah and sons—all mythic story is libidinally present. Partnership was now needed if there was any chance left to make good the world. In Abraham, then Moses, this God and good would be constituted. Unification and reconciliation of God and the world had begun.

What Hinduism and Hellenism would one day understand as "the One and the many" were now made synergetic in purpose. The dialectic that Pythagoras and Plato would understand as the interplay of matter and spirit would now begin to collapse into integrated dynamic tension and movement known as the Spirit of God in the world. The eternal and earthly breach, symbolically affected by fallen angels, would now begin to be healed as redemptive, repairing process began within earthly process. The world had turned the corner. As filmmaker Krzysztof Kieslowski would show with his planes and angles, singularity now began to yield meaning and unity. God was the One for the world. Leviathan of sea and land was given notice.

Oneness with the Fellowship
As in Judaism, the declaration of faith in Christianity also focuses on the Oneness of God and Christ with the fellowship. John remembers Jesus saying:

> "There will be one flock, one shepherd" (John 10:16).
>
> "The Father and I are One" (10:30).
>
> "Holy Father, protect them in your name that you have given me ..." (17.11b).
>
> "... so that they may be one, as we are one ..." (17:11b).
>
> "that they may all be one . . . so that the world may believe you have sent me" (17:21).

Again Paul writes to the congregation in Corinth:

> . . . there is one God, the Father . . . and one Lord, Jesus Christ . . . (1 Cor 8:4-6) there is one bread . . . one body, for we all partake of the one bread (10:17)
>
> . . . all the members of the body, though many, are one body . . . (12:12)

The Christian tradition summarizes:

> . . . One Lord, one faith, one baptism, one God and Father of all . . . (Eph 4:5–6)

In Romans 3, Paul further focuses this Oneness motif:

> Is God for Jews alone?
> Is he not for the Gentiles too?
> Most certainly for Gentiles too!
> If, indeed God is "One," who will set right the circumcision from faith? and the uncircumcision by the faith? (Rom 3.29–30)[10]

In its three movements, the Abrahamic faiths perform the symphony of divine singularity and unity. In symphony, particular instruments are meant to play together in timed entrance, occasionally in solo, other times in concert—often in dissonance then resonance, B minor then C major, Shostakovich then Brahms. God's unity both composes and evokes reciprocity among the three movements and instruments. Therefore all boasting and blasting must cease so that each voice may be heard in its solitary and solidarity beauty. Here we can entertain the suggestion of Peter Ochs that trinity may not only be a cacophony and stumbling block in the "bosom of Abraham," but in some mysterious sense a *munus triplex*—a binding and releasing of all of the faiths into a higher sublimity.

Such concord or harmony is seen to be essential if the world is to believe. That divine oneness demands human unity is found when Christianity rebukes Israel's exclusivism and affirms Abrahamic universalism: "I will multiply thy seed as the stars of the heaven and as the sand which is upon the seashore." (Gen 22.17) When Christianity is tempted to exclusivism, both Judaism and Islam serve as monotheistic checks. The end and purpose of Torah is the world, not Israel alone. But what if the world remains committed to eliminate Israel? Here arises the controversy of Jimmy Carter's book on Palestine and the outrage it provokes. One God as a force in history means to make right—circumcision, uncircum-

---

10. See Jewett et al., *Romans: A Commentary*.

cision, then circumcision again—what's going on? Somehow these three faith/works, working/faiths are involved, but how?

This One God (*eis theos*) formula—which, we remember, is divine and worldly reality to the Jewish-Christian Paul—points back to the Egyptian amulet's formula, "There is One God who heals every illness"(15th-century b.c.e.), and was already deeply imbedded in Pythagoras, Plato, and Aristotle. Oneness was connected with righteousness through mediation of Word and Wisdom. Messiah, *Mediato*, and *Mahdi* are representations woven into the fabric of this Oneness. These manifestations, at root, are also one.

The unity of God elicits the focal unity of faith and the derived unity of humanity. As Augustine sharply advocates in *The City of God*, only one God, one faith, and one body can guarantee one world. Though Augustine, like the Fathers, seems to feel that the Jewish *ecclesia* will eventually dissolve into *corpus Christianum*, Aquinas—if only because his Napoleatan origins were in *dar al-Islam* and the theological seriousness with which he takes thinkers like Maimonides and Averroës—takes Judaism and Islam into account in his thinking about One Body. In my view, the communal spiritual body of the three monotheistic Abrahamic faiths weaves interpenetrably into the one world body.

Affirmation of Divine and Human Unity

Islam, as well as Judaism and Christianity, affirms this divine and human unity. *Al'Islam* (surrender) is submission to this singular loyalty. The sacred Qur'an is, in the words of Sura 2 (136), a rendition of the communicative Word of God through "Abraham, Ishmael, Isaac, Jacob, the tribes and Jesus." The creed, "there is no God but Allah" codifies a universe of God, humanity, and the world that will decisively shape theology, human history, and science—not only for *dar al-Islam*, the Muslim realm and reality, but for the entire world. Philosophy and science come to modern Europe and then the whole world from the Muslims. The lasting truth of this medieval revolution is found in its convictions of unity and universality. In my recent study, *An Abrahamic Theology for Science*, I show that such theology is woven into the very conceptual and ethical substance of modern science itself.[11]

A Qur'anic text that reflects this monotheistic synthesis and synergy is Sura 17:

11. See Vaux, *An Abrahamic Theology for Science*.

> Do not set other gods alongside Allah;
> Honor the parents and family as God's gift;
> Have mercy on the weak and poor;
> Wounding or killing others imposes bloodguilt;
> Respect the Earth; and
> God knows all and holds all responsible for their acts.

This text is suffused with the Spirit of Israel's *Shema* and Decalogue and Jesus' Sermon on the Mount and high priestly prayer. It is an ascription to the same God.

Human action in the world is extrapolated from the nature of God. God is holy, just, good, and merciful. To maintain communion in righteousness with and before God, we must be similarly holy and just. Many passages from *hadith* and the great commentaries from the eighth century onward focus on the unbrokenness and unity of God, and of the association of God with humanity and the world. These teachings document our first assertion that there is only one God—the same for all the faiths of Abraham.

Historical Derivation and Continuity

See pages 82–107 in section three for a discussion of the historical continuity of the three traditions.

Experience of Interfaith Dialogue

A final corroboration of the same-God thesis comes from the experience of interfaith dialogue. Theologians, pastors, and laypersons of all persuasions—Jew, Christian, Muslim—must now make this experience, as you do so well in this university, a norm of your learning, study, service in the world, and prayer. This experience has yet to seep into the tissues of the provincial parish—urban or rural. You must make that happen.

David Ford has written in the highly informative issue of *The Promise of Scriptural Reasoning* that Scriptural Reasoning may be the clue in our time to wisdom-seeking and wisdom-making.[12]

I have offered an argument that the three faiths of Abraham do, in fact, worship and serve the same God. It is a conclusion at once so obvious and so unlikely. The recovery of that common bond alone, I've argued, can heal the current fratricidal tribulation we witness from London to Lebanon, Iraq, Bosnia, Chechnya, Philippines, Sudan, Somalia, Kashmir,

---

12. See Ford, "An Interfaith Wisdom."

Afghanistan, and Pakistan. Only a spiritual unity and concord anchored in our One God and Lord can transmute current strife into justice on the ground, on the streets, and in the sanctuaries. Only such hard fought-for-struggle and care can mute the strident voices of fanatic and violent rabbis, priests, mullahs and, worst of all, politicians, those today at the beck and call of such unworthy court jesters.

Should this dawning arise, then will come to pass the prophetic dream:

> "But this is the covenant that I will make with the house of Israel after those days," saith the Lord, "I will put My law in their inward parts, and in their heart will I write it . . . and they shall teach no more every man his neighbor, saying, 'Know the Lord' for they shall all know Me from the least of them to the greatest of them. . . ." (Jer 31.32–33)

And again as the sacred scripture of one tradition ends, another begins with the same words: In that wonderful and dreadful day, "I will turn the hearts of the parents to the children and the children to the parents, Lest I come and smite the Earth with a curse." (Jer 31:33, Mal 4:5–6, Luke 1:17).

CONVERSION AND RELIGIOUS FREEDOM

This essay is part of the course reading for the "Doctrine of God" class at Garrett-Evangelical Theological Seminary, Spring 2009.

In an earlier essay presented at the Divinity faculty in Cambridge in early 2007, we walked through the rudimentary interfaith question: Do we worship and serve the same God? As I now field-test that study guide, persons offer a recurring response: Though the arguments that Jews, Christians, and Muslims have the same God are convincing, we have been told, people cannot bring themselves at a gut level, to assent to this premise. Attributing the same God to Jews and Muslims would seem to invalidate their own Christian faith. I often ask in response to this reticence what they think it would imply if these three sibling communities, indeed, were not the children of the One God of Abraham. After the initial shock, a terror sets in at the thought that we then might be perpetually condemned to spiritual incompatibility, irreconcilable apartheid, unending strife, perhaps even mutual destruction. So the matters become urgent and of supreme moment. This essay therefore begs the question of intramural conversion and proselytism (voluntary, not coercive) between these sibling- or stranger-faiths, as the case may be.

My own persuasion is that we are not only sister faiths, but we lose our own identities when we live in alienation and animosity toward each other. Today, in the wake of the war on terrorism, we are witnessing a frightful turn of events among the three faiths. It is a slight but very significant mutation from Huntington's "Clash of Civilizations" (Islam vs. the West). Today, it appears to me that we are coming to live in a bipolar faith world with America, the global evangelical and Pentecostal community and world Jewry (95 percent in Israel and the U.S.) on the one hand and Europe and the Islamic world on the other. Let us submit this issue to deeper analysis.

Case Studies

- In 1998, 30 Filipino Christians were arrested for distributing Bibles in the closed Islamic state of Saudi Arabia. Only a concerted effort by the U.S., the Philippines, and other European embassies was able to secure their release later that summer. Under Saudi law, you can bring in one Bible in your suitcase, but smuggling 20,000 presented a challenge to the theocratic state. The Western value of free religious expression was at loggerheads with the Islamic value that conversion amounted to apostasy—a sin and crime— meriting severe, even capital, punishment.
- This sanction became clear in the second case. In 2005, the case of Afghan Abduhl Rahman, who had served for years in a Christian relief agency, came to public light. He had converted and become a Christian 15 years earlier, a quite common experience in the heyday of Christian missions in Afghanistan in the early decades of the 20th-century, before American, British, and Russian political machinations led to the Taliban state and the endless strife that endures to this day.

  Five years earlier, Rahman had appealed for custody of his children from their Muslim mom. He was accused of apostasy, disowned, and turned into civil authorities who accused him of breach of the first commandment (no other gods), was therefore a heretic and was given the death penalty. Again, only frantic diplomatic efforts and bald Euro-American economic threats (let's get down to the real gods of our time) saved his skin. Like the celebrated Nigerian woman who also was condemned to death by stoning, in this case for adultery, the simple Rahman was exonerated, exiled, forever removed from his family, and the case was dropped.

- The third case also occurred in Afghanistan just this year (2007). Pastor Park Eun-Jo of Samuel Presbyterian Church was arrested in Afghanistan by the Taliban along with 20 of his parishioner-evangelists. They were held captive for some weeks; the pastor and another elder were killed. They were finally released after delicate negotiations with the South Korean government, with a large ransom reportedly involved. Rather than being greeted as martyr heroes, their homecoming was shrouded in shame for bringing disgrace on the government, a fascinating case of evangelism and freedom of religious expression.

These cases, admittedly dramatic and quite atypical, raise a specter of issues for pan-Abrahamic interfaith study, including: conversion and proselytizing; ecclesial and civil suppression or assertion of evangelism; public policy issues of religious freedom and expression; the sociopolitical endorsement of particular faith traditions; and, perhaps behind all these quandaries, the inner biblical-theological meanings of the phenomenon of witness and martyrdom. This essay explores the set of questions that must be raised to carefully broach these matters.

I first explicate some of the meanings and parameters of evangelism. Secondly, I look at several interpretations of the expansion and contraction of the particular faiths of Judaism, Christianity, and Islam. Thirdly, I consider what seem to be the possible postures of the state toward the issues of evangelism and how these might bear on ecclesiological policies of synagogue, church, and *masjid* and their broader judicatories. Finally, I offer what I hope will be received as scriptural-theological-political imperatives to live together in this troubled world in truth and righteousness.

Meanings of Evangelism

I begin with the world I know best as a trainer of Christian leaders in a theological seminary. The "evangelistic cosmos" of Christianity sees the whole inhabited world as a realm to be won to Christ. I interpret this Abrahamic mission, "a light to the Gentiles," as mysteriously integral to the destiny of Israel and Islam in the world as well as to the Jesus movement. World history, I believe, is the concourse of Messianic *Logos* into the world through Abrahamic witness. The faiths we call Christianity and the broader family of fraternal faiths of Abraham now constitute nearly three quarters of the peoples of the world. Buddhism, Hinduism, Confucianism, indigenous movements, and secular humanism as spiritual philosophies and ethical schools of conduct complete the roundtable of faith and life commitments we can survey.

To stay with the great monotheisms, my view is that evangelism or proselytizing is inherent in each of the Abrahamic faiths, so much so that it would violate the very substance of each movement to become non-converting. This leads me to propose the concept of intramural evangelism as a process of mutual enrichment and edification. The only alternative to this, it would seem, is the ever-increasing tendency to draw caricatures and to demonize each other's faith. For example, the sadly and stupidly discriminatory inclinations of the U.S. at present lead us to see the Islamic world as a seedbed of hatred toward our country, places where terrorism festers so that we are more and more inclined to preemptively strike Muslim countries—Afghanistan, Iraq, Iran, Syria and Palestine—thinking that such belligerence or show of force will discourage the enemy. We now even have a military acronym for this "realm of the enemy"—MOPAK—the lands from Morocco to Pakistan, with Iran and Syria in between.

My ideal political backdrop to provide the salience for peaceful and just interaction among these several faiths would be the Western Protestant, religiously tolerant and democratic state, assuring all the freedom of religious expression and allowing vital dialogue and lively cross-fertilization such as that which existed in the first centuries of the Christian era, in Medieval *Al-Andalus* in Spain and in present-day Canada, Western Europe, India, and Singapore. This would seem to be the best governmental format to ensure religious vitality and the common good.

Missiologists have sketched various rationales and strategies for these grand designs of faith interactions. Four examples would be Arnold Toynbee, Kenneth Cragg, Vinoth Ramachandra, and J.Z. Smith.

Arnold Toynbee

Arnold Toynbee has ventured a theology of history that sees religions as transcending realities overarching the rise and decline of empires. The quadrilateral of Hinduism and Greek Idealism on the one hand, and Judaism/Christianity and Islam on the other, arise as antidotes to destructive empire, forming an "anti-imperialist matrix of spiritual and ethical truth."[13] Faiths in dialogue offer the best hope for deliverance from mutual destruction. Faiths are the transcendent gifts of God to the transience of world history, allowing the leavening of the eternal kingdom of God to the fleeting empires of this world. Of the 22 empires that have risen and fallen in world history, 19 were less advanced in decadence than the U.S. is at present. Christianity and Islam, and, of course, sister Judaism in particular, share a common heritage and destiny having been pilgrim peoples, living in catacombs and tents, in a world they had not created and in which they could never be at home. Even the invasions and conquests, crusades and holy wars, could not, for Toynbee, mute the salutary effect of "high religion" in world history. These cultures become citadels of truthful and righteous energy, in a world destruction bound by imperial fury.

If the U.S. can avert its collapse as an empire by shunning materialism, sustaining liberty, striving for diversity and ecumenical cooperation, and supporting theological and ethical values, it may yet achieve that state of cultural vibrancy that Toynbee asserts achieves universality and a certain transcendence and become again a "light to the world," the "city on the hill" that beckons the world's huddled masses yearning to breathe free.

In my thesis, such divine blessing will only be achieved if we become an interfaith society by:

- sustaining a strong and dynamic Jewish community at home in America, in Diaspora and in Israel, all the while cleansing this body from the sins of savage capitalism and dispensational Zionism;
- rebuilding a vital Christian witness that again radiates

---

13. Toynbee, *A Study of History*, vol. 12.

throughout culture, while cleansing the sins of manifest destiny and global hegemony; and

- welcoming Islam, supporting its global *Ulama* (community of legal scholars) and its present "greater *jihad*" of striving for its historic pluralism and toleration for all *Ahl al-Kitab* (peoples of the book). Zion in Abrahamic vision is the earthly and divine representation of homecoming after exile and tribulation. As Emmanuel Levinas said once in a lecture in Jerusalem, "Israel's universal vocation and Zion's only purpose is to make possible a discourse addressed to all men in their human dignity so as then to be able to answer for all men our neighbors." This interfaith testimony, welcoming the other world faiths in an atmosphere of respectful and reciprocally edifying witness, is, I believe, the will of God for our time. In this way, America could take its place among the other great world civilizations: Europe, Russia, the Middle East, Africa, India, Asia, and China—together fashioning that cosmos lyrically envisioned by George Herbert where "all the world in every corner sings, my God and King."

Kenneth Cragg

In a massive and monumental work, Bishop Kenneth Cragg, perhaps the most insightful contemporary theological commentator on Islam, professor at Oxford and long-time resident in the Middle East, offers another missiological thesis—not as sweeping and triumphalist as Toynbee—but equally thoughtful and provocative. He spoke of his overarching conviction at a meeting of the Middle East Council of Churches (MECC) in 1999 on the subject of "Judaism, Christianity, and Islam: Divinity in a Political World."

In this address, Cragg reflected on the future of Christian missions in the Muslim world. He noted that missions had evolved through three stages: 1) the era of evangelistic conversion; 2) the period accenting social services, hospitals, and schools; and 3) programs with an emphasis on pastoral and liturgical issues.

Today, as the need for social services has been assumed by indigenous governments, the focus has returned to evangelism—now defined as faith-tradition formulation and formation enriched by intense and profound interfaith dialogue. The emphasis is no longer the conversion of Jews or Muslims, which remain intractable and frustrating, much as Christian and Muslim missions to Japan. Now evangelism accents the formation of discipleship and inculcating communities—in the sociopolitical context of religious freedom. When asked about individual conversion in the American voluntaristic mode, Cragg hesitated, suggesting that we work with "educated villagers," accenting concerted interfaith community development. His main emphasis is on the upbuilding of various Christian communities, all the while calling on the public order for the human right of "free religious expression and the freedom to move among religions." The October 2007 letter of world Muslim leaders to World Christian leaders reflects this "Fatherhood of God/Brotherhood of Man" approach.

Vinoth Ramachandra

Vinoth Ramachandra resonates with Cragg's theme from an "evangelical" purview and J.Z. Smith from an "ecumenical" perspective.

Ramachandra's thesis is that a lively companionship of Word and work is the only viable witness in the world today. Verbal proclamation and social action go hand in hand. His charter is that Christian witness is "about what God has done, is doing, and will do for the world He created and loves."[14] With Cragg, he sees vital mission in the making and nurturing of disciples. Social witness comprises in not perpetuating our cultural norms (*e.g.*, Americanism), but in honoring, attending and loving the poor, oppressed and "least of these." The terrible liability of trying to do this as Westerners and Americans nowadays shifts major responsibility for Christian evangelism in the hands of non-Westerners. With Bishop Cragg, Ramachandra feels strongly that indigenous churches must assume the mantle of leadership in building viable and vital faith communities—engaging in dialogue and concerted social action with other faith communities in order to redeem and transform society.

J.Z. Smith

An "ecumenical" version of Cragg's conviction can be found in J.Z. Smith, the landmark religion scholar of the University of Chicago. In *Relating Religion*, Smith explores, in the mode of his mentor, Mircea Eliade, the

---

14. See Ramachandra, "What is Integral Mission?"

descriptive phenomenon of religion, along with a more normative quest to examine the new interfaith dialogue between Jews, Christians, and Muslims—seeing what this adds to the contemporary phenomenology of religious experience.[15] Smith's own normative thesis contends that the search towards faith (religion) must be *exempli gratia*—an exercise in the thankful participation in the recognition of "new being" (Tillich) in this new world. This renewal can only come from a comparative exploration in which all parties are open to transformation.

Following his master, Eliade, in his eclectic enamorments, yet with an intrigue for the ascending monotheisms and their compelling urgency for new transformative religious conviction, Smith shakes the dust from his abandoned New York City Jewish roots and examines freshly the Abrahamic faiths in their reciprocal complementarity as well as the salutary condemnation and commendation they offer each other for mutual purification. Smith's analysis provides fresh ground for vital religious witness. In several essays, he lays the foundation for a more wholesome mode of intramural witness among the Abrahamic faiths, especially vis-à-vis Israel, replacing the more insidious anti-Semitic and supercessionist view of Judaism implied in the traditional "Israel-as-sign" eschatology of evangelism.

In this view, widespread in Christian theology and dominant throughout Christian history, and now present in a new, virulent form which may be the prevalent Darbyesque heresy of our time, the conversion of the Jews becomes the signal for the inception or culmination of the evangelical "end times" of world history. As antidote to this pernicious understanding, Smith's view, along with recent repentance confessionals by Roman Catholics and other Christian bodies on our anti-Semitic, even genocidal past, put the Jewish and Christian bodies, at long last, on a sound dialogical footing. The challenge of coming centuries will be to extend this rapprochement to Islam.

My own view, developed in *Jew, Christian, Muslim*, finds hope, indeed mutual correction and fulfillment, in what I call "faithful unification" of the three traditions and by contrast, global war and calamity in continuation of the present "fateful trifurcation." For now, the antagonist theorists like Huntington prevail.

---

15. See Smith, *Relating Religion*.

Political Formats

Finally, some comments on the conversion-seeking witnessing and evangelism of religious bodies within various sociopolitical formats. The laws of individual nations can enhance or stifle the evangelistic witness activities of religious bodies. The political ethos also influences the freedom of persons to convert or change faiths, a position all faiths embrace by affirming that conversion can never be compulsory. The societal format also influences the maintenance or sustenance of a particular spiritual/ethical salience in the society. The hard rub comes when each intense monotheism sees perdition in disbelief and apostasy in conversion.

Different political formats include: 1) the model of Roman Catholicism and historic European Christendom; 2) the model of *Al-sharī'ah* states and (*dar al-Islam*) regions; and 3) the model of religious freedom, pluralism, and separation of church and state in modern Protestant and Jewish communities. Each of these political theories has advantages and disadvantages according to differing views of the virtue of liberty and uniformity.

A Policy Proposal

I have surveyed the contemporary crisis in religious unity and witness, noting that our splintered and often irrelevant religious organizations often fail to command attention and loyalty in our time. Such formal organizational structures therefore provoke and persistently spin off fundamentalist reactions such as Christian Zionisms and political dispensationalisms. Muslim *madrassas*, the historic medieval universities in Muslim lands, the textual content that Tony Street of Cambridge has historically examined, often today seem to purvey fanatic certainties and prejudices that cannot stand the light of day of intellectual examination. These defy the remarkable Christian/Muslim concordat that David Ford and others have reached, with Muslim leaders finding common ground and common word between the faiths in the "love of God and love of fellow human beings." Finally, sectarian Jewish organizations often forsake the noble theological and ethical substance of that faith while turning to political maneuverings both defensive and offensive that create strife in the world. So now, in the tent of Abraham, we face a company of unbelievers and pretending believers together hell-bent on setting fire upon the Earth. As a trainer of Christian ministers, I offer a mournful "I'm sorry."

Defensive and simplistic religion is the *soup du jour* of Jews, Christians, and Muslims, but, surprisingly and shockingly, the faithful clamor for more. Meanwhile the moderate (should we say lukewarm?) and those who seek aesthetic and intellectual excellence sit in empty pews. But we yearn for truth, conviction, and righteousness and someday soon, I believe, we will cease slaking our thirst at these "broken cisterns that can hold no water." (Jer 2:13) It is my conviction that these prophetic "days that are coming" (Malachi) will occur when the better impulses of our faith traditions encounter authentically and creatively the spiritual phenomenology of our times.

Today, parochialism and xenophobia seem to have won the contest over conviviality and mutual encouragement. As Christianity further splinters into agonizing schisms and antagonisms, and as alienation from our parental faith, Judaism, and our offspring faith, Islam, intensifies after the Holocaust and into the "war on terrorism," a careful reading of the "signs of the times" and the theological meanings of our history will be an imperative for survival. While Americo-Israeli hegemony seems to command the support of Judaism and Catholic, Protestant, and Orthodox Christendom, at the same time, suicidal and terroristic resistance and martyrdom defending homelands from invasion and occupation appears to have achieved the authority of *mitzvot* and *fatwa* within Islam. All the while beneath the chaos, the epidemiology of faith and the phenomenology of world religious history and hope seem to point in more irenic directions.

Despite the events of September 11th, the ethos today seems to be irrepressibly interreligious. If this is the global spiritual and ethical salience within which our witness must occur in the interfaith context, we will need to recover the brilliant cultural sensitivity of the 14th-century Andalusians, 16th-century Jesuits, or the 19th-century Dutch who understood the great river of Abrahamic faith—now departing into tributaries, now joining in mighty confluence.

Today as *madrassas* near the Red Mosque in Islamabad, Pakistan infiltrate the sanctuary with truckloads of weapons, as the Roman Catholic Archdiocese of Los Angeles settles for $660,000,000 in victim awards and legal fees for 70 years of priest abuse of 500 children, and as Jewish rabbis continue to foment righteous disdain by using the title of "terrorist" for *Hamas* and *Fatah*—the rightful and duly-elected government and elymosenary arm of the Palestinian people—we verge on self-induced, not God-induced, apocalyptic fury.

The essay therefore can conclude by offering an appropriate rationale and practical program for evangelism today in light of what we have proposed to be the intrinsic logic of theology and the extrinsic epidemiology of religion in the world today. To illustrate our point, we first consider the July 6, 2007 announcement of the Vatican on the subject of "the true faith"—a document revisiting and clarifying the pre-September 11th document, "*Dominus Jesus*: A Declaration on the Unicity and Salvific Universality of Jesus Christ and the Church." Alongside this, we will comment on the response of the World Alliance of Reformed Churches (July, 2007) and a concurrent document of "*Dominus Jesus*"—"*Dabru Emet*" of September, 2000.[16] This latter piece, offered by Jewish leaders around the world, including Peter Ochs of our interfaith program, again affirms our position that religious witness today (conversion and religious speech policy) is best formulated with respect to our sister Abrahamic faiths and in light of the global crisis to which animosity these faiths have contributed. As Karl Barth taught, as believers, we must read the world with the Bible in one hand and the newspaper in the other.

Pope Benedict's 2007 announcement was meant to allay perplexing uncertainties that have been vexing the beliefs and life patterns of the faithful in recent years. The times, as we have noted, seem to be demanding greater clarity and conviction while the ecclesial and civil environment has thrown up greater doubts. An assault is felt by the rampant disinvolvement in church caused by an underlying cultural secularism both in America and Europe. Like Protestants, Catholics simply are not observant in Europe. Benedict, however futilely, seems intent on calling Europe back to its Catholic heritage, arguing that neither society nor church can long endure without some renewal of the medieval synthesis. His confrontation with insurgent Islam—which seems to transit throughout Europe into the so-called "clash of civilizations" and the surge of conversions away from mother church into evangelical and Pentecostal communities, especially in Asia, South America, and Africa—constitute a further erosion. Though Catholic faith remains vital in China, it is being outstripped by neo-evangelical house churches always suspect of being

---

16. "*Dabru Emet*" is a Jewish statement that articulates eight principles to guide Jewish-Christian relations/ for more information, see the Jewish-Christian Relations Web site, http://www.jcrelations.net/en?item=1014.

less than loyal to the "sacred state." In China, the Christian upsurge is evidenced not only by the reported 50,000 new converts reported weekly, but also by the fact the Professor K.K. Yeo, of our Garrett-Evangelical faculty, has been asked to form a program in Christian Studies at the distinguished University of Beijing with offerings at the Masters and Doctoral level, along with continuing education for pastors and lay leaders. While the new Roman Catholic Bishop, also approved by the State, has been ratified by the Vatican and now foresees steady growth, most of the dynamic evangelism in the world comes from movements related to the Protestant revolution in Europe—Calvinist, Baptist, evangelical, and Pentecostal. These developments in China pose special political challenge to the magisterial Roman Church and the authoritarian state.

When *"Dominus Jesus"* appears either in origin (2000) or update (2007), this tableau reflects on the Catholic mind as it is challenged by the inescapable interfaith reality. The World Alliance of Reformed Churches, an affiliation of some 100 million Calvinists and Baptists, registers its own dismay to the document. General Secretary Dr. Setri Nyomi comments on the 10 July, 2007 statement of the Congregation of the Doctrine of the Faith that it "seems puzzling at this time in the history of the church and society" and that the "signs of the times" would rather encourage "common witness in our oneness in Christ" and our "commitment to the unity and peace of the world."[17] Though ecclesiastical structures are far less prominent in Protestantism than in the Roman Communion, Reformed Christians—in my view, as a theologian in that heritage—would ask whether in any land and any time the "Word of God" is "rightly preached" and the sacraments are "rightly administered." Only under such conditions is "truth" and "civil righteousness" possible. Amid the plethora of evangelistic efforts and power moves effecting free expression of religion, the Reformed faith seeks to preserve in history free range for biblical-evangelical faith in an atmosphere of religious toleration. As index of the seriousness of this matter, it has often gone to the wall of martyrdom to preserve this freedom of testimony.

At the very least, evangelical Protestantism will insist that absolutist ecclesial/civil forms such as Islam and Roman Catholicism guarantee the rights of religious freedom, expression, and toleration for all citizens. The deal struck between the Afghan Taliban and the government of South

---

17. World Alliance of Reformed Churches document of July 7, 2007.

Korea (binding on its Presbyterian missionaries)—to desist from evangelism activities in that land after the kidnapping of some 20 and the killing of two—becomes problematic in the light of this principle.

"*Dabru Emet*" furthers this understanding in its first principle:

> Jews and Christians worship the same God. Before the rise of Christianity, Jews were the only worshippers of the God of Israel. But Christians also worship the God of Abraham, Isaac, and Jacob; creator of heaven and Earth. While Christian worship is not a viable religious choice for Jews, as Jewish theologians we rejoice that, through Christianity, hundreds of millions of people have entered into relationship with the God of Israel.[18]

My view within the project of interfaith exploration is that the Church, Abrahamic Faith and certainly the State, have not yet reached ultimate truth about who is included and excluded from the kingdom of God and that therefore political programs should remain open. Further proliferation and elaboration of movements within the three Abrahamic families of faith are to be expected. Indeed this openness to the spirit (*semper reformanda*) is the inherent original ethos of each faith tradition at its best. In my view, the *Heilsgeschichte* (holy/salvation history) of our time is still alive and well. Within the Christian movement, it is found in the national baptismal and missionary witness of the Roman, Anglican, and Lutheran churches, in the ethnocentric upholding ministries of the Eastern and Orthodox communities, and in the dynamic evangelical witness springing from the Protestant and para-church movements—the beat goes on. World history remains a process of personal and public transformation in the theological and ethical realms. Throughout the inhabited world and on into the future history of this planet, the concourse of the *Logos*-Gospel, the Messianic-Torah, the synthetic and innovative *Taurut/Injil* of Islam, and the sublime wisdom of the faiths of India (Hinduism and Buddhism) glimmer through the facets of the one jewel of the presence of God in the world. This light radiates into the darkness of our own persistent injustice and violence. Yet, we believe and hope for "The light shines in the darkness, and the darkness did not overcome it." (John 1.5).

---

18. "*Dabru Emet*," 1.

What Do We Do Now?

The final move of this bizarre exercise—surely the strangest course on God ever undertaken—belongs now to each of us. As Gilkey has shown, we are inextricably wrapped up in the reality and meaning of the creation. Verging on heresy, I am still tempted to assert that without God we do not exist nor, if Christ is truly God, does God exist without us. The Triune God is God for and with the Creation where Jesus came to live and die and live evermore in Spirit—with and for this world. Divinity and humanity deeply and inextricably intertwine. During this Spring term that begins in cold and darkness and ends in the high and brilliant summer, we will chart our theology of God and our answer to the question: so what? So let's set sail. Bon Voyage!

INTO GOD'S WORLD

The following is the text of a sermon delivered to the First United Methodist Church, Park Ridge, Illinois on the second Sunday in Easter (April 19, 2009).

Following Karl Barth, I headline my sermon and public lecture at Park Ridge with two texts—from the newspaper on the one hand:

> ... Economics is the greatest challenge facing this country (and the world) in our generation, since the great depression, in the last 100 years. ...[19]

> "The patient has atherosclerosis—vessel blockage. He is on the verge of heart-attack." No alarmist, Princeton Professor and Fed Chairman Ben Bernanke went on with the deft scalpel of a heart surgeon, suggesting that $1 trillion now invested in revascularization and a stent might spare us a myocardial infarction—the heart attack to come.[20] What the doctor failed to mention was that Bush/Greenspan deregulation (lack of preventive medicine) allowed "fast-buck seekers" to take on $40 trillion in debt with only $1 trillion in the bank—hypertension and plaque build-up, to say the least, and an exhausting deflation of the balloon to come. As of Thanksgiving 2008, the American people had lost $12 trillion in

---

19. At a Chicago news conference on November 7, 2008, Barack Obama said "We are facing the greatest economic challenge of our lifetime ... ," and in subsequent speeches, he reiterated the serious economic hurdles facing the U.S.

20. See Isidore, "Hopes Grow for Emergency Rate Cut."

wealth and assets—$5 trillion in housing values and $7 trillion in the stock market. By Easter of 2009, that had risen to 15 trillion. "Moral hazard" already has set in, wherein financiers take risks because of support forthcoming from taxpayers exposing themselves to acute breakdown. We need "jolt" and jar—stability and security. We're in the ICU.[21]

And the Bible in the other:

> Now the whole group of those who believed were of one heart and soul, and no one claimed private ownership of any possessions, but everything they owned was held in common. With great power the apostles gave their testimony to the resurrection of the Lord Jesus, and great grace was upon them all. There was not a needy person among them, for as many as owned lands or houses sold them and brought the proceeds of what was sold. They laid it at the apostles' feet, and it was distributed to each as any had need. (Acts 4.32–35)

Let's take it a little deeper: first, the news on economics. In his book, *The Great Inflation*, Robert Samuelson records some of these elusive facts:

- Venture capital rose from $18 billion in 1997 to $107 billion in 2000.
- NYSE trading volume rose from 5 million shares a day in 1980 to 2 billion in 2006.
- Morgan-Stanley in 1950 had one office of 100 employees; in 2007 the company was in 333 countries with 47,000 employees.
- In 1946, household debt was 23 percent of family income; in 2006, 134 percent.
- Home ownership in 1940 was 44 percent; in 2007, 68 percent.[22]

As President Obama said on Tuesday at Georgetown, it is not sustainable that 40 percent of our national economy comes from speculative financial sectors.

And the corresponding Bible material:

---

21. This section is excerpted from Vaux, *America in God's World*, 18.
22. Samuelson, *The Great Inflation and Its Aftermath*, 218.

> Therefore everyone who hears these words of mine and puts them into practice is like a wise man who built his house on the rock. The rain came down, the streams rose, and the winds blew and beat against that house; yet it did not fall, because it had its foundation on the rock. But everyone who hears these words of mine and does not put them into practice is like a foolish man who built his house on sand. The rain came down, the streams rose, and the winds blew and beat against that house, and it fell with a great crash. (Matt 7.24–27)

Economic behaviors have been influenced by misguided religious convictions—such as those of the so-virtuous Enron executives—that have led to unethical imperatives: rebellious and ungracious religiously animated greed, presumption of righteousness (idolatry), injustice, and contempt for the poor, all on a grand scale. This combination of corporate vice and the consumptive consumers behind it constitutes the evil at the root of the economic crisis.

> ... they that will be rich fall into temptation and a snare ... For the love of money is the root of all evil: which while some coveted after, they have erred from the faith and pierced themselves through with many sorrows" (I Tim 6.9–10).

In salient theological/ethical insight, Judaic conviction at the time of Jesus (*e.g.*, Qumran) perceived evil ("the snares of Belial"/the devil) as threefold: blasphemy (false gods/idolatry), *porneia* (false loves/immorality), and riches (false possessions/injustice).[23]

John Calvin, the great progenitor of the Protestant, Puritan, and Wesleyan faiths, wrote of our biblical passage in his commentary on the manna passage in the Corinthians correspondence. He invokes the image of the peoples of Israel in the desert of Sinai when God alone was their sustenance and guidance. With direction provided by pillars of cloud and alimentation by daily quail and manna, Calvin spoke of all resource and supply of our existence coming from the one provider—the One was the giver of every good gift in oasis and desert, who opened His hand, "satisfying the desire of every living thing." (Ps 145.16)

Manna, a provident and perishable gift was profusely available for all. It was abundant to be shared with all; if it was cordoned off and hoarded, if insatiable greed led anyone to exploit the commons, the manna rotted

---

23. This section is excerpted from Vaux, *America in God's World*, 19–20.

away. Calvin's teaching conveys Acts 4 into what would become the bread of modern economy—Adam Smith and Marx, John Keynes, and Milton Friedman. He put it this way:

> God wills that there be equality among us; that is, none should have too much and none too little (from each according to his bounty and to each according to his need).[24]
>
> Hereby it appeareth what that meaneth, that no man counted anything his own, but they had all things common. For no man had his own privately to himself, that he alone might enjoy the same, neglecting others; but as need required, they were ready to bestow upon all men.[25]

As Easter people, we carry the riches of resurrection life out into the farthest corners of God's world. As he who was rich for our sakes became poor that through his poverty might be rich—so we, like Andrew Carnegie, Bill Gates, or Warren Buffett gave it all away. In Wesley's words, "earning all we can allows us to save all we can and give all we can."[26]

We have various sorts of societies on Earth:

- high capitalist and consumerist;
- high communalist; and
- high crisis and poverty.

America and, to a lesser extent Great Britain, are societies that epitomize the capitalist, free-enterprise economic model.

- In America, nine percent of all people work in the finance industry; in England, it is 20 percent (40 percent floating free capital in finance—can this be channeled into human needs?)
- In America, the top one percent of the population holds 20 percent of the world's wealth.
- America has five percent of the world's population and consumes 30 percent of the world's oil and gas.
- In America, that top one percent pays 30 percent of the public taxes.

24. Calvin, *Commentary Upon the Acts of the Apostles*, Acts 4.32–37.

25. Calvin, *Commentaries on the Second Epistle of Paul the Apostle to the Corinthians*, Chapter 8.

26. Wesley, "Serving God with Mammon, A Sermon on Luke 16.9."

Most of the advanced, civilized societies on Earth provide education, health care, and retirement for the public commonwealth. The present crisis in America has left us with depleted 401Ks and pensions, and we swing in the wind.

Even worse, the poor of our national experience grueling poverty—the average home in Detroit now sells for $6,000. Globally, the poorest also are hit the hardest.

Returning to the Bible, we see that we also follow the evangelical/ethical line of belief and action of 1 John. Call the main points to mind:

- We are in the light. . . . let us walk in the light.
- If we say we have no sin . . . we lie.
- If we say we live in him and do not keep his commandments . . . we lie.
- But if we live in his love, we keep his commandments. (1 John 1.5–10)

Recall also at this point that the commandments include prohibitions against stealing, lying, craving, and coveting.

So basic to the real world of economy, many presidents in the past have condemned greed-mongers. Jefferson and Jackson—and both Roosevelts—denounced "unscrupulous money-changers," what today we might call loan sharks, mortgage brokers, and investment bankers. At the Christmas season of Thanksgiving and giving, Jimmy Stewart (George Bailey) in *It's a Wonderful Life* and Scrooge in *A Christmas Carol* lend voice.

This mentality creates a strong ambivalence: We want to be generous, but we also hope to prosper and provide for family, church, and community. In his inimitable style, Mike Royko once pointed out that the motto of Chicago, *Urbs in Horto* (city in a park), had now become *Ubi est Mea* (where's mine?). Today's class warfare—Main Street vs. Wall Street?—is counterbalanced by a common desire in the president's word to achieve "the American dream."

In all of this confusion, faith leads us to:

- *Acknowledge our interdependence.* If is any one of us is to get rich, it most likely involves someone else getting poor.

- *Recognize that our blessings are God's intentions to bring good for others from our responsible stewardship.* "To whom much is given, much will be required." Those whom God loves, he chastens, and a tree that is to grow needs pruning.

I conclude with a story—you know it well. Two scenarios in Afghanistan. The president, much like his predecessor, says that we must root out terrorists in Afghanistan and their support areas in Pakistan. Terrorists include *Al Qaeda*, the Taliban, the Pakistani partisans who killed Benazir Bhutto, perhaps even the bold young people who attacked Mumbai. Indeed, the Taliban even claimed responsibility for the shooting at a U.S. Immigration Center in Binghamton, New York (April, 2009).

In Obama's words, "When I am president, we will wage the war that has to be won, the first step must be getting off the wrong battlefield in Iraq and taking the fight to the terrorists in Afghanistan and Pakistan. We will disrupt, dismantle, and defeat." May his life be defended, and his policy be just. Now I'm a strong supporter of Barack Obama. I played a role in his campaign, and my pledge was to support him all the way to the White House, though I would be his hardest critic all the way and thereafter.

But it is the other story that interests us this evening of Easter—Greg Mortenson tells the story in his classic book, *Three Cups of Tea*.[27] Left for dead after his companions died in a climb of Pakistan's K2, the world's second-highest mountain in the Kakakoram range, he stumbled near-dead into the small Muslim village of Korphe. Greg's dad was a Christian missionary in Tanzania, where he founded the Kilimanjaro Christian Medical Centre and loved the people of these mountains with all his heart.

The local children embraced Mortenson, as did the Muslim leader of the town who nursed him back to health. One day, he saw the kids writing with sticks in the sand and promised one day to build them a school. Today, 15 years later, 80 schools serve 30,000 children, including 20,000 girls.

We are Easter-ascension-Pentecost people. We are commissioned to go into God's world. Look into your heart and mind, into the life and soul of this great congregation. Find afresh that Great Commission, and go with free confidence as the cosmic Lord Christ, who promises, "I am with you always, to the end of the age" (Matt 28.20).

---

27. See Mortenson and Relin, *Three Cups of Tea*.

THE BREAD OF ANGELS

The following is the text of a sermon delivered to the Murchison Isom Temple CME Church in Chicago on Good Friday, 2009.

Like Judge Judy, Pastor Judy will tell you that when I teach, I ask that you hold the Bible in one hand and the daily newspaper in the other. I teach my students first to do scripture reading and reasoning. We are to mull over, chew on, munch on, digest the word of God. God in Christ is *panis angelica*, the bread of angels, like the Medieval monks of Munich (Munchen), we munch on the Word—we are companions who break bread together. With Jacob, we wrestle to the ground the messenger coming down the ladder from heaven. With Ezekiel, we "open the book and eat it." (Eze 23) With the psalmist, we "taste and see that the Lord is good," "the Lord is God." (Ps 34.8) *Gott* and *gut* in all languages are the same word: God and good; *Dieu* and *donne*; man and manna.

The scripture portions and servings for us this week are Passover, Holy Monday and Thursday, Good Friday. The events Monday are cleansing the temple from those who abuse the animal sacrifice (those who sell the pigeons by gouging the poor then demanding temple cash while Passover folk have their own tender) from the false money changers. The widow's mite belongs here. Now penniless, she offers her last haypenny, a copper silver and the crooked temple lawyers, watching her keenly—now she is bankrupt, her last coin, now they can foreclose on her small shack, her roof and floor, her little security. Now, as in Isaiah, they can join house to house and field to field (Isa 5.8). They had given her bad money, a subprime mortgage that rapidly becomes super-prime, and they knew that she would soon be desperate and helpless (in Detroit today, the average home for sale is $6,000, and Chicago's South side is getting just as bad!), and the scheisters gather like vultures they snatch up foreclosures at auction. These—the pay-day loan sharks, Father Michael Pfleger's drug and paraphernalia peddlers, those who grow rich by devouring the poor, by trampling on the widows and children—are alive and well.

Then, on Thursday in the garden, there is the other thief in the night—the one with 30 pieces of silver in his pouch, reading to betray his own rabbi, the beloved Son, the one sent over by his own choice to die as ransom, to bear the debt. Remember Joseph in the pretty coat, like "Little Joe" with his dream coat. Joseph is betrayed by his own brothers, kidnapped and thrown in a hole, abandoned and sold into slavery. The drama of the seventh commandment, "do not steal." If they only knew he would become vizier of Egypt, chancellor of the Exchequer, dispenser of the great stores of grain, ruler from the throne (Pss 84, 87), that he would become their savior from starvation—*panis angelicus*.

Then comes the day, the grotesque Friday we dare call good, like many days in those days, hundreds of trees and cross logs dotted the Palestine skies. It's what you do with zealots and terrorists, life and vitality poured out, water and bread, blood, sweat, and tears given over, and that thief on the next rugged cross—the only one ever who could truly say, "I am crucified with Christ." Then the still descent from the cross in the cool of evening, the rich guy from Arimathea, Joseph, a counselor, an *advocatus*, a solicitor, a lawyer, one good and just, for a change. And then the tumultuous events of Holy Saturday and Sunday, the long journey to the gates of hell, the release of captivity of humanity—of all the fallen creation—and then . . . But that's the next chapter.

This mid-week drama I address in *America in God's World* under the rubrics of security and economy. So, as we shift to the hand of the daily news (which, by the way, is the literal meaning of *gospel*) and move to discussion time, there are a few extracts for us to chew on this evening. Let me collapse these two themes security and economy: how do we secure the economy so that we can give to the poor? How can we get the bread on its way to Mombassa, Kenya?

I conclude this message with some remarks from this book:

Security and Economy

Security
In exploring America's place in God's world, we consider initially the realm of militarism and might—policies to insure national safety at home and vested interests abroad (*e.g.*, energy to run the nation's engine). As people of God, we are to be advocates of all national sovereignties in a world that we share as a commonwealth. God "has made of one blood all nations to dwell on the face of the Earth, determining the times and bounds of their habitations" (Acts 17.26). We are the advocates of nation Israel and nation Iran, even though certain exigencies may make us temporarily adversaries. National and global security are therefore mandates. Homeland security in a safe, respectful, and peaceful world is the right of all nations. In addition to defense of motherland, this means protection

from attack, invasion, and occupation. Security, then, is the first thematic topic explored in all four sections of this book.

Economy
Economy is the second cross-cutting theme. Resources, work, commerce, trade, and livelihood are perquisites of the well-being of all peoples in God's world—including America. Theologically conceived, work is the blessing and curse of existence. It is the task that both animates and ages our being, bestowing joy and drudgery. Writ large, economy is the management and stewardship of the local, national and global house—*oikos*—the habitation and cohabitation of our space/time being in the world. Economy, a cultural phenomenon with deep theological resonance, is proffered providence and the sphere of justice and sharing. Now it has become secular in meaning to the danger point of losing its ethical and theological charter.

For good and ill, economy is the enclosing envelope of our co-humanity—inciting both virtue and violence. Crisis has ensued as *ora et labora* has become tedious, hand labor has been converted to industry, then business, then management, and finally into abstract systems such as finance. Do such virtual powers exist? Virtually, yes. Should they?—a legitimate question. This fall from face-to-face and hand-to-hand dealings to "virtual finance" is highly problematic. "Finance," a new entity created by entrepreneurs seeking profits and fees, is made up of an array of phenomena called hedge funds, leverage, securitization, and bundled liquid assets. It is, in large, a human fabrication in the past few years, perhaps a demonic structure in the biblical language of "the powers of the world."

In the fallen world, these exist over against the power of God.[28] This unjust and inhuman system of virtual transactions culminates in the sad spectacle of no one in the world knowing who owns my mortgage. We also see it when General Motors Corporation pleads for financial bailout from the only still viable financial entity—the Federal Government—that pale facsimile of the sacred body politic. Economics rightly belongs to *ecumene*—the one God-derived habitation for all humanity—so it must not become a demonic human construal bringing injury and death to humanity and the world itself.[29]

---

28. See Wink, *Engaging the Powers*; *Naming the Powers*; *The Powers That Be*; *Unmasking the Powers*; and Migliore, *The Power of God and the Gods of Power*.

29. This section is excerpted from Vaux, *America in God's World*, 3–4.

Idolatry, Immortality, and Injustice

Economic behaviors have been influenced by misguided religious convictions—such as those of the so-virtuous Enron executives—that have led to unethical imperatives: rebellious and ungracious religiously animated greed, presumption of righteousness (idolatry), injustice, and contempt for the poor—all on a grand scale. This combination of corporate vice and the consumptive consumers behind it constitutes the evil at the root of the economic crisis.

> . . . they that will be rich fall into temptation and a snare...For the love of money is the root of all evil: which while some coveted after, they have erred from the faith and pierced themselves through with many sorrows" (I Tim 6.9–10).

In salient theological/ethical insight, Judaic conviction at the time of Jesus (*e.g.*, Qumran) perceived evil ("the snares of Belial"/the devil) as threefold: blasphemy (false gods/idolatry), *porneia* (false loves/immorality), and riches (false possessions/injustice).[30]

Sharing or Stealing

Theologically and ethically speaking, economy is a matter of sharing and/or stealing. At present, we watch a spectacle on this matter in the seas off East Africa. Somalia pirates have commandeered hundreds of international ships and held their crews and cargo for ransom. Left without options, companies usually pay up. The U.S. and NATO cry to spend millions and send vast security and attack flotillas into the waters to break the barbarous and brazen acts of stealing. One wonders whether the outlay of funds might better be used to create jobs in the desperate economies of the horn of Africa. Do the pirates steal because we stole from them in the first place, *i.e.*, the colonial enterprise of extracting precious minerals (didn't the nativity gift of Frankincense originate in Mogadishu?) Sharing or stealing? Perhaps one prevents, provokes, or ameliorates the other.[31]

Primacy of Distributive Justice

Genesis 1 juxtaposes creation and Sabbath. The priests who compose this material know that making the world "good" is holy gift, worthy of worship. Creation means sacred art and act. Though sublimely free and cre-

---

30. This section is excerpted from Vaux, *America in God's World*, 19–20.

31. This section is excerpted from Vaux, *America in God's World*, 24–25.

ative, it is not haphazard trial and error. It is restful contemplation—from everlasting to everlasting. It is evocative and beatific: Praise is shown forth and exultation is offered in return.

The essence of Sabbath is the pause to glorify as one is glorified: "God opens his hand and satisfies the desire of every living thing" (Ps 145.16). The striking aspect of God's self-rest is that it is shared with each and every creature: ". . . your slaves, your children, your donkey and goat, even the refugee in your town" (Deut 5.14). It thus becomes a work of justice and equality. Indeed justice is the substance of creation as creation is the vehicle of justice.

The meaning of this crucial point for my thesis is that power is profuse and diffuse—meant to be shared, not concentrated.[32] Distributive justice is the divine gift enabled through human implementation. Power is in service to redemption: It exists for the empowerment of the creation, of each creature. It cannot be restricted to personal or national purpose. It cannot be contorted from edification to domination. Here the nuance of my thesis becomes clear. Empire is not, *per se*, wrong. It becomes wrong and dangerous as it betrays the purpose of power—which is divine justice showered and distributed on each and every creature.[33]

Call to Sacrifice and Service or Destruction and Death

". . . Once to every man and nation comes the moment to decide, In the strife of Truth with Falsehood, for the good or evil side . . ."[34] This occasion of decision is called temptation or the "valley of the shadow." In the paradigmatic depiction of the people of Israel (or Buddha, Jesus, the Church, or Islam) the Mount of temptation or valley of the shadow is the moment where decision is made about how to live and die.

- Do we live or die to God or the self?
- Do we live or die to justice and for others or to violence and harm?
- Do we live reconciled to family, neighbor, even our enemies?
- Do we live in self-contempt, unforgiving guilt, and destruction or to grace and life?

---

32. See Migliore, *The Power of God and the Gods of Power*.
33. This section is excerpted from Vaux, *America in God's World*, 37–38.
34. Lowell, "The Present Crisis."

Clint Eastwood's film, *Gran Torino*,[35] culminates his life-long and searching quest for these issues of meaning (ontology) of existence in God's world (If indeed, there is a God!). His masterpiece embraces all of these dimensions of *Why? What for? And where to?* (*cf.* Heidegger)

The film is set in the job-starved, refugee-inhabited (Hmong, Palestinian, and Southern slave descendents, etc.) Detroit of the early 21st century. Eastwood portrays and directs the late-life story of Walter Kowalski, a veteran of Korea with an unbearable memory. He's one of the last white-ethnic residents in a Hmong and poor-black neighborhood. Drinking and smoking his already blood-expectorating lungs toward death in a frame house somewhere—it could be out along 100 Mile road—he struggles as a profane, bigoted widower to find some meaning in his life.[36] Estranged from his neglected and petty sons and daughter-in-law, his saucy granddaughter tells him she craves his vintage 1972 Gran Torino after he dies.

The life/death moment rises when the two Hmong teen-agers next door, who have changed his bigoted heart and become his friends, are brutally bullied, raped, and intimidated to the point of shooting up their home. Walt and Thao contemplate revenge. The boy-priest, Father Janovich, who has confronted Walt's salvation destiny at the behest of his deceased wife ("He must come to confession"), shadows him to the gangster's home, but is forced by police to leave just before Walt's denouement—having made his terrible choice.

He confronts the four gang members as night falls in a *chiaroscuro-*Rembrandt-like profile—reminiscent of Eastwood's early westerns and his *Unforgiven*. He reaches into his breast pocket and they riddle his already moribund body with AK-47s. As his deposed body exsanguinates in the dust, the hand falls from his breast-pocket with his Zippo lighter—an award for his service in Korea. As we glimpse the lighter, we see in the darkness that covers the Earth the crystal sparkle of received confession and pardon of Walt's Cain/Abel crime in which he had shot and killed 13 boys—the last one in the face. The film ends as the gang is put away for life, Walt's white Lab Daisy is with Thao as they drive along Elysian green fields on Jefferson Avenue with his newly inherited Gran Torino, and Eastwood sings at his Jazz piano.

35. *Gran Torino*, produced by Clint Eastwood, Warner Bros. Pictures, 2008.

36. "Candide" (Libretto), lyrics by Richard Wilbur, score by Leonard Bernstein, 1956.

Conclusion

I have followed through on my thesis that the present crisis of America's place and activity in God's world has deleterious aspects provoked by underlying deficient theologies. I have probed corrective theologies offered by the best minds on the matters under discussion, and these have supplied my constructive theological proposals. It is now up to all of us to see what can be done to right the course of our beloved nation—in church, synagogue and mosque and in the corridors of public life—especially politics, economics, and environment. By God we can do it, yes we can![37]

JEWS AND CHRISTIANS

Many questions remain as we conclude this study. Some remain between Christians and Jews. These will serve as an indicator of important unresolved matters that we are challenged to address in an anticipated endeavor entitled "Project Interfaith."

In an important volume of theological reflection, the eminent secular philosopher and self-designated methodological atheist Jürgen Habermas explores the intricacies and profound dangers evoked in the relationship between Christians and Jews throughout history. A salient essay, "Israel or Athens: Where Does Anamnestic Reason Belong? Johann Baptist Metz on Unity Amidst Multicultural Plurality," looks at Father Metz's incisive analysis of what has gone wrong in the interactive theological history between Christians and Jews.[38]

Metz, a protégé of Karl Rahner (both of whom were my colleagues in 1972 when I was on sabbatical at Max Planck Institute of Economics in Strasbourg), waged a career-long engagement with his Bavarian Catholic tradition and with the broader Christian (Protestant) heritage—urging Christians to come to terms with a modern secular perspective. Enlightenment thought has had to top intellectual priority of healing the scandal of the diminishment and distancing the relation and affinity with Jews. Cultural anti-Semitism and Judaocide has fashioned a grievous schism, which threatens to irreparably harm both faith bodies.

Habermas agrees with Metz that the crucial moment for rapprochement with Judaism comes in recovering the rational social-justice ethos

---

37. This section is excerpted from Vaux, *America in God's World*, 150–51.
38. See Habermas, "Israel or Athens: Where Does Anamnestic Reason Belong?"

of the Enlightenment—both philosophical and religious—as this ethos is supplied not only by Greece and Rome (Hellenism), but also by a robust Hebraism draw from Torah and prophets:

> If the biblical vision of salvation does not mean simply liberation from individual guilt, but also implies collective liberation from situations of liberation and oppression . . . then the eschatological drive to save those who suffer unjustly connects up with those impulses toward freedom which have characterized modern European history.[39]

Freedom and justice, truth and peace, are the synthetic gift of reason and revelation, Athens and Jerusalem. These synergies constituitive of civilization, also portend the resolution of the agony of discrimination, ghetto, and ultimately holocaust—which has driven Christianity from the bosom of Abraham, Isaac, and Israel.

Habermas is a keen enough historian to know also that the Enlightenment itself has contributed to the cultural mind that caused the *Shoah*. Not only Medieval Catholicism and Martin Luther's vitriolic grace vs. law anti-Semitism, but systemic rationalism all add to the cultural poison.

My student, Darrius Hills, proposed today in an excellent homily in Garrett's chapel that the prophetic imperative in Joel 2—"'Then afterwards, I will pour out my Spirit on all flesh; your sons and daughters shall prophesy, your old men shall dream dreams, and your young men shall see visions. Even on the male and female slaves, in those days, I will pour out my spirit.'" (Joel 2.28–29)

In this pivotal scripture, which becomes the signpost of *Shavuot* and Pentecost, we see the power of the spirit of Torah, which insists that all flesh—great and small, male and female, are emancipated in the Decalogic grace of God, and are therefore bearers of divine Word and Spirit. By tracing the memory of the courageous pioneering spirit of Sojourner Truth, Rosa Parks, and other saints in feminist ministry of the spirit, Hills drew in the universal political impulse of freedom and emancipation, a gift in part of the Kantian and Hegelian esuality doctrine of the Enlightenment, anchored squarely in the prophetic traditions of Israel. To this spirit of the rational Enlightenment, he joined the prophetic spirit of Numbers 11, its eschatological and earthly celebration of Torah, flames of fire and tongues of spirit, a synthetic and synergistic whole, and he got it right.

39. Ibid., 130.

In the same universal, rational, and emancipatory spirit, Habermas affirms with Father Metz a Judaocentric and retrieval of law and prophets where the Christian posture of *ecclesia triumphans* is chastened and transformed into justice and equality through the Hebraic prophetic spirit of "listening to the cry of the oppressed and the demand for universal justice."[40]

In this rejection of Hellenism and recovery of Hebraism, Metz finds Christianity able to rediscover sacred "remembrance." When the faith is confined to the categories and capacities of Hellenized philosophy, it cuts itself off ("is halved") from the constituting memory that is the theological and ethical substance of the faith, while the faith is aided by a handmaiden philosophy—in the way that early Christianity prospered within the rational envelope of neo-Platonism. Metz asks if there is an Hebraic rational, philosophical, wisdom package to house modern Jewish and Christian thought.

Metz offers a complex of faith factors to solve the malaise of animosity between Jews and Christians. Factors embraced include memory, saving healing, sympathy to suffering, and redemption. The broad complex of theodicy—God, justice, mercy, and reconciliation—is woven into the fabric of active personal and collective faith. This coalescence overcomes bias and discrimination, reestablishes the faith as a universal conviction, and relieves the necessity of anger, animosity, violence, death wish—and eventually the desire to demonize and destroy the other. Only in this manner can the psychology, sociobiology, and theology of lethal prejudice be overcome. Only a new access to the One God of the world—the God of Abraham, of *Logos*, the second God in heaven, the One who comes to the world and in Spirit pervades the world. Only when this cache of meaning is joined to reason and public action can such pathology find healing.

Recovery of this vital and theological and ethical impulse is mediated through what Metz calls "*anamnestic* reason." This *memoria* reaches back for "Word" mediated through Moses and the prophets. "God" in this living memory is not a philosophical concept but a dynamic power in life experience. In my view, the sustaining strength of thought and belief is here joined to the companionship of the being and "way" of God—expressed in self-verifying and validating faith. Venturing confession conveys confirmation. The God confronted in Abraham's venture,

---

40. Ibid., 130.

Moses' adventure, Job's trial, and Jesus' journey to Golgotha and Emmaus is "saving remembrance" (Metz) which, when "pondered" (Luke 2.19) in heart and mind becomes sustaining faith.

Such remembrance also is hope. Passover also is Easter. From their mentor Karl Rahner, protégés Metz and Moltmann glimpse a new theological anthropology of proleptic reason where God as beyond and ahead dwells as care in our being as hope: knowledge becomes prescience as in sound and sight we feel reverberations and reflections—perceiving again the Yahweh Moses and Abraham first premonitored: "I will be whom I will be." (Exod 3)

In the great ages, when reason was applied as handmaiden to revelation—neo-Platonism and Aristotelianism, Augustine, Aquinas, Calvin, Kant, Hegel, Barth, Levinas, and Derrida, to name a few—there was a full complement of belief and intellectual formulation.

In terms of this essay on interfaith associations among the branches of Abraham, I argue that recovering the pathways of both revelation and reason has a chance to heal the breach between Christians and Jews and therefore perhaps eventuate ultimately in better relations of these two foundational bodies and the faith heritage (Islam) that arises from Judaism and Christianity. The "parting of the ways" between Jews and Christians has had grievous and distorting effect on both bodies. Islam, in part, steps into that breach to perpetuate what might be called the faith/ethics import of a Jewish Christianity that disappeared from the world in the Roman holocaust (66–70 c.e. and following). In sum, interfaith reasoning helps save faith and reason in the interfaith world.

Bibliography

Ali, Kecia and Leaman, Oliver. *Islam: The Key Concepts*. New York: Routledge, 2008.
Armstrong, Karen. *A History of God: The 4,000-Year Quest of Judaism, Christianity, and Islam*. New York: Ballantine, 1993.
Arnold, Matthew. *The Great Prophecy of Israel's Restoration: Isaiah, Chapters 40–66*. London: Macmillan, 1875.
Augustine, *The City of God*. New York: Penguin, 1984.
Berger, Peter. "Between Relativism and Fundamentalism," The American Interest Online (September/October 2006), www.the-american-interest.com.
Bloom, Harold. *Jesus and Yahweh: The Names Divine*. New York: Riverhead, 2005.
Bonhoeffer, Dietrich. *The Cost of Discipleship*. Norwich, UK: SCM-Canterbury, 2001.
———. *Ethics*, Internet Encyclopedia of Philosophy, www.iep.utm.edu/b/bonhoeff.htm.
———. *Letters and Papers from Prison*. New York: Touchstone, 1997.
Borg, Marcus. *Jesus: Uncovering the Life, Teachings, and Relevance of a Religious Revolutionary*. New York: HarperOne, 2006.
Borowitz, Eugene B. "The Torah, Written and Oral, and Human Rights: Foundations and Deficiencies." *Concilium, The Ethics of World Religions and Human Rights*, eds. Hans Küng and Jürgen Moltmann, 1990.
Boyarin, Daniel. *Border Lines: The Partition of Judaeo-Christianity*. Philadelphia: University of Pennsylvania Press, 2004.
———. *Dying for God: Martyrdom and the Making of Christianity and Judaism*. Palo Alto, CA: Stanford University Press, 1999.
Breslauer, Daniel S. *A New Jewish Ethics*. Lewiston, NY: Edwin Mellen, 1983.
Brockopp, Jonathan E., ed. *Islamic Ethics of Life: Abortion, War, and Euthanasia*. Columbia, SC: University of South Carolina Press, 2003.
Buber, Martin. *On Zion: The History of an Idea*, trans. Stanley Godman. Syracuse, NY: Syracuse University Press, 1997.
Calvin, John. *Commentaries on the Second Epistle of Paul the Apostle to the Corinthians*. Grand Rapids, MI: Christian Classics Ethereal Library, www.ccel.org/ccel/calvin/calcom40.html.
———. *Commentary Upon the Acts of the Apostles*, Volume 1. Grand Rapids: MI: Christian Classics Ethereal Library, www.ccel.org/ccel/calvin/calcom36.html.
Chittick, William C. *The Heart of Islamic Philosophy: The Quest for Self-Knowledge in the Teachings of Afdal al-Din Kashani*. Oxford: Oxford University Press, 2001.
"The Christian Definition of the Four Virtues." Grand Rapids, MI: Christian Classics Ethereal Library, www.ccel.org/ccel/schaff/npnf104.iv.iv.xvii.html.

Delaney, Carol. *Abraham on Trial: The Social Legacy of Biblical Myth*. Princeton, NJ: Princeton University Press, 1998.

Dorff, Elliot N. *To Do the Right and the Good: A Jewish Approach to Modern Social Ethics*. Philadelphia: The Jewish Publication Society, 2002.

Facultés jésuites de Paris, *L'exégèse patristique de Romains 9–11: Grâce et liberté: Israël et nations; Le mystère du Christ*. Paris: Centre Sèvres, 2007.

Feldman, Noah. *After Jihad: America and the Struggle for Islamic Democracy*. New York: Farrar, Straus, and Giroux, 2003.

———. *What We Owe Iraq: War and the Ethics of Nation Building*. Princeton, NJ: Princeton University Press, 2004.

Fitzmyer, J. *Romans: Anchor Bible*. New York: Doubleday, 1993.

Fish, Stanley. "Religion Without Truth," the *New York Times*, March 31, 2007.

Ford, David F. "An Interfaith Wisdom: Scriptural Reasoning Between Jews, Christians, and Muslims," in *The Promise of Scriptural Reasoning*, David Ford and C.C. Pecknold, eds. Hoboken, NJ: Wiley-Blackwell, 2007.

———. *Theology: A Very Short Introduction*. New York: Oxford University Press, 2000.

Forell, George Wolfgang. *Ethics of Decisions: An Introduction to Christian Ethics*. Philadelphia: Muhlenberg, 1955.

Gelb, Leslie H. "Dual Loyalties," *The New York Times*, September 23, 2007.

Habermas, Jürgen. *The Divided West*. Cambridge, UK: Polity, 2006.

———. "Israel or Athens: Where Does Anamnestic Reason Belong? Johann Baptist Metz on Unity Amidst Multicultural Plurality" in *Religion and Rationality: Essays on Reason, God, and Modernity*. Cambridge, MA: MIT Press, 2002.

Harkness, Georgia. *Christian Ethics*. Nashville: Abingdon, 1958.

Hauerwas, Stanley. *The Hauerwas Reader*. Durham, NC: Duke University Press, 2001.

———. *The Peaceable Kingdom: A Primer in Christian Ethics*. Notre Dame, IN: University of Notre Dame Press, 1991.

Heschel, Abraham. *God in Search of Man: A Philosophy of Judaism*. New York: Farrar, Strauss, and Giroux, 1976.

Hollinger, Dennis P. *Choosing the Good: Christian Ethics in a Complex World*. Grand Rapids: Baker, 2002.

"Islamic Ethics," Wikipedia: The Free Encyclopedia, hypertext, http://en.wikipedia.org/wiki/Islamic_ethics.

Illich, Ivan. *In the Vineyard of the Text*. Chicago: University of Chicago Press, 1993.

Isidore, Chris. "Hopes Grow for Emergency Rate Cut," *CNN Money*, September 26, 2008, http://money.cnn.com.

Jenkins, Phillip. *God's Continent: Christianity, Islam, and Europe's Religious Crisis*. New York: Oxford University Press, 2007.

Jewett, Robert and Lawrence, John. *Captain America and the Crusade Against Evil: The Dilemma of Zealous Nationalism*. Grand Rapids: Eerdmans, 2004.

Jewett, Robert, et al. *Romans: A Commentary-Hermeneia: A Critical and History Commentary on the Bible*. Minneapolis: Fortress, 2006.

Goodman, Martin. *Rome and Jerusalem: The Clash of Ancient Civilizations*. New York: Knopf, 2007.

Grelot, Pierre. *Une Tosephta targumique sur Genèse xxii dans un manuscrit liturgique de la Geniza du Caire*, in *REJ*, xvi (cxvi), Ms. T-S, B 8/9, 1957.

Johnson, F. Ernest. *Patterns of Ethics in America Today*. New York: Harper, 1960.

Juul, Donald. *Messianic Exegesis: Christological Interpretation of the Old Testament in Early Christianity*. Minneapolis: Fortress, 1992.
Kant, Immanuel. *The Metaphysics of Morals*. Cambridge, UK: Cambridge University Press, 1995.
Kerner, J. *Die Ethik der Johannes—Apokalypse in Vergleich mit der des 4 Esra*. Berlin: Walter de Gruyter, 1998.
Kierkegaard, Søren. *Fear and Trembling*, Alastair Hannay, trans. New York: Penguin, 1985.
Kravitz, Leonard and Olitzky, Kerry M., eds. *Pirke Avot: A Modern Commentary on Jewish Ethics*. New York: UAHC, 1993.
Levenson, Jon D. *The Death and Resurrection of the Beloved Son: The Transformation of Child Sacrifice in Judaism and Christianity*. New Haven: Yale University Press, 1993.
———. *Resurrection and the Restoration of Israel: The Ultimate Victory of the God of Life*. New Haven: Yale University Press, 2006.
———. *Sinai and Zion: An Entry Into the Jewish Bible*. New York: HarperOne, 1987.
Lowell, James Russell. "The Present Crisis," 1844.
Luther, Martin. *D. Martin Luthers Werke; kritische Gesamtausgabe (1883)*. Vienna: H. Böhlau, 1908, www.archive.org/details/dmartinlutherswo7luthgoog.
Mayer, Arno J. *Why Did the Heavens Not Darken? The 'Final Solution' in History*. New York: Pantheon, 1998.
Meeks, Wayne A. *The Origins of Christian Morality: The First Two Centuries*. New Haven: Yale University Press, 1993.
Melville, Herman. *Moby Dick*. London: Collector's Library, 2004.
Migliore, Daniel L. *The Power of God and the Gods of Power*. Louisville: Westminster John Knox, 2008.
Miles, Jack. *God: A Biography*. New York: Alfred A. Knopf, 1995.
Moltmann, Jürgen. *The Crucified God: The Cross of Christ as the Foundation and Criticism of Christian Theology*. Minneapolis: Fortress, 1974.
Murad, Abdal Hakim. *Bombing Without Moonlight: The Origins of Suicidal Terrorism*. Bristol, UK: Amal, 2008.
Naqvi, Syed Nawab Haider. *Ethics and Economics: An Islamic Synthesis*. Leicester, UK: The Islamic Foundation, 1981.
Niebuhr, H. Richard. *Radical Monotheism and Western Culture: With Supplementary Essays*. Louisville: Westminster John Knox, 1993.
Niebuhr, Reinhold. *The Nature and Destiny of Man: A Christian Interpretation—Human Nature*. Louisville: Westminster John Knox, 1941/1964.
Mortenson, Greg and Relin, David Oliver. *Three Cups of Tea: One Man's Mission To Promote Peace...One School at a Time*. New York: Penguin, 2007.
Ochs, Peter. Introduction to "The Rules of Scriptural Reasoning," in *The Journal of Scriptural Reasoning*, no. 2.1 (May 2002), http://etext.virginia.edu/journals/ssr/issues/volume2/number1/ssr02-01-e01.html.
———. *The Return to Scripture in Judaism and Christianity: Essays in Postcritical Scriptural Interpretation*. Mahwah, NJ: Paulist, 1993.
———. "Speaking the Truth (*Dabru Emet*)," October 14, 2007 (Jewish Responses) and Kenneth L. Vaux, "Comment on the Document 'Common Word,'" October 2007 (Christian Responses) on the Web site of A Common Word, www.acommonword.com.

O'Donovan, Oliver. *Resurrection and Moral Order: An Outline for Evangelical Ethics.* Grand Rapids: Eerdmans, 1986/1994.

Pelikan, Jaroslav. *Mary Through the Centuries: Her Place in the History of Culture.* New Haven: Yale University Press, 1998.

Peters, F.E. *The Children of Abraham: Judaism, Christianity, Islam.* Princeton, NJ: Princeton University Press, 2004.

Polkinghorne, John and Welker, Michael. *The End of the World and the Ends of God: Science and Theology on Eschatology.* Harrisburg, PA: Trinity Press International, 2000.

Pope Benedict, Paraphrase of Pope Benedict XVI's First Encyclical Letter, December 25, 2005, www.vatican.va/holy_father/benedict_xvi/encyclicals/documents/hf_ben-xvi_enc_20051225_deus-caritas-est_en.html.

Ramachandra, Vinoth. "What is Integral Mission?" (unpublished paper).

Sacks, Jonathan. *Faith in the Future: The Ecology of Hope and the Restoration of Family, Community, and Faith.* Macon, GA: Mercer University Press, 1997.

———. *To Heal a Fractured World: The Ethics of Responsibility.* New York: Random House, 2005.

Samuelson, Robert J. *The Great Inflation and Its Aftermath: The Past and the Future of American Affluence.* New York: Random House, 2008.

Saarinen, Risto. "Ethics in Luther's Theology: The Three Orders," in *Moral Philosophy on the Threshold of Modernity*, J. Kraye and R. Saarinen, eds., 195–215, www.springerlink.com/content/n3728v67747v8267/fulltext.pdf.

Schweiker, William, Johnson, Michael A., and Jung, Kevin, eds. *Humanity Before God: Contemporary Faces of Jewish, Christian, and Islamic Ethics.* Minneapolis: Fortress, 2006.

Schweitzer, A. *The Quest for the Historical Jesus*, W. Montgomery, trans. New York: Macmillan, 1968.

Segal, Alan F. "He who did not spare his own son," in P. Richardson and J.D. Hurd (eds.), *From Jesus to Paul.* Waterloo, ON: Wilfrid Laurier University Press, 1984.

Sherwin, Byron L. *How To Be a Jew: Ethical Teachings of Judaism.* Northvale, NJ: J. Aronson, 1992.

———. *Jewish Ethics for the Twenty-First Century: Living in the Image of God.* Syracuse, NY: Syracuse University Press, 2000.

Sherwood, Yvonne. "Binding–Unbinding: Divided Responses of Judaism, Christianity, and Islam to the 'Sacrifice' of Abraham's Beloved Son," in *Journal of the AAR* 72:4 (Dec. 2004).

Smith, Jonathan Z. *Relating Religion: Essays in the Study of Religion.* Chicago: University of Chicago Press, 2004.

Spiegel, Shalom. *The Last Trial: On the Legends and Lore of the Command of Abraham to Offer Isaac as a Sacrifice—The Akedah 1899-1984.* Woodstock, VT: Jewish Lights, 1993.

Stark, Rodney. *Cities of God: The Real Story of How Christianity Became an Urban Movement and Conquered Rome.* New York: HarperOne, 2007.

Stassen Glen H. and Gushee, David P. *Kingdom Ethics: Following Jesus in Contemporary Context.* Downers Grove, IL: InterVarsity, 2003.

Teilhard de Chardin, Pierre. *Le Phenomena Humaine.* Paris: Editions du Seuil, 1955.

Telushkin, Joseph A. *A Code of Jewish Ethics, Volume 2: Love Your Neighbor As Yourself.* New York: Random House, 2009.

Toynbee, Arnold J. *A Study of History: Abridgement of Volumes I–VI*. New York: Oxford University Press, Inc. 1946/1974, Volume 12.
Trimingham, J. Spencer. *Islam in Ethiopia*. Oxford: Oxford University Press, 1952.
Van Buren, Paul Matthews. *According to the Scriptures: The Origins of the Gospels and of the Church's Old Testament*. Grand Rapids: Eerdmans, 1998.
Van Hooft, S. "The Meaning of Suffering," *Hastings Center Report*, 28 (5).
Van Leeuwen, Arend Theodoor. *Christianity in World History: The Meeting of the Faiths of East and West*. New York: Scribner, 1966.
Vaux, Kenneth L. *An Abrahamic Theology for Science*. Eugene, OR: Wipf & Stock, 2007.
———. *America in God's World: Theology, Ethics, and the Crises of Bases Abroad, Bad Money, and Black Gold*. Eugene, OR: Wipf & Stock, 2009.
———. *Birth Ethics: Religious and Cultural Values in the Genesis of Life*. New York: Crossroads, 1989.
———. *Death Ethics: Religious and Cultural Values in Prolonging and Ending Life*. New York: Continuum, 1996.
———. *Ethics and the Gulf War: Religion, Rhetoric, and Righteousness*. Oxford: Westview, 1992.
———. *Ethics and the War on Terrorism*. Eugene, OR: Wipf & Stock, 2002.
———. *Jew, Christian, Muslim: Faithful Unification or Fateful Trifurcation? Word, Way, Worship and War in the Abrahamic Faiths*. Eugene, OR: Wipf & Stock, 2003.
———. Syllabus for Christian Moral Theology class, Fall 2008.
Vermès, Géza. *Scripture and Tradition in Judaism: Haggadic Studies*. London: Brill, 1962.
Walzer, Michael. *Arguing About War*. New Haven: Yale University Press, 2006.
———. *Just and Unjust Wars: A Moral Argument With Historical Illustrations*. New York: Basic, 2006.
———. *Spheres of Justice: A Defense of Pluralism and Equality*. New York: Basic, 1984.
Watts, Isaac. "Jesus Shall Reign Where'er the Sun," paraphrase of Psalm 72, www.hymnary.org/hymn/PHW/Ps.156.
Wesley, John. "Serving God with Mammon, A Sermon on Luke 16.9," www.cambridgestudycenter.com/giving/wesley.htm.
Wilson, Rodney. *Economics, Ethics and Religion: Jewish, Christian and Muslim Economic Thought*. Washington Square, NY: New York University Press, 1997.
Wink, Walter. *Engaging the Powers: Discernment and Resistance in a World of Domination*. Minneapolis: Fortress, 1992.
———. *Naming the Powers: The Language of Power in the New Testament*. Philadelphia: Fortress, 1984.
———. *The Powers That Be: Theology for a New Millennium*. Minneapolis: Fortress, 1998.
———. *Unmasking the Powers: The Invisible Forces That Determine Human Existence*. Philadelphia: Fortress, 1986.
Winter, Timothy. "Qur'anic Reasoning as an Academic Practice," in *The Promise of Scriptural Reasoning*, David Ford and C.C. Pecknold, eds. Hoboken, NJ: Wiley-Blackwell, 2007.
Yancey, Philip. *The Bible Jesus Read*. Grand Rapids: Zondervan, 1999.
Yoder, John Howard. *The Politics of Jesus*. Grand Rapids: Eerdmans, 1972.
Yoder, John Howard, Cartwright, Michael G., and Ochs, Peter, eds. *The Jewish-Christian Schism Revisited*. Grand Rapids: Eerdmans, 2003.

www.ingramcontent.com/pod-product-compliance
Lightning Source LLC
Chambersburg PA
CBHW070338230426
43663CB00011B/2372